# IN

TRAVELS

# PURSUIT

ACROSS

# OF

PATRIOTIC

# FREEDOM

LANDS

# IN

TRAVELS

# PURSUIT

ACROSS

# OF

PATRIOTIC

# FREEDOM

LANDS

PRADEEP DAMODARAN

HarperCollins *Publishers* India

First published in India by HarperCollins *Publishers* 2024
4th Floor, Tower A, Building No. 10, DLF Cyber City,
DLF Phase II, Gurugram, Haryana – 122002
www.harpercollins.co.in

2 4 6 8 10 9 7 5 3 1



P-ISBN: 978-93-6213-895-8
E-ISBN: 978-93-6213-832-3



Typeset in 12/15 Arno Pro by
HarperCollins *Publishers* India

Printed and bound at
Thomson Press (India) Ltd

# Contents

## THREE



## FOUR

# Introduction

MY FASCINATION WITH THE WORD 'FREEDOM' planted that first seed. The intricate, evocative images that exploring the idea of freedom triggered in me soon became an urge I couldn't resist. I'm neither the first nor will be the last one to pursue this; I could even argue that the pursuit of freedom has remained the most fundamental quest of mankind since the time the human race began to appreciate the value of free will. In modern nations, though, freedom comes with such clearly defined boundaries that often contradict the meaning of the word.

'Right to freedom' is a fundamental right enshrined in the Constitution of India. Article 19 guarantees that all citizens shall have the right to freedom of speech and expression; right to assemble peacefully; right to form associations and unions; right to move freely; right to reside and settle anywhere in the country; and right to practise any profession, occupation, trade or business.

This freedom that we take for granted today came after a long period of turmoil. India's struggle for independence remains one of the most fascinating narratives of the modern world and is like none other. From armed revolts to peaceful, non-violent satyagrahas to waging a conventional war by raising a private army—the road to India's independence was laced with tales of valour and sacrifice.

However, the freedom that generations of Indians had fought for and achieved for us has transformed significantly over the past seventy-seven years. As we are on course to complete eight decades as a sovereign nation, this book attempts to track that change—the freedom they fought for and the freedom that we enjoy (or not) today.

Like most other countries, India has its fair share of iconic locations that have played a crucial role in its freedom movement. Many of those have been glorified in history books, films, school curricula, etc.; but there are also places where equally important struggles took place, and yet, those have been forgotten and erased from public memory. This book also traverses through those lands.

My year-long travel itinerary in pursuit of freedom began in February 2022 at the Sabarmati Ashram in Ahmedabad and concluded at the Gandhi Memorial in Kanniyakumari, after criss-crossing the length and breadth of the country. I have segregated my journey into four sections.

In the first, we explore the relevance of Gandhism in today's India by following the footsteps of the Mahatma from the serene riverfront at the Sabarmati Ashram in Ahmedabad through acres and acres of swank, identical villa communities owned by NRIs in Sardar Vallabhbhai Patel's Bardoli, past the grey sands of Dandi beach and all the way down to the remote town of Dharampur on the Maharashtra–Gujarat border, where young tribal men and women still apply Gandhian principles to fight injustice.

The next section of this journey begins in the dusty, dry plains of Rani Lakshmibai's Jhansi in the Bundelkhand region of Uttar

Pradesh, veers into the dark alleys of Unnao, where rural women are still afraid to step out of their homes after sundown, then heads farther east to Gorakhpur and Motihari in Bihar, the birthplace of the Indigo protests—one of the most important farmer agitations during the freedom struggle—where today's farmers discuss their year-long agitation on the outskirts of New Delhi and what it means to be an agrarian in twenty-first-century India.

The third section, my favourite, unravels those forgotten narratives of the freedom struggle that have helped in shaping the country we live in today but are largely absent in our history books. From Bilga in the Doaba region of Punjab to Jim Corbett's Ramnagar to the abandoned palaces of Tamluk in West Bengal, the section is full of those tales that we have either lost or have chosen to ignore with the passage of time.

The concluding section of this book is a deep dive into the origins of dissent in the deep south of the country. This leg of the journey begins in Panchalankurichi in Thoothukudi district, hometown of Veerapandiya Kattabomman—one of the earliest freedom fighters in the country—revisits the eventful life and times of V.O. Chidambaram Pillai, founder of the country's first steam navigation company in Ettayapuram, before delving into how those early protests Pillai organized have paved the way for the most recent anti-nuclear and other agitations that have rocked the nation.

---

As had been the case with my earlier books, I have used travel writing as a tool to explore the idea of freedom—recording my observations and conversations with people I encountered along the way. To provide a context to those experiences, I have also referred to other books on the Indian freedom struggle extensively. However, I wish to clarify that this book does not aspire to be an authority on the history of our land, and I am no historian.

These travels in pursuit of freedom rank among the most rewarding and enlightening journeys I have undertaken in my life. They have humbled and transformed me. I hope you find something to take away from this book too.

# ONE

# Sabarmati Ashram, Ahmedabad District

I WAS LOOKING AT THE THE PORTICO OF HRIDAY KUNJ, home of M.K. Gandhi and Kasturba Gandhi between 1918 and 1930 at the Sabarmati Ashram. There was an elderly man with a silver-grey beard and silky white hair, clothed in an off-white khadi kurta-pajama and a light blue Nehru jacket, sitting cross-legged behind a wooden Bardoli charkha and lecturing to a group of about six or seven eager tourists. The audience, ranging from a doe-eyed three-year-old girl to a Gen Z teenage boy in a striped blue shirt and jeans to a much older, clean-shaven man in a white dhoti-kurta with a huge pot belly, who looked like he could be Lalu Prasad Yadav's younger brother, was also sitting cross-legged and paying earnest attention to the man behind the spinning charkha. To the left of Gandhi's former residence (he never stayed there after the Salt March) was a glowing graphite-grey statue of a cross-legged 'Father of the Nation' on a granite slab surrounded by a lush, well-maintained lawn. Three teen girls—with straightened, shiny hair and bright red lips (all of them)—giggled playfully while resting on one knee and posing for a portrait with the Mahatma. The girl to Gandhi's left covered both her eyes with her fingers; the one next to her hid her mouth with both her palms; and the girl to Gandhi's right blocked both her ears with her palms. All three of them tried hard to stop grinning but couldn't, as a young man made several attempts to capture that perfect Kodak moment.

Leaning on a wide compound wall facing Hriday Kunj, I was observing the last batch of visitors walk in and out of the various rooms of the historic house against the backdrop of a setting mid-February sun. Just a few feet away from me, a dozen-odd chirpy parakeets landed smoothly on the surface of the wall, whistling at each other rather noisily; an adolescent squirrel cautiously sneaked up a sleek lamppost clamped to the wall and stole grains from a bird feeder attached to the post, even as a couple of mynahs tried to scare him away. Behind me, the picturesque Sabarmati Riverfront—pride of the Gujarat government—fed mostly by water diverted from the Narmada river, remained as still as a photograph. To my right, a fleet of pigeons flapped their wings and took flight from the wide riverside pavement for yet another sortie before darkness would force them to return to their nests; a young cyclist pedalled casually along the river with his hands off the handlebar. A little farther away, a steady stream of vehicles clogged the concrete bridge built across the Sabarmati. The quiet river, the multi-storey buildings on the other bank of the river, mirror images of which glowed in the still greenish-grey water, the birds and small mammals in the ashram premises, and even the tourists relaxing on the waterfront—they all glowed in a sepia tone in the diminishing twilight, transporting me to a different time and space. Rivers often remain sole testimony to everything that unfolds on their banks, and the Sabarmati has been witness to her fair share of monumental events.

On a similar evening ninety-two years ago, a day before Mahatma Gandhi began his historic Salt March from this exact spot outside Hriday Kunj on 12 March 1930, at least 10,000 people had gathered here to listen to Gandhi's speech.[1] Under the shade of the tall trees that still surround Hriday Kunj, Gandhi was known to hold his regular meetings. Chaos, excitement and apprehension had prevailed among the audience as he had addressed the gathering that evening. 'Either we shall win the goal for which we are marching or die in the attempt to win it. There can be no turning back for us hereafter. We will keep on our fight till Swaraj is established in India. This will be the last fight. The soldiers who accompany me must note that there is to be no retreat. Those of them that are married should take leave of their wives, and the wives should congratulate their husbands on their being the first soldiers of the country's freedom battle. We are as good as parting from the Ashram and from our homes. Only with complete victory can we return to this place. In all probability, this will be my last speech to you. Even if the government allow me to march tomorrow morning, this will be my last speech on the sacred banks of the Sabarmati. Possibly these may be the last words of my life here,' Gandhi told the large gathering during the prayer meeting held at the ashram.[2]

The Sabarmati Ashram was the centre of all activity in Gujarat as well as the rest of India during that period. When Gandhi had chosen the site for this Ashram after deciding to shift from the Kochrab Ashram, he called his choice of venue '... the right place for our activities to carry on the search for truth and develop fearlessness, for on one side are the iron bolts of the foreigners, and on the other, thunderbolts of Mother Nature.' In February 2022, as I began my journey from the Sabarmati Ashram that balmy evening, the 'thunderbolt' river had been tamed into a perennial, sepulchral waterway: A mute spectator to the cacophony of a burgeoning city.

---

1 Thomas Weber, *On the Salt March: The Historiography of Gandhi's March to Dandi* (New Delhi: HarperCollins Publishers), 1997, p.148.

2 *The Collected Works of Mahatma Gandhi* (The Publication Division, Government of India), vol. 48, p. 403.

Since I reached the ashram at eleven that morning, a steady stream of visitors had been walking in from across the country. They perused the museum and photo galleries, and walked in and out of the various homes that have been maintained just as they were a hundred years ago, except for a coat or two of fresh paint or varnish. Obviously, the busiest was the residence of the Mahatma. At least twenty pairs of slippers were always present outside the large veranda of Hriday Kunj. While I had expected a lot of khadi kurtas and pajamas at the ashram, I could identify just one or two men during the course of the entire day. When I brought it up with Atul Pandya, director of the Sabarmati Ashram Preservation and Memorial Trust, at his office later that evening, he simply laughed. I asked Atul, a Gandhian who was raised in a family who believed in the man and his wisdom, if he thought Gandhi was still relevant in today's Gujarat and India.

He laughed again. 'The question, is are we relevant to Gandhi?'

Like most people of my generation, my introduction to Mohandas Karamchand Gandhi, a.k.a. Gandhiji, a.k.a. Bapu, etc., was through textbooks referring to him as the Father of our Nation: An ethereal projection of a man labelled a mystic, freedom fighter, philosopher and leader of the masses—all in one. In 1982 came the Ben Kingsley-starrer *Gandhi*, which I was forced to watch during the Gandhi Jayanti celebrations at the convent school I went to. If anything, the movie helped me form a more distasteful image of the man as a scantily clad, unappealing older person who walked and talked animatedly and refused to fight back even when he was attacked. During higher secondary and undergraduate college years, 'Gandhi' was the word used to ridicule the weak. If someone wore a particularly wrinkled shirt or any other clothing that was extremely old-fashioned, he would be promptly called 'Gandhi' that day. Physically weak or studious boys who were too scared to bunk classes or drink beer at parties were the 'Gandhis' of our school and college. As I grew older, more words and phrases, such as 'sathyameva jayathe', 'satyagraha', 'ahimsa' and civil disobedience, got associated with Gandhi, who had by now gradually transformed into a man of principle to those who sought to know more about him—but the vagueness still prevailed. Now, in my late forties, when I announced to my family that I would travel from the Sabarmati Ashram to Dandi Beach like Gandhi did, my college-going daughter laughed and asked if I would also dress like him (wearing just a langot) while I travelled. Perhaps it was this aspect of Gandhi that had made those three girls posing for a selfie at the Sabarmati Ashram laugh uncontrollably.

When I shared my daughter's comment and the general opinion about Gandhi among the post-millennials, Atul said that he would not blame the younger generation for ignoring Gandhi. 'But I would blame parents, teachers and the education system for projecting Gandhi in such a way that the younger generation gets confused. Our Indian pedagogy is such that youngsters need a medium to reach Gandhi, that is, through teachers, mentors, etc., and that has created many issues. In photographs, textbooks and statues, Gandhi is projected as an old, impoverished man. His youth is not celebrated as much as it should be. At eighteen, he went to England, and by twenty-five, he was a successful lawyer in South Africa. He knew so many languages, he was proficient in most world religions—but nobody has put forward that Gandhi in front of the youth. What is portrayed is the image of a daridra Narayan, champion of the poor, to the younger generation.

'We should identify and interpret Gandhi to the younger generation as a voracious writer, orator and successful lawyer. He was an extremely hard-working and health-conscious person. He worked sixteen hours a day, was adept at multitasking at an age when it wasn't even talked about. A look at his correspondences will reveal how sophisticated he was. But that is not what reaches the younger generation, and so they naturally stay away,' Atul clarified.

Browsing the visitors' book at the ashram earlier that morning, I had been surprised to find a significant number of abusive comments. One visitor had written that Gandhi will continue to rot in hell forever for what he has done to Indians: 'Even after 75 years of Independence, still we are crying, dying because of you Mr. Gandhi. I realized why BABASHEB B.R. AMBEDKAR DID NOT CALL YOU MAHATMA. Because of you, more than one crore plus have died during partition. Only soldiers dead in Kashmir as of today's count is 90,000 [no idea how he arrived at that figure]!' the visitor vented. Some of the other comments left by visitors were even more vile, irrational and unworthy of being reproduced. When I pointed this out to Atul, he quipped that this freedom to freely criticize Gandhi in his ashram was exactly what the man had fought for. 'Let them try to openly criticize today's leaders and see if they can get away with that.'

---

On my way from Sardar Vallabhbhai Patel International Airport to my hotel near the Sabarmati Ashram the previous night, I had witnessed a beautiful scene unfold from the window of the cab. By the spectacularly illuminated Sabarmati Riverfront, which seemed to stretch across most of the city, a young man and a woman had embraced each other and kissed. It was just around 8 p.m. and the air was crisp. The woman with long flowing hair was facing away from me. She walked towards the man who stood before her with open arms, hugged him and kissed his lips without a care for the world around her.

I've always noticed that such acts attract all eyes. Besides me, the kiss also drew the attention of my Uber driver, Usman Bhai. 'Amdavad has changed a lot,' he had observed, returning his gaze to the steering wheel.

Usman is fifty-one and has a jovial face, the kind that disarms you the moment you see him burst into a smile, despite his flowing grey beard. Originally from Rajasthan, his family has lived in Ahmedabad for seventy-five years. Like most cab drivers who drive around a newcomer in their city, he began chatting from the moment I got in his vehicle and had an opinion on just about everything in the world. For most of the journey, Usman bitched about the corruption in the city. 'A policeman makes at least Rs 10,000 every day through just bribes. You don't wear a mask ... he will charge you Rs 500. If you don't wear it properly, he will take a picture and then charge you the same. Drive an out-of-state vehicle and you're fined, no helmet, you're fined. For everything there is a fine,' he said while cruising along the Riverfront. As we neared the Sabarmati Ashram, I was surprised to find him vouch dearly for his Amdavad—perhaps it was the 'kiss' effect. 'Even at 2 a.m., a woman can step out alone in Amdavad and no one will bother her in any way. This is one of the safest cities and people are really nice. Usually, if you ask someone politely for directions, it's likely that they will drop you wherever you want to go if they are free. If you're impolite, then it's a different story, but generally, people are nice here,' he said.

'Looks like there is some Gandhigiri still left in Gujarat, isn't it?' I replied, just to provoke him.

'Not Gandhigiri, sir, insaniyat ... there is still insaniyat in this city, unlike in Delhi or Mumbai,' he said as we parted for the evening.

I liked that. And 'insaniyat', humanity, was what I went looking for in Usman's Amdavad for the next few days along with him.

---

8 April 1919

> The standing complaint of the Hindus against the Mussulmans is that the latter are beef-eaters and that they purposely sacrifice cows on the Bakr-i-ld day. Now it is impossible to unite the Hindus and Mahomedans so long as the Hindus do not hesitate to kill their Mahomedan brethren

> in order to protect a cow. For I think it is futile to expect that our violence will ever compel the Mahomedans to refrain from cow slaughter.[3]
>
> I believe myself to be an orthodox Hindu and it is my conviction that no one who scrupulously practises the Hindu religion may kill a cow-killer to protect a cow.
>
> M.K. Gandhi

The above lines were written more than a hundred years ago.

---

My first halt was at Juhapura, labelled by Google and Wikipedia as a modern-day ghetto of Ahmedabad, located approximately 11 kilometres from the ashram. Those familiar with the Dandi March might recall that Gandhi and his followers, when they set out on their historic journey, made their first halt at Aslali village about 18 kilometres from their ashram. But my search for insaniyat in the land of Gandhi led me to this congested and expansive suburb of Amdavad, also known as the headquarters of the Muslim population in the city.

The tranquil atmosphere surrounding the Sabarmati Ashram, occupied largely by former institutions of the ashram, such as the Goshala and the Khadi Emporiums, dissipated gradually as we drove past the Ashram Road, taking a few turns here and there before merging with the majestic Riverfront Road, flanked by the Sabarmati on one side and corporate buildings, multi-storey boutique hotels and posh residential properties on the other. After staying on the Riverfront Road for a few minutes, Usman veered off onto a dusty narrower road towards Juhapura.

---

3 *The Collected Works of Mahatma Gandhi*, vol. 17, 'The Vow of Hindu-Muslim Unity', pp. 400–02.

The view from the passenger seat of the Indica I was in was rather strikingly different now, with a sudden rise in the number of auto rickshaws and two-wheelers scrambling for the limited space available on the narrowing road. As we inched closer to Juhapura, the number of burkhas and skull caps I could spot also increased significantly. The roads were dusty, bumpier, but still comfortably motorable, especially for auto rickshaws packed with people, their limbs jutting out, that navigated their way past open load vehicles, motorists and the occasional bus or large van. The plush office spaces with transparent glass windowpanes and the residential buildings with tall iron gates of Riverfront Road were now replaced by smaller, dirtier commercial buildings whose colourful, vibrant name boards were coated with a thick layer of brown dust. Restaurants offering Chinese noodles with chilli chicken and chicken Manchurian and roadside butcher shops with deskinned torsos of goats hanging off iron hooks now began to appear along the road, as Usman Bhai deftly manoeuvred his Indica through one congested road after another. After about five more minutes of driving through dusty roads, he turned into a quiet lane lined with large two-storey homes shielded by high compound walls. 'We are in Juhapura. It's a large area stretching 5–6 kilometres,' he announced. 'Where do you want to go in Juhapura?'

Looking around at the posh, insulated bungalows, I asked him to take me to a neighbourhood where I could interact freely with the people. 'Then we have to go to the poorer parts of Juhapura. The bungalow residents do not open their doors to strangers. They don't have the time to talk to people like you either,' he suggested.

I agreed and we drove again past more walled bungalows that were followed by smaller apartment complexes as the tar road became narrower and narrower, until we reached a point where there was just mud road ahead, wide enough for a car to pass besides one or two two-wheelers. The sprawling bungalows were now replaced by dirty little row houses leaning against one another, often sharing the same wall which was in a semi-dilapidated condition. I also found that most homes, or at least portions of the homes, here were painted in various shades of yellow, tainted by varying layers of dust. The almost absolute absence of trees or any form of green cover in the neighbourhood made the entire area resemble a poor Mexican suburb in a Hollywood film, often achieved by using camera filters.

'This neighbourhood used to be a jungle just twenty years ago,' Usman said as he continued to drive. 'All this development happened after the Godhra incident. After the riots, most Muslims felt unsafe in other neighbourhoods and moved here, abandoning their homes for safety. This is a fully Muslim neighbourhood now and we feel very safe in Juhapura. Back then [before Godhra] land used to be sold for just a lakh per ground, about 2,400 square feet, and yet, there were no takers. Look at it now—there is hardly any land left to build on. This settlement has come out of nowhere in the past two decades.'

The narrow dirt road ended abruptly before the crumbling, unplastered walls of a modest one-floor house. In front of the house was an open drain, about 1-foot wide, filled with greenish-grey stagnant water with gas bubbles rising up to the surface and exploding amid split-open packets of Lays and Kurkure, besides cigarette butts and other plastic bags. A swarm of flies hovered over little mounds of garbage collected from the drain to pave way for sewage to flow. A bony child with burnt dry hair, aged about five or six and wearing just a half-pant with his bare torso exposed, stood in front of the drain and threw a stone into it, probably trying to hit a frog or insect. The sewage water splashed all around, dampening the walls of the building as well as his hands, chest and legs before he ran off to join other children like him at the end of the street, their bony torsos also exposed. Usman parked the car just ahead of the gutter. We got down and walked to a grocery shop about three buildings behind us and asked the shopkeeper if he would be willing to talk to us about his neighbourhood. The middle-aged man with a neatly trimmed silver-grey beard said he had no time to talk and asked us to talk to a certain Sameer Khan instead. 'He is an influential person in this area,' the shopkeeper said and left for his house behind the shop. We spoke to a couple of other shopkeepers, who also pointed us towards Sameer Khan's bungalow a little farther away.

Behind the sprawling, pale green gates of Sameer Khan's residence was not just a home but a line of bungalows to my right, with a wide-tiled central pavement and a modest office building to my left, where half a dozen men stood facing each other, engaged in an animated conversation. When Usman asked one of them for Sameer Khan, we were told that he was busy with his daughter's wedding and might not be able to talk to us. 'But I'll still check,' said a young man, directing us to an air-conditioned office.

A fair, older-looking man with a wrinkled face smeared with talcum powder walked in and occupied the chair facing us a few minutes later. He wore a blue polyester full-sleeved shirt and matching trousers. The man introduced himself as Wazir Khan Pathan and added that Sameer Khan was his son. A lawyer from Visnagar in Mehsana district, Wazir and his family had been living in Juhapura for the past twenty years. He's an active Congressman and was recently appointed as the chairman of the minority department in the Gujarat Pradesh Congress Committee.

After basic introductions were done, I told him about my quest. 'When I was a student', there was still some insaniyat left in this city, but I am now convinced that life has only become worse. Politicians have driven Hindus and Muslims away from one another in Gujarat. The situation was much better when I was growing up,' Wazir recalled and began reminiscing about the not-so-distant past. Back in the late 1970s, when Wazir was studying at a college in Visnagar, there were 6,000–7,000 Hindu students and just about 100 Muslim students on the campus. Despite the overwhelming number of Hindus, he claimed that he managed to win the students' union elections with a thumping majority.

Several years later, during the municipal elections in Visnagar in the '80s, Wazir claimed that he was elected as councillor in a Hindu-majority constituency and remained in office for fifteen years. 'It is unthinkable now. I feel that politics of religious identity has widened the rift between Hindus and Muslims in Gujarat. In my opinion, this began sometime in the mid-1980s, when certain religious outfits with an extreme ideology decided to consolidate the anti-Dalit and anti-Muslim votes because they were not getting any support from these two communities. After that there were minor tensions between the two communities, but since the 2002 riots, the split has been total. After the train-burning incident in Godhra, the Hindu groups attacked Muslims at will. A storm raged across the state, with no visible action to curtail it. Even in tiny villages with just a handful of Muslim families, we were isolated and attacked. Muslim homes were burnt down, stones were hurled at us and we were basically chased away from our ancestral lands. So people living in villages across Gujarat felt unsafe and wanted a secure place where they could be safe from Hindu communalists, and even the police. They just left everything and came away to this part of Ahmedabad. Many of them have not returned to their homes even twenty years later,' he said.

Sweets, savouries and heavily sweetened tea were brought and placed before us. Urging us to try out the sweets and munching a little serving of the savoury himself, Wazir Khan continued. 'Now, there is a clear segregation between Hindu and Muslim areas. While we can freely go and come to any part of Ahmedabad, no Muslim wants to live in a Hindu area, nor a Hindu in a Muslim area. People are afraid to return to their homes in Ahmedabad itself; their multi-storey bungalows remain unoccupied even twenty years later. The sad result is that this division has crept even into the schools of this city. Muslim children now study mostly in schools present in Muslim neighbourhoods and Hindu children remain confined to schools in their neighbourhoods. Both Hindus and Muslims are afraid to go out of their comfort zones to schools because they are either afraid, denied admission or charged more fees. The reasons may be many, but the truth is even children aren't allowed to mingle freely anymore the way it was during my school and college days. If Hindu and Muslim children aren't allowed to sit next to each other, be friends with one other, what will be the future of this country when these children grow up? This was not the case when we grew up,' he said.

Wazir Khan must be at least a dozen years older than me, but I could still relate to him. When I was growing up in the '80s in Chennai, my best friend in class six was a Muslim boy, Shahul Hameed. He lived in Pudupet, right next to our school, and went home during lunch breaks. Whenever his mother cooked biryani, he brought back a tiffin box filled with it, which we eagerly waited for and gobbled up in seconds. Since Shahul and I were among the shortest in class, we shared the first bench along with Eldridge, an Anglo-Indian. All three of us shared our meals. I used to take idlis, curd rice or some form of mixed rice, Shahul used to bring biryani and Eldridge brought meat sandwiches, pork chops, etc. During Christmas season, we often went to Eldridge's to eat pork chops, which his mother cooked so well. During Eid, we spent time hanging out in Pudupet with Shahul. But he wasn't great at studies and stopped coming to school when we were in class eight or nine, and I haven't been in touch with him since. Before Shahul, there was a Suhail Ahmed and his sister, Sameena. We were known as the 'Hindi' students, as our second language was Hindi, and we bonded in the language classes. Suhail and his sister also discontinued their studies midway. But those classmates introduced me to a culture that was so unlike mine and made my childhood colourful. To even imagine children growing up in a monolithic culture in this day and age, celebrating the same festivals, sharing the same food and fearing/loathing anything that isn't theirs, makes me sad and worry if Wazir Khan was, in fact, right.

Before parting, I asked him if, as a politician, he thought the situation could change and if Muslims and Hindus could live together in the same colony, at least in the future. 'I don't think it's possible anymore, not in the near future. In Gujarat, any issue, even if a boy elopes with a girl, is given a communal angle and made into a Hindu–Muslim problem. People have been so communalized by politicians that I don't see the two communities living together again, unless there is a law against religious politics. No one should be allowed to campaign/contest elections in the name of religion. Perhaps, that will make the situation better,' Wazir Khan fancied.

From Wazir Khan's home we drove to a slightly less congested neighbourhood in Juhapura, past more homes and shops painted yellow, off-white and occasionally in darker shades of pink and other bright colours, through barely motorable roads, to the housing society built by the Gujarat Sarvajanik Welfare Trust for the rehabilitation of the 2002 riot victims. The Congress leader wanted me to meet some families who had been rehabilitated to Juhapura after abandoning their homes, which brought us to this more breathable neighbourhood. The row houses built by the Welfare Trust were sturdier and better maintained than the homes we had encountered on the way to Wazir Khan's home, but they were also cramped next to one another. The clothesline belonging to one home overlapped with the clothes drying in the next home, making the apartment complex look like a multi-storey dhobi ghat. The street was empty but for a frail old man with a cone-shaped white beard, who was seated on a parked motorcycle and appeared to be lost in deep thought. His sunburnt dark complexion enhanced the shine on his beard.

Usman parked the car next to the bike and asked the man for the head of the society. The old man didn't even bother to look back at him. Usman then went closer and told him that an officer had come from Delhi to find out about their condition to prepare a report. Turning towards me, Usman winked and asked me to wait by the car. About five minutes later, another frail but younger man with a weepy face walked towards to us. He was wearing a white cotton kurta-pajama and a white cap. Although he extended his hand and introduced himself, his voice was so feeble that he was barely audible and his soft fingers trembled as we shook hands. Since I could barely hear him talk, I invited the man inside the cab to cut down the background disturbance and introduced myself again. 'I'm Feroze Mohammed Guzzar Mohammed Pathan,' the man said, and claimed that he was the head of that society of about 180 families, who had migrated here from different parts of Gujarat after the 2002 riots. 'I'm from Gulbarg Society in Chamanpura,' he emphasized.

I had read about the Gulbarg Society massacre just that morning before leaving for Juhapura and had been shocked by the outrageous brutality of what had taken place. The site was on my list of to-be-visited spots, along with Naroda Patiya, where a larger, more violent massacre had taken place on 28 February 2002. After his introduction, I understood his frozen look and trembling hands better.

Looking at my reaction, the forty-eight-year-old said sixty-nine people, including women and children, in his society were killed in one day, between 10 a.m. and 5 p.m. 'I lost my mother, father, sister and two brothers [aged twenty-five and nineteen] right before my eyes,' he recalled, probably for the thousandth time over the past twenty years, as tears flowed down his cheeks—he broke down even after all these years.

Despite my temptation to probe further on what transpired that day, I refrained from asking anything more. But as if he had read my mind, or since he was used to recounting the events that unfolded that day again and again to so many different people, or perhaps as that was the only incident from his life that instantly attracted strangers' attention, he delved into the details. 'We had already received a phone call early that morning from Ehsan Jafri [a former Congress Member of Parliament and resident of Gulbarg Society, who was also killed] warning us that a mob was planning an attack on our society and asking us to be prepared to retaliate. We had gathered together and prepared ourselves to resist if attacked. Ehsan had even called the police for help, but we did not receive any protection,' Feroze said, recounting the events as they had unfolded that day. 'When the mob came with swords and fire torches, hurling stones at us, around 11 a.m. or so, our men tried to fight back. I remember receiving a blow to my head and a knife cut on my hand before blacking out. They probably thought I was dead and moved on to attack the others. When I regained consciousness, the mob was on a rampage inside our home. I crawled into the apartment complex opposite our home [the gated society had around eighteen individual homes and eight flats in a single complex] and climbed onto the rooftop with six others. From there, we watched my parents, sister and brother get butchered and later burnt to death,' he said, before breaking down again.

As the mob continued to raze homes and burn the dead, Feroze and a few others climbed down through the rear entrance of the apartment building and escaped to a nearby mosque, from where he was rushed to a hospital. The only survivors in their seven-member family were he and his younger brother Mohammed Arif, who survived because he wasn't at home at the time of the massacre.

Twenty years had gone by since the incident, yet when I met Feroze, his shivers and nervousness refused to go away. Usman, who was sitting in the driver's seat and listening to Feroze, remained frozen in his seat, unable to speak. Even I had forgotten to turn on my voice recorder. After I turned it on, I asked Feroze why he had not gone back to his home. 'I never went back to the house, nor can I ever go back again. I cannot bear to see our home the way it is now. My family was wiped out right before my eyes. How do I go back there?'

In 2006, Feroze married Shabnam and the couple now have a son, Mohammed Khan, and daughter, Tehsin. The children go to Ankur School and study with children of different religions, Feroze pointed out. 'I deliberately did not put them in a Muslim school. I want them to grow among children of different religions.' Feroze and his wife intend to educate both their children as much as possible and hope that they have a better future. 'My brother and I were allotted a house here after the riots, and I now live with my wife, children and brother, who runs a garage in the neighbourhood. All the past residents of Gulbarg Society have left for good, except Qasim Khan, who lost nineteen of his family members but still lives there with the remaining members,' Feroze continued. Some of the victims' kin now visit Gulbarg Society on 28th February every year to participate in a memorial service and pray for the deceased.

Before leaving, I asked him my staple and silly question that I asked everyone on that journey. '*Azadi Ka Amrit Mahotsav ka kya matlab hai apke liye*? (What does the government's celebration of seventy-five years of Independence mean to you?)' He laughed for the first time in almost an hour and looked at Usman Bhai, who also laughed. '*Ab mein kya bataoon apko?* (What do I tell you now?)' Feroze said. And I left it at that.

---

With Feroze's impassioned rendition of his ordeal still playing in my head, I headed straight to Gulbarg Society in Chamanpura to meet Qasim Khan. While Juhapura had all the tell-tale signs of a poor and rundown neighbourhood, the landscape on my way to Chamanpura, another poor and thickly populated part of Ahmedabad, was strikingly different. The roads were still dusty and crowded with two-wheelers, auto rickshaws, tempo travellers and other types of dirt-coated, badly maintained vehicles puffing out carbon dioxide, but were also distinctly wider and properly laid with tar topping. There were many people on the road, but hardly any burkhas or skull caps could be spotted. Instead, women draped in bright, colourful sarees and salwar suits and men sporting tilaks of various sizes and colours on their foreheads occupied the street corners and front doors of homes, and even crowded the balconies of row houses in Chamanpura. Kachori stalls, mobile juice carts and ice cream vendors occupied road corners every 50 metres or so. Numerous roadside temples that appeared to have sprouted up in random junctions ate into the limited space available for the vehicles, forcing them to take detours, resulting in traffic chaos. I also spotted several idols of Goddess Durga in white paint parked near the temples. Just about 100 metres ahead of the tall, freshly painted pale green compound wall of Gulbarg Society, a young man rode an elephant draped in a dark blue silk sheet embellished with gold embroidery. A crowd comprising mostly children, along with a few young women and men, tailed the elephant and were so amused that they refused to let it pass without fiddling with its trunk, tail and other body parts. The rhythmic drumbeats of a dholak player who accompanied the elephant perfectly blended with the jubilant mood of the crowd—the religious colour-coding of the Chamanpura area was complete that Sunday evening.

As we drove through the large iron gates and walked inside Gulbarg Society, an eerie silence engulfed us. The entire gated community was desolate and lifeless. At least five or six auto rickshaws were parked at the far end on the right side of the complex. A few mini lorries and smaller load vehicles were also parked in random corners. At the entrance, to my right, were sprawling two-storey homes with spacious balconies, porticos with round pillars and tiled flooring completely blanketed by dust, soot and scars of burnt human flesh and blood. Doors and windows had been ripped off, probably stolen by anti-socials. Fans and furniture in areas not destroyed by the fire were also missing. Spacious living rooms and bedrooms were bereft of furniture; burnt clothes and glass pieces lay scattered upon piles of other debris, mostly burnt wood. A multi-storey apartment that lay amid the row villas was also unoccupied and in shambles. Sunshades of some villas had developed cracks and even given way in a few cases, while grill gates had collapsed and were buried under overgrown weeds. The entire gated community resembled the site of a World War II battlefield left untouched since.

The house to our left, upon entering the compound, was occupied. A fair, young woman wearing a bright pink suit sat cross-legged at the entrance, stitching a piece of fabric. When I tried to talk to her, she directed me to a middle-aged man lying on a cot out in the open about 50 feet away from me, close to the rear compound wall. He was petting a grey-white kitten, while a meek little lamb with extremely dirty fur was tied to one of the legs of the cot. The man appeared to have emerged straight out of a '90s Hindi movie set, wearing camouflage trousers, a black T-shirt and dark sunglasses, although the sun had already begun its descent for the day. His long, silky black hair and an equally black handlebar moustache completed the look. Despite his aloof appearance, the man was friendly and offered me a seat next to him on the cot when I approached him. I told him I was looking for Qasim Bhai and about my meeting with Feroze. 'I'm his son Rafiq Qasim Mansoori. Papa has gone out,' he said. Looking around, I asked him if he was present during the massacre. Rafiq immediately took off his sunglasses and inched closer to show me his right eye, which appeared completely mashed up, with no semblance of an eyeball or presence of any life in it. 'This happened on that day; a stone hit me in the eye,' he said, and wore the coolers again. 'I lost nineteen family members that day, including my wife and infant son.'

Yet again, an oral narrative of the horrors of the day played out as Rafiq guided us through each home in the society and revealed in excruciating detail where and how different families were butchered by the mob. The nonchalant manner in which Rafiq narrated the sequence of events made them even more chilling. When we returned to the cot after his massacre tour, Usman asked him about the young woman we had tried speaking to at their home. 'She's my wife,' he said. 'When the incident happened, my son was just five months old. He was also killed along with my then wife. Since I was in the hospital for several weeks, I had no clue. Now I have three children with my second wife, whom I married in 2005. She is from Indore,' he clarified.

Usman asked him if he wasn't afraid to live alone in a Hindu-dominated area without any other Muslim family to support them after all they had gone through. 'Why don't you go to Juhapura, where we were given free homes, and live with other Muslim families?' he asked Rafiq.

'Why should I be afraid?' Rafiq shot back. 'What is there to be afraid of anymore? They have killed nineteen members of my family. What more is left for them to do? Many of those who attacked my family are roaming around freely right here. When they can do that, why should I run away? I feel perfectly safe here and am not going anywhere,' he asserted. Usman had no answer to that, and neither did I.

---

If the ruined, uninhabited homes and apartments at Gulbarg Society show the devastating effects of a communal riot even twenty years after it took place, the more impoverished, congested bylanes and streets of Naroda Patiya, which endured an even harsher streak of violence during the same period, unveil a tale of resilience. Its residents have overcome the devastating effects of the communal storm that splintered their lives with greater courage and bravery by staying put on their lands. The details of the Naroda Patiya massacre and the events that followed are too well-documented for me to get into the details. Around a hundred men, women and children (there is still some confusion over the exact number) were butchered and burnt in what was the worst massacre in India in recent times. But over the past two decades, this neighbourhood has bounced back to fully normalcy.

When I stopped by at Naroda Patiya on the way back from Gulbarg Society that Sunday evening, there was hardly any indicator of the horrors that shattered this quiet, predominantly Muslim neighbourhood exactly twenty years ago. Almost all the homes are now occupied, which include some two-dozen-odd Hindu families, mostly from south India, who are now living in harmony with their Muslim neighbours. The edges of the narrow streets were lined with old cots, sofas and reclining chairs, on which shirtless elderly men sat with newspapers, mostly to ward off flies and other insects that attempted to land on them. Little children scampered around happily dodging motorcycles and auto rickshaws while screaming out to one another. Women sat on their balconies oiling their hair, while roosters and hens pecked at grains, insects and other dirt from the gaps in the tiles before sundown, just like in any other low-income, congested neighbourhood anywhere in the country. Most of the 700-odd residents who currently live in Hussain Nagar and Jawan Nagar have been living here for the past several decades and have been eyewitnesses, often lost family members too, to the massacre in February 2002, but have decided not to move out. 'Today, we have come past it. Most men are going to work, earning for their families, and children are going to school. We are now living in total communal harmony with our Hindu neighbours,' said seventy-two-year-old Nazim Khan Rahim Khan Pathan, fondly known as 'Master' in this neighbourhood. 'The only problem we face now is that there is no development in this area.'

Nazim Khan is originally from Kantharia in Anand district and moved to Naroda Patiya in 1990, when he got a job here as a schoolteacher. A few years later, he joined a local primary school as headmaster and has also been tutoring students privately in maths and economics, thus earning the title of Master. He now runs a tutorial centre, where he coaches weak students, often free of cost, besides helping youth with English and other subjects to crack competitive exams.

On 28 February 2002, when a Hindu mob ransacked their neighbourhood, Master was alone at his home, hiding inside a water tank, after sending his wife and son to a relative's home in a different neighbourhood. 'We knew that something was going to happen soon after the train-burning incident. A mob came to Naroda Patiya with weapons and petrol to attack us, but the police were present here in large numbers, so they went back. Later that evening, I sent my wife and son off to our relative's home in a safer neighbourhood and stayed back to protect the house. When the mob returned the next morning, the police were gone, and so they had a free run. The rioters walked into every home and attacked the residents. When they came to my street, I could hear the men say my name and that I was a school headmaster and should be killed without fail,' he recalled.

Master had anticipated that and had devised a plan. He immediately got inside the water tank, partially closed its lid and sat inside until late that night. The 5'5" water tank had saved his life, but his neighbours Taskar Bibi, who was seventy back then, and Ayub, who was just thirty-four, weren't so lucky. They were dragged out of their homes and chopped into pieces, alleged Master, who said he had heard it all from inside the water tank. According to him, most of the perpetrators are either in jail or dead already. 'A lot of innocent people were killed. Some innocents got arrested too.'

Despite having witnessed the most horrific form of communal violence, Master still believes that religious harmony will prevail in

India. 'I don't consider all Hindus satanic. At the same time, I have found some Muslims to be extremely evil,' he said. 'I am a teacher and I don't discriminate between my Hindu and Muslim students. Even now I visit the homes of my Hindu students and they welcome me, discuss their problems with me. I help them in whatever way I can. Most of the Hindus living here have come from the southern states and do not know Gujarati. So they come to me to fill out any forms or write letters for them in Gujarati, which I'm glad to do. Just last week, a Malayali man came to me with the application form for a job and I filled it out for him. They trust me so much that I even write letters for them.'

Of the 1,044 people killed in the 2002 communal riots in Gujarat, 790 were Muslim and 254 Hindu.[4] Although most of the neighbourhoods that suffered this horrific violence had a Muslim majority, several Hindu neighbourhoods were also targeted: Homes were razed, families butchered. At least 10,000 Hindus, mostly from Muslim-dominated localities like Shahpur, Jamalpur, etc., were also reported to have taken refuge in makeshift camps and stayed put for several days, as Muslim mobs were also out on a rampage, targeting the most vulnerable caught in the crossfire while the state boiled.[5] According to media reports, several Hindu families

---

4 'Gujarat: After Naroda Gam Massacre Acquittal, Here Is How Other Gujarat Riot Cases Stand', *Outlook*, 21 April 2023, https://www.outlookindia.com/national/gujarat-after-naroda-gam-massacre-acquittal-here-is-how-other-gujarat-riot-cases-stand-news-280252

5 Sanjay Pande, 'Riots hit people all classes, people of all faith', *The Times of India*, 17 March 2002, http://timesofindia.indiatimes.com/city/ahmedabad/Riots-hit-all-classes-people-of-all-faith/articleshow/4007683.cms

were attacked with acid bulbs, petrol and crude bombs. Following the riots, hundreds of Hindu families in Muslim-dominated areas shifted to neighbourhoods where they were in a majority. Some even relocated completely to other cities, such as Chennai, Mumbai and other metros, following the riots, scars of which remain fresh in their minds to this day.

# Godhra, Panchmahal District

I WAS OUT FOR A CASUAL WALK ON MY FIRST MORNING IN Godhra, one of the several congested, insignificant small towns in Gujarat that became notoriously infamous after the 2002 train-burning incident and subsequent riots, when I discovered its Lal Baug, a public park. Godhra had been a disappointment since I had arrived the previous evening, after switching two poorly maintained Gujarat State Road Transport Corporation buses from Ahmedabad. The road outside GSTRC bus terminus was bumpy, the tar topping carved off the surface of the road completely except in random patches. Sewage from the surrounding eateries and sweetmeat shops overflowed into these potholes, where flies and mosquitoes bred aggressively, only to return to the shops and harass the customers. Traffic was chaos, with two-wheelers, auto rickshaws, minivans and even swank cars competing with buses and other larger vehicles for road space. To add to all that, the hotel I had booked was not even remotely as clean or well-maintained as in its photographs online, almost reflecting the general condition of the city.

Having spent a restless, resentful night in a grimy room, I stepped out around 8 a.m., when there was still a mild chill in the late February air, and walked vigorously along the road past the GSRTC terminus to overcome my general bitterness about the place through physical exertion. This road was also filled with tiny shops on both sides that were yet to open for the day; sweepers assigned by the local municipal body were busy clearing plastic sachets, teacups and other garbage off the roads along the way. Towards the end of the stretch near the railway lines, I noticed a miniature replica of the Himalayas with artificial fountains and a statue of a goddess. Next to those was a statue of Swami Vivekananda, beyond which lay the entrance to a sprawling park with tall trees, neat lawns and ornate greenery all around. Like a starving man stumbling upon a feast, I stormed into the park just to breathe some fresh air and began walking even faster on the neatly paved walkway that almost surrounded the perimeter of the park.

Lal Baug was so unlike the chaotic city it was surrounded by. Neatly paved walkways served as a boundary to the well-maintained lawns of the park, where tall gulmohar, mango, ashoka, ponytail palm and a few other trees and shrubs belonging to the Arecaceae family grew. The trees provided adequate shade for those who preferred to stretch their muscles or perform yoga on the grass, while neatly trimmed ficus plants, ornamental banana plants and other flowering shrubs bordering the walking path formed a green wall separating the grassy areas. Even at that hour, the park was brimming with morning walkers: Middle-aged men and women wearing tight T-shirts and sweatpants, out of which protruded every excess pound of flesh even as they tried their best to conceal the bulges; senior citizens wearing neatly stitched-to-size shirts and trousers who took a gentle stroll without much exertion; dozens of women covered head-to-toe in burkhas of various shades and with only their sneakers exposed, mostly accompanied by their men dressed in white or other light-coloured kurta-pajamas. Interestingly, all the T-shirts, sweatpants and salwars walked from left to right of the park alongside me, while the burkhas and kurta-pajamas with skull caps walked right to left. There were a few exceptions, but I couldn't help notice how dress codes determined the direction of the morning walk, by and large.

As I made several laps around the park, I began to notice the other characters there. Seated on the benches along the pavement were little groups of two to three men facing each other, holding copies of *Rajasthan Patrika* and other Hindi dailies and chatting in loud Gujarati. The kurta-pajamas sat with other kurta-pajamas, while the T-shirts and sweatpants sat with others of the same dress code. On the leftmost end of the lawn, a small group of middle-aged men who appeared to belong to a shakha (as they took some pledge in unison at the end of the session, raising one of their hands) practised yoga and meditation, while a bunch of college students gathered in a circle on the right end of the lawn and kept exchanging notebooks and other paperwork among themselves.

At the centre of the park was a huge open hut with a thatched roof where a couple was performing yogic breathing seated in the lotus position. Besides the lawns and walking path, the park also had an open-air fitness centre filled with calisthenics equipment, an acupressure walking track, an amphitheatre and a children's play area, most of which were unoccupied when I was walking. Lal Baug also had its irregulars that morning, including a beggar-sanyasi with a flowing beard and long hair who probably lived on one of the benches. As clumsy and appalling as he was when I started the walk, the man turned out to be smartly dressed, with oiled, groomed hair, a washed, clean kurta and bright red kumkum smeared on his forehead, by the time I finished walking. There was a young couple, runaways perhaps, too: A small-made man with an unkempt beard, wearing a headscarf, perched himself on one of the remote benches close to the railway line that passed behind the park, and next to him was a younger, much smaller girl who stuck to him as if she were in constant fear.

On the stretch of the lawn facing the entrance gate to the park, about a dozen Muslim youngsters, aged between fifteen and twenty-five, played cricket using a leather chappal for a bat and a plastic ball. They were so loud and cheerful that they naturally attracted my attention as well as that of others. While the boys cheered, argued and played fervently, a middle-aged man, probably a relative of one of them, sat a few benches away and kept an eye on the game and the boys, discreetly. All of them were clothed in white or light-coloured polyester kurta-pajamas and wore white skull caps. The players also sported beards of different lengths.

To the left of the cricketers were three other boys, almost of the same age as the younger Muslim boys, engaged in catch practice using a tennis ball. These boys were clothed in full-sleeved sweatshirts and trousers; one of them even sported a sikha, or kudumi (as we call the long tuft of hair grown at the back of the skull down south).

After walking for about forty-five minutes, by when the sun was shining bright and the temperature was warm, I sat on a bench facing the boys playing cricket. Despite using one of their chappals as a bat, the boys were engaged in a pretty intense game. The stumps at the edges of the wicket were also two pairs of chappals and the bowler chucked the plastic ball as forcefully as he could, aiming for the chappals at the batsman's end. The batsman swung his chappal-bat as hard as he could, and if there was a hit, the two batsmen ran between the wickets to the cheering of the rest of their team. Although the boys had neither regular bats nor balls, they did have a straight umpire and a leg umpire, with whom they argued for every possible catch or LBW, which was whenever the ball was in line with the chappal-wickets. To their left, the three catch-practisers stood in a triangle and played their game. While one of them swung a tennis ball high in the air, the other two tried to catch it. The boy who caught the ball now swung it in the air as the other two tried to catch. When compared with the intense cricket match that was underway just about 100 feet away, these three boys seemed to be simply doing some activity to get over their boredom.

While watching the two groups of boys, I wondered why they wouldn't play together. Even when the plastic ball got in the way of the catch-practisers, the kurta-pajama players cautiously walked towards the other side of the lawn, sought permission and picked up their ball. The catch-practisers, too, followed the same protocol and hardly got in the way of the cricketers. I sat and watched both groups of boys play for at least half an hour before returning to my room. To me, that image—of boys of the same age dressed so differently and playing separate games right next to each other in a public park, extremely cautious not to disturb the other group—defines Godhra. I decided to visit the park every morning while I was there, to see if this was a one-off affair or a regular activity.

---

In the afternoon, I took an auto rickshaw from the GSRTC bus stand to Godhra Junction Railway Station, a ten-minute ride past the busy and congested Polan Bazar, a Muslim-dominated area with very few non-Muslim shop owners. Despite the excruciating heat of the afternoon sun, the market was busy with men loading and unloading mini trucks and other carts that jammed the narrow streets. The dust, garbage and open drains that I had noticed near the bus terminus were also prevalent here, but the railway station appeared deserted when I reached. Except for a long line of green-and-yellow auto rickshaws parked outside the station, whose drivers, all of whom were clad in flowing kurta-pajamas and chitchatted with each other in little groups, there was hardly anyone at the entrance. The reservation and current booking counters were also empty. I had expected the presence of more security personnel and some vigorous checking because the twentieth anniversary of the Sabarmati Express S-6 coach-burning incident that killed around fifty-nine passengers, including several kar sevaks, was just two days away.

On the main platform, a small group of about twenty or thirty Muslim men sat next to each other on the steel benches facing the track with their duffel bags and small suitcases. Two Railway Protection Force (RPF) personnel were seated on a bench to my right and engaged in an animated discussion. Food vendors, also belonging to the minority community, selling vada pav, tea and coffee, pushed their carts to shaded, cooler parts of the platform and got busy preparing for the arrival of the next train, which was expected soon. A few other passengers, mostly young men and women, dragging heavy suitcases, kept trickling onto the platform, while I sat on a steel bench near the station master's room and watched. At exactly 1 p.m., the calm, deep voice of the muezzin from a nearby mosque, calling for afternoon prayers, silenced all other clatter at the railway station. Muslim men spread out large sheets of cloth on the railway platform and offered namaz. Even as the men were praying, the station loudspeakers announced the arrival of the Haridwar–Bandra Express, which rolled in gently on platform number one about ten minutes ahead of its scheduled arrival. All the passengers at the station had come for that train and soon got busy loading their luggage onto their respective coaches. The vada pav vendors also got busy as passengers from the train got down and crowded around them. The train halted for a good ten minutes, when all the vendors made brisk business, even as the RPF personnel walked back and forth, keeping a close watch on the passengers.

After the train departed, there was nobody left on the platform, except for me and the two RPF personnel, who were still busy discussing something. An eerie silence prevailed. About half an hour later, two saffron-draped mendicants walked into the railway station, with large cloth bags on their backs. The two quietly settled down on the same spot on the floor where the Muslim men had performed their namaz, placed their bags next to each other and lay down with their heads resting on the bags. Soaking in the monastic silence of Godhra Railway Junction that afternoon, I could not relate to the violent atmosphere that must have prevailed on the station premises twenty years ago, as more trains rolled in and out and more passengers arrived and left.

---

On 27 February 2002, at around 7.40 a.m., the Sabarmati Express had rolled into Godhra Railway Station, filled mostly with kar sevaks who were returning home from Ayodhya after participating in the Purnahuti Maha Yagna organized by the Vishwa Hindu Parishad in Ayodhya.[1] The train had halted for about five minutes when several passengers got down to buy tea, coffee and snacks from vendors who were mostly Muslim, as is the case even now in this town where Muslims constitute over 51.3 per cent of the population, according to the 2011 Census. Reports state eyewitness accounts of kar sevaks and the vendors having arguments that escalated into minor scuffles before the train left the station. Soon, the locomotive engines came to a grinding halt just outside the station, near an area called Signal Falia,[2] allegedly due to a mechanical snag, when a huge mob attacked the passengers with stones and Molotov cocktails.

---

1 Aviral Virk, 'Revisiting Sabarmati Express Fire That Englulfed Gujarat in 2002', The Quint, 1 March 2018, https://www.thequint.com/explainers/gujarat-riots-2002-godhra-sabarmati-express-fire-explained

2 Uday Mahurkar, 'Godhra massacre: Forensic report come in handy for rival politicians', *India Today*, 22 July 2002, https://www.indiatoday.in/magazine/states/story/20020722-godhra-massacre-forensic-report-come-in-handy-for-rival-politicians-794762-2002-07-22

The rest of the story has multiple versions depending on one's point of view. But the irrefutable facts of the case at the time of writing this book are that fifty-nine people, including several women and children, died in the carnage and thirty-one persons have been sentenced to life in connection with the crime, while sixty-three others, charged by the police, were acquitted. The horrific riots that followed also brought to national limelight Narendra Modi, a first-time chief minister who later rose to the highest elected office in the country and became one of the most popular Prime Ministers the country has ever had.

From the railway station, I got into an auto rickshaw and asked the driver to take me to what I was told was the latest mall in Godhra, about 8 or 9 kilometres away, just to beat the intense heat even at that time of the year. The auto rickshaw driver, a middle-aged Muslim man with a wooden leg, who referred to Godhra as his 'gaon', drove me to a DMart supermarket on the Godhra–Dahod highway. On my way, I noticed that this part of Godhra appeared so different from the busy bazar area where my hotel was located. Neat two-storey bungalows lined both sides of the highway, resembling a posh suburb you'd find in any Indian city. We also passed a boutique star-rated hotel, which boasted a banquet hall and two fine-dining restaurants, a Pantaloons showroom, Mahindra and Bajaj vehicle showrooms, and at least a handful of swank pizzerias. Despite all this, the auto rickshaw driver, whom I now came to know as Sheikh, still referred to Godhra as a his gaon. 'This is the largest mall of our gaon. This is the latest star hotel in our gaon. People are living very peacefully and there is no tension in our gaon ...' he kept repeating.

---

If one has to put the communal tension prevailing in Godhra into perspective, it is requisite for us to take a tour of the past history of communal violence in the region. This town, which is also the headquarters of Panchmahal district, has a long history of religious strife that dates back to the pre-Independence era, which the country's partition was expected to put an end to. But it didn't. An *Economic and Political Weekly* report published more than forty years ago, in October 1981, points that out.[3] Back then, Godhra town had a population of about 86,000, of whom 39,000 were Hindus and 35,000 were Muslims, while other communities made up the rest of the population. Muslims in Godhra were mainly Ghanchis, who are different from other Muslim communities like the Syeds and Bohras. In Godhra, Ghanchi Muslims remain poor, have large families and generally lack the education and progress achieved by the Bohras, who are the more affluent among Muslims and have smaller families. During Partition, a large number of Sindhis (Hindus) migrated from the Karachi area in Pakistan and settled down in Godhra. They belong to the Bhaiband sect, who are mostly petty traders, less educated and conservative when compared to the Amils, who are the more affluent Sindhis.

The Sindhis who came to Godhra during Partition with horrendous tales of suffering at the hands of Muslims added to the already volatile communal relations in the region. The communalists among the Hindus present in Godhra took advantage of this Sindhi resentment and directed it against the Ghanchis in 1948, resulting in a large-scale communal riot. According to news reports, over 3,500 properties belonging to Muslims were burnt down in Godhra town alone, forcing several Ghanchi Muslim families to flee the country, and their homes were occupied by the Sindhis who had arrived during Partition. Even at the time, arson was top choice for rioters in this region.[4]

---

3 Asghar Ali Engineer, 'Communal Riots in Godhra: A Report', *Economic and Political Weekly*, vol. 16, no. 41 (10 October 1981), pp. 1638–40.

4 Ibid.

After the 1948 riots, the next major communal flare-up happened in 1965, when around sixty Muslim homes, according to the *EPW* report, were burnt down by Sindhis and four Ghanchi Muslims were killed, including two by police, during the riots. After about fifteen years of relative peace, the Sindhis and the Ghanchis, both coming from poor and conservative backgrounds, clashed again in October 1980 after a petty quarrel between a Sindhi and Ghanchi hawker flared up uncontrollably. Arson was yet again the preferred act of violence to attack the enemy. Both Sindhis and Muslims set fire to each other's homes in rival pockets, even in far-flung areas. During that violence, a Sindhi family was burnt alive in the Signal Falia area, following which more homes were burnt and entire colonies gutted. According to reports, hundreds of homes belonging to both Hindus and Muslims were razed during this period. While minor skirmishes and outbreaks of violence continued between the Hindus and Muslims in this region, those born in Godhra and surrounding villages in Panchmahal district believed that the wounds of Partition had healed and that the region would probably not witness gruesome incidents of violence anymore.

Mehboob Yusuf Dedki, a primary school teacher from Ranipura village, approximately 25 kilometres from Godhra, also believed that such violence was buried in their past and would never happen again in his village. He is now forty-five and his large family has been in Ranipura for generations, since even before Independence. During those days, there were quite a few Dedki families spread out across villages in Panchmahal district. Mehboob vividly remembers his father frequently recalling violent memories of Partition. 'Hundreds of Muslim homes were set on fire and the families chased away. Along with the thousands of Muslims who fled to Pakistan during Partition were several of my extended family members, leaving behind just one Dedki family in our village,' the teacher told me when I caught up with him at a restaurant on the highway to Ranipura from Godhra.

But the villagers lived in peace after Partition and the Dedkis—Mehboob has five brothers and four sisters—prospered in Ranipura. At the time of the Godhra riots, the family owned two flour mills and a kirana store, besides some agricultural land, and employed at least a dozen workers for their operations. Within a span of a few hours, fifty years of hard work by the whole family was razed to the ground on 8 March 2002 by an angry Hindu mob. Mehboob clearly recalls the events that unfolded on the days preceding the attack. 'Soon after the Sabarmati Express burning happened, riots broke out all over Gujarat, but our village remained untouched as there was just one other Muslim family besides ours. Still, we sent off all the women and children to relatives' homes in Godhra, and my father, one brother and I stayed back to guard our home and businesses. Since we had the full support of our Hindu neighbours in the village, we got information on the morning of 8th March that a group was planning to attack our home that night. Soon, at least twenty-five of our Hindu neighbours accompanied the three of us in a van all the way to Godhra and returned to the village only after ensuring we were in a safe house. Later that night, our home and all our shops were burnt down, just as we had been warned,' Mehboob recounted.

From being a business owner employing about a dozen people, Mehboob was forced to work as a primary school teacher for Rs 1,350 per month in Godhra to survive, following the riots. Though the family was allotted a home by the Islamic Relief Committee, he had to work several jobs to make ends meet and ensure his children received a good education. In 2005, Mehboob started giving private tuitions to students in the evenings. When the income from that job also turned out to be insufficient, Mehboob took up another job as a front office manager for a hotel in Godhra for a salary of Rs 3,000. In 2010, his wife got a job as an Anganwadi worker, following which the family could breathe a little easier. Mehboob's salary at the primary school also increased consistently and is now at Rs 12,000. Using the little savings he had put aside for a rainy day and banking on his experience at the hotel, Mehboob has now set up a dhaba about 2 kilometres from Ranipura. Just six months ago, after two decades of staying away, Mehboob's extended family returned to their ancestral home in Ranipura. 'Now, my parents and brothers have shifted back to our village and look after the dhaba. As of now, I'm still in Godhra for my children's education, but I visit the dhaba every day,' Mehboob clarified.

I asked him if he felt safe now to move back to the village and Mehboob responded with an emphatic nod. 'It was a different time then and the entire state was in turmoil. While growing up in the village, I studied in a government school in Ranipura until class eight. In my class of about thirty students, only two of us were Muslims. But we never felt any different—we played, ate and studied like siblings. I used to help a lot of Hindu boys with their homework and they did the same for me. Even during the riots, we were able to stay in our home until the mob attacked due to the support from our Hindu neighbours. We were that close; it was their assurance that made us feel comfortable during that period. The mob that attacked our home was from outside, and we were alerted about it ahead of time. There was no enmity among our villagers then, and I don't think there is any rivalry or enmity even now. It's just that political parties try to separate us in the name of religion, and sometimes, they succeed.'

While the violence in Ranipura could be seen as an outcome of just petty politics and not borne out of organic hatred, what Mehboob and his family lost were the fruits of a lifetime of hard work. He is among the thousands of Muslims as well as Hindus across Gujarat who lost everything they had earned over several generations within a few weeks and had to rebuild life from scratch. Unlike him, many were not lucky enough to get the right opportunities to put their lives back on track. They continue to live impoverished, insecure lives even twenty years after the riots, like Feroze from Gulbarg Society.

As for Mehboob, while both his daughters have been married off, his two sons are still at school in Godhra. His eldest is in a Gujarati-medium school, while the younger one is in a private school, where he was admitted under the Right to Education Act.

---

The next morning I returned to Lal Baug a little early, as the mornings were already getting sultrier. There were many more people in the park than the previous day, and the walking path was full of middle-aged men and women walking briskly, swinging their arms and legs as wide as they could while thrusting their chests forward. The connection I had noticed between the attire of the walkers and their direction remained consistent with my earlier observation. All the skull caps, kurta-pajamas and burkhas marched right to left, while the T-shirts, shorts, sweatpants and salwars progressed in the clockwise direction. The older men with their *Dainik Jagrans* and *Rajasthan Patrikas* were seated on the benches; the yoga practitioners were on the lawn with their mats; and also present were the park's cleaning staff, along with some more volunteers wearing reflective jackets and gloves. On the left side of the lawn, the shakha was underway in exactly the same corner as before, and the couple who were meditating in the hut the previous day were seated in the lotus position again. The only folks missing at the park since my last visit were the 'runaway' couple and the beggar-sanyasi. Though it was just my second day at the park, I was already getting some friendly smiles and subtle nods of acknowledgement from other walkers whom I had seen the previous day, mostly from those coming in the opposite direction. The park's speaker system was operational and AIR FM programmes were being aired. As I walked, a soft-spoken RJ played '90s Bollywood hit songs, which were interrupted by two-minute news bulletins. About half an hour later, the Muslim boys, who had been playing cricket the previous day, arrived again as a group and hung around the children's play area. I counted them today and found there were eleven players, of whom at least three or four must have been in their early to mid-twenties. The middle-aged man who had kept a keen watch on them the previous day was, however, missing. Before I could finish my walk, the boys returned to the same part of the lawn and resumed their chappal-plastic ball cricket. Once again, I sat down on a bench to watch them play after completing my walk. Ten minutes later, the other three boys also arrived and started their catch practice session with the tennis ball. The two groups of boys played their games cautiously, aware of each other's game just as the previous morning. A little later, a group of youngsters wearing Reliance Trends T-shirts arrived at the park and sat in a circle to discuss animatedly what seemed like pertinent matters.

By around 9 a.m., the morning walkers had dwindled down to one or two in each direction but more kurta-pajama and sweatpants-T-shirt combos had settled on the benches. One thing was clear: The kurta-pajamas chatted only with one of their own, and the sweatpants-T-shirts also did the same. A little later, the four men practising yoga had signed off and gone to the juice stand at the entrance of the park to buy some fresh juice before heading home. An older man who was practising sirsasana (headstand) the previous day was again on his head, wearing the same pale yellow T-shirt and shiny blue tracks. I had also identified more tree species in the park, including wild almonds, teak and flame of the forest, as well as more ashoka and portia trees, besides the palms. Thousands of bats hung from a tall portia and a flame of the forest tree right above me, chirping violently and letting go of droppings mercilessly every time someone threw the ball high in the air. The three boys playing with the tennis ball disappeared from the park earlier than they had the previous day and were replaced by slightly older boys and girls, probably college students, who sat in a circle under a large portia tree and chatted. I sat on the bench for some more time watching the young men play cricket until the heat forced me to return to the comfort of my air-conditioned room.

In Godhra, if you like to eat good non-vegetarian food, Polan Bazar near the railway station is your destination. While there are one or two restaurants in other parts of the town serving non-vegetarian food too, good and authentic non-vegetarian food is available only at the restaurants in the Polan Bazar area, where most of the lower-income group Muslims work and live. With my craving for meat reaching a crescendo after just a few weeks in Gujarat, I took an auto rickshaw to Polan Bazar later that afternoon. Unlike at Lal Baug, kurta-pajama-skull caps are the most preferred attire among men in and around the Polan Bazar area. Like the rest of Godhra, the bazar was noisy, dusty and full of cheerful people going about their day as usual. At the central junction of the bazar, a giant, magnificent Indian tricolour waved atop a tall flagpole of about 50 feet or so. With long, flowing beards making a resurgence as the in-thing in men's fashion globally, hair stylists could take a trip down to Polan Bazar to draw inspiration on innovative shapes and colours for facial hair, as beards of almost every possible size, density and shade were sported there. I spotted thick, well-groomed, flowing black beards that could be used to advertise hair oils, trimmed salt-and-pepper beards shaped like an ice cream cone, free-flowing silver-white beards that almost brushed the huge paunches of older men, thin, barely visible noodle-string beards, even brownish-grey henna-dyed goatee beards and adolescent facial hair that was just sprouting off the smooth faces of young boys. Finding a man without a beard would be a challenge out in this bazar. A few women were also around, dressed in black or brown burkhas, busily arguing with vegetable cart vendors and other roadside shop owners. At the restaurant where I had butter naan and kadhai chicken, just about one or two men wore trousers and shirts/T-shirts like me.

After relishing my first meat dish in weeks, I approached a few business owners in the bazar to talk to them about their town, but most of them shooed me away, claiming they were either too busy or not interested in speaking to media people. Considering that the twentieth anniversary of the Godhra train burning was just two days away and one of the prime accused in the case, who had been absconding all these years, was arrested from Signal Falia just about a week before my visit, their reluctance was understandable. I kept walking in and out of every shop in that stretch, trying to strike up a conversation with someone, when a young man running a travel agency told me to my face that no media, including social media, was allowed in Polan Bazar. He even warned his friend, a hotelier who was present with him and seemed more friendly, to stay away from me. But the hotelier asked me to go and meet a maulana, who was also the principal of the Polan Bazar Urdu School, located at the central junction of the bazar, where the national flag fluttered in the breeze from atop a giant pole. He also offered to call the maulana and put in a word.

The Polan Bazar Urdu School functioned out of a robust concrete multi-storey building on a moderate-sized campus. A middle school with classes up to eight, it accommodated about 500 students, both girls and boys. As I entered, about 100 children from the lower primary classes, seated on a long, cemented corridor of the ground floor, recited the days of the week in English, Urdu and Gujarati one after another. While all the boys were clothed in their traditional kurta-pajamas, the little girls wore colourful dresses with headscarves.

Maulana Iqbal Hussain Bokda was just forty-nine but already an accomplished scholar and a respected man in the community. Besides working as the principal of the school, he was pursuing his PhD in history at Shri Govind Guru University in Godhra and had also earned the title of Maulana for his accomplishments in Islamic studies. Bokda was also an author of two books on the contribution of Muslims to Gujarat and on the role of Muslims in the 1857 Sepoy Mutiny. Both the books have been published in Gujarati and Urdu. Unlike other community leaders I had approached, the maulana readily agreed to talk to me.

Against the backdrop of the tiny tots reciting Urdu rhymes and numerals sonorously after their teacher as if they were musical notes, the maulana and I chatted for almost half an hour, touching upon various aspects of Muslim life in Godhra, specifically in the Polan Bazar area, which was '100 per cent Muslim and being ghettoized', according to him.

In our discussion, we touched upon many topics, but the one aspect of my observations that I wanted more clarity on was the scenes I had witnessed at Lal Baug: The clear separation between Muslims and non-Muslims in every aspect, including the games children played. Coming from Chennai, I had never noticed such stark discrimination, although there are predominantly Muslim neighbourhoods in my hometown too. Both adults and children mingle freely and often there; one cannot even find any distinction between members of the two communities until names are called out. But in Godhra, and in the rest of Gujarat too, the situation was very different, and I wanted the maulana's take on it.

'Muslims here continue to remain poor and uneducated, and that is the core of the problem,' he said, and went on to add that despite the presence of quite a few Urdu schools in and around the city, just about 1 per cent of the Muslim population are postgraduates and hardly 4–5 percent are graduates even in 2022. Girls from Muslim neighbourhoods hardly continue their education beyond class eight and are often married off even before they turn eighteen. With most Muslim parents admitting their children only to Urdu-medium schools, inter-religious mixing among children remains a pipe dream. Hindus and students from other religions mostly study at schools in Hindu neighbourhoods. As a result, the segregation among children happens at a very early age in Gujarat and, according to the maulana, the scenes I had witnessed at Lal Baug were an outcome of that exclusion.

Since most Muslim students study only in Urdu-medium schools and there is a shortage of Urdu-medium colleges and higher education centres, as opposed to Gujarati- or English-medium institutions, the Muslim youth hardly has any scope for pursuing quality higher education. So they are forced to discontinue studies and take up the family business, often at a very young age, according to the maulana. And for those few scholars who continue higher education in Urdu and Gujarati, such as himself, job opportunities are very few in the rapidly evolving and globalized economy. They are then forced to look for opportunities only within the community, which isolates them even more.

I realized that these problems were quite clear to community leaders like the maulana, but how would they address them? Besides, this is not an issue with the entire Muslim community, for there are affluent Muslim neighbourhoods in Godhra and its surrounding areas, where children go to private schools, adults either run large businesses in swank complexes or leave for jobs in Mumbai, Surat and other big cities, and they do not exist as isolated communities. It is the poor Muslims who are often at the receiving end of this social exclusion. The core of the issue is the lack of economic growth among the community that forces adults to continue familial occupations and children to study in religious or free community schools, as the maulana pointed out. To me, the lack of economic growth and lack of a solid political space go hand in hand. I had discussed this with other Muslim leaders like

Wazir Khan in Juhapura too: Why don't the Muslims in this region consolidate their vote bank and get their demands fulfilled?

Despite having a sizeable population of over 50 per cent of the 1,62,000 population in Godhra, Muslims have not been able to consolidate the community votes and produce a leader to take up their cause in a democratic space that is theirs. When I asked the maulana about it, he said, 'The Muslim community here has not paid attention to it until now. The problem is that nobody has really thought of it yet, and that is mainly due to lack of education. We have still not understood how to use our vote bank.'

While a vast majority of Muslims, especially from Godhra, have no grasp over any language other than Gujarati or Urdu, which is a major deterrent in taking their cause forward, those like the maulana, who have received a good education and have sound political awareness, have also not come forward. When I asked him about it, he said that it requires a lot of effort to take steps in that direction. 'It is a problem, a vast problem.'

Before the maulana could elaborate on his response, the 1 p.m. muezzin's call for prayers blared from the loudspeakers of the mosque on the other side of the market junction and the schoolchildren immediately began reciting out loud religious hymns in Urdu. As he prepared to leave for his afternoon prayers, I asked him if he or the other residents of Polan Bazar regretted not having left for Pakistan during Partition, like many of their neighbours or relatives had.

A little disturbed by the question, the principal walked me to the corridor and pointed at the tricolour flying high. 'You see that tiranga? Since 2005 that flag has been hoisted every day at 7 a.m. and is brought down at 5 p.m. You tell me if you can find this anywhere else in India. The tiranga hoisted every single day! If one person cannot do it, someone else does, but the tiranga is hoisted every day. You know why? It is because we are Indians and we believe in this country,' he asserted as we walked out of the school.

After he left for his prayers, I waited under the awning of a tyre puncture repair shop outside the school for my auto rickshaw driver, Mehboob, who had also gone to the same mosque for his afternoon prayers. Ahead of me, dozens and dozens of men and boys of different ages came out of the mosque one after another and headed towards their homes and workplaces. As they walked past me, most of them stared at me, and some even spoke among themselves while looking at me.

Standing there, I recalled how unusual and out of place I had found those boys clad in kurta-pajama-skull caps playing chappal-cricket in that lush green park. Here at the busy Polan Bazar junction, I was the odd one out, dressed in a maroon cotton T-shirt and jeans, sporting a sleeveless fishing jacket on top of it. It was clear that my presence was making at least a few people curious and concerned.

And that is probably our biggest failure as a nation. Hindus and Muslims have been coexisting in this country for so many centuries, and yet, at that very moment, I felt like I was in a different world—a world that made me uncomfortable. That is probably also how the Muslims in Godhra feel when they go to Hindu-dominated areas. Perhaps the fact that we still exist in different worlds, so oblivious to the presence of the other, is at the core of the problem that Gandhi spoke about a hundred years ago. Or it could just be a problem of perception and our inability to see the world the way others do.

# Bardoli, Surat District

> The Bardoli triumph was unique in that it compelled not only the nation's but the whole Empire's attention, and the justice and moderation of the people's demand won practically the nation's sympathy. It was unique in that it was fought by perhaps one of the meekest of the talukas in India, in that it affected the Revenue Department whose dispositions, it was up to now believed, not even the gods may question, and it compelled a mighty Government, pledged to crush the movement, to yield within a fortnight of the pledge.[1]
>
> —*The Story of Bardoli,* Mahadev Desai.

MY TRIP TO BARDOLI WAS A SWEET ONE, QUITE literally. The air I breathed began to dulcify within minutes after the MEMU train to Nandurbar rumbled out of the ever-busy Surat Railway Station, thanks to the acres and acres of sugar cane crops popping out of green fields on both sides

1 Mahadev Desai, *The Story of Bardoli: Being a History of the Bardoli Satyagraha of 1928 and Its Sequel* (Ahmedabad: Navajivan Publishing House, 1929), p. 232.

of the railway line. The spectacle of ripe black-and-yellow canes as far as the eye could see, in contrast to the arid lands surrounding Ahmedabad and Godhra, mollified my senses all the way to Bardoli. A little after Chalthan station, the pleasant odour became stronger and sedating as sugar factories dotted the landscape. In dry Gujarat, this was the closest I could get to satiating my craving for alcohol.

At around 7.30 p.m., the MEMU reached Bardoli Railway Station, a modest two-platform stopover with neither an auto rickshaw stand nor a taxi stand. Beyond the station, this historic town resembled the congested suburb of any big city: Shops with flashing neon name boards lined both sides of the Surat–Bardoli Road; cars, two-wheelers and auto rickshaws jostled for the limited road space available; pavements were narrow and dirty as in most other suburbs; and people seemed so busy even at that hour. I fixed an auto rickshaw to take me to the hotel I had booked a room at, next to the main bus terminus, and was on my way, when a young woman waved her hand and also got into the vehicle—a common practice in this part of the country, where even if you have agreed to pay the auto driver full fare for the ride, he still picks up and drops off people along the way to make a little extra and nobody really complains.

The lady, who was slightly on the heavier side, was wearing a red cotton top and black jeans and had straight shoulder-length hair. She also had a matching red mask covering her nose and mouth. From her looks, I thought she must be a student or a young intern, as we had just passed a chartered accountants' training institute. But soon after getting into the auto rickshaw, the lady called someone on her mobile and kept talking all through the journey, and I couldn't help but eavesdrop. She made three calls, and from her conversations, I deduced that she was working either in a bank or some other financial institution. Her first interaction was with a client, then she talked to a car dealer and later to her boss. All three conversations were in such drastically different tones that it made me curious about her.

Her first conversation was with a male client regarding his application for a car loan that was getting very delayed. She spoke to him in an extremely humble voice and with the most respectful salutations. '*Haan ji ... haan ji ... bilkul ji ... maaf kijiye ... sorry ji ... bilkul ... bilkul.*' Besides apologizing at least half a dozen times during the conversation, she told the client that there was nothing to worry about. If his last application did not work out, she would put him with another dealer who could finish the sale for him. After ending that conversation, the woman spoke to someone from a car dealer's office. This time, she was as rude as her age and sophistication would allow. She curtly informed the dealer that she wanted a response by Saturday evening (this was a Friday) or she would go with someone else and blasted him for directly contacting the client and updating him with the details, instead of getting back to her. From what I heard, I gathered that the loan was getting processed for a pretty expensive car. After ending the second call, she called her boss, again a male voice, to whom she was very casual and friendly. She told him that both the buyer and dealer were trying to screw them and asked for his advice. Unfortunately for me, the girl reached her destination and got off the auto rickshaw while still on the call with her boss.

Two minutes later, the auto rickshaw driver stopped outside a building complex that flashed the name of my hotel on its second floor. Since I could not find a reception area or any kind of entrance beyond the huge parking lot, I asked the driver again if that was the hotel. He pointed at the neon board, asked me to get out and left. On the ground floor of the building was a non-vegetarian restaurant with an open dining facility and right next to it was a kulfi shop, both full of people. To the right of the restaurant was a retail outlet for the menswear brand Killer, while on the other side of the road was a Food King outlet claiming to serve 'the best chicken in town' on a flashy hoarding. Next to Food King was Chai Sutta Bar. Was I still in Gujarat? Was this the land of the famous satyagraha? During the past two weeks that I had spent in Gujarat, finding a non-vegetarian restaurant had always been a challenge and had required effort. Here in Bardoli, the area surrounding the main bus terminus was full of outlets selling fresh chicken kebabs, mutton biryani and every other non-vegetarian dish except those with beef. I also noticed there was a certain finesse in the décor of all these outlets, which clearly wasn't small-townish.

But more surprises were in store within my first hour in Bardoli. As I couldn't find the entrance to the hotel, I went to the restaurant on the ground floor and asked for directions. The man at the reception told me that the hotel's entrance was on the other side of the building. 'Go by the road,' he said. So I went to the road and started walking. Before I could take a few steps, an auto rickshaw almost rammed into me and its driver asked me if I needed a ride. Tired after the long journey from Godhra and struggling with my luggage, I agreed even though I knew the hotel entrance was just on the other side of the building, about 100 metres of walk by road. 'Will cost you Rs 100,' said the middle-aged auto driver. I was shocked and told him that I just wanted to get to the other side of the building. He gave detailed directions of a route spanning 5 or 6 kilometres to reach my destination. 'Take it or leave it. You're not going to get another auto rickshaw here at this hour,' he threatened. When I took out my phone, opened Google Maps and showed him the distance to my destination, the man suddenly realized that I could just walk the distance and said that he had mistaken the name I had mentioned for some other hotel, before scooting.

Such experiences must be familiar to anyone reaching an unfamiliar town at odd hours with luggage in hand, but perhaps I was not expecting that in Bardoli—land of the most famous satyagraha that arguably changed the course of India's freedom struggle. To put my experiences into perspective, let's travel through the history of Bardoli.

---

The year was 1926. Bardoli, the easternmost taluk of Surat district, comprising 137 villages with an area of 222 square miles, was bound in the north by the Tapti river, Mandvi taluk in the east, the kingdom of the Baroda Gaekwads in the west and Jalapur taluk in the south.[2] The majority of Bardoli's population, of around 87,000, were farmers and agricultural labourers.

Back then, the British government periodically reviewed the revenue assessment for agricultural lands in their territory by forming a committee that would suggest a hike in the taxes to be paid by the farmers, based on the prevailing economic conditions, crop yield and the economy in general. The last land settlement due for Bardoli taluk had been calculated in 1896 and a fresh reassessment was due in 1926. The settlement officer who was entrusted with the job in 1924 recommended an increase of 25 per cent over the existing rates, while also raising twenty-three villages from a lower taxation group to a higher one. Thus, their taxes were increased by over 30 per cent.

The farmers of Bardoli opposed this unreasonable hike in taxes, petitioned the government for a review of the new tax rates and began agitations against the hike in mid-1926. When their representations to the government failed to yield any success and the revised settlement was fixed as final, the agitators held a conference in Bardoli in September 1927. It was attended by thousands of farmers who resolved to withhold payment of the revised amount, which invariably led to a chain of events that culminated in the famous Bardoli Satyagraha of 1928.

---

2 Mahadev Desai, *The Story of Bardoli*, p. 11.

What is a satyagraha? It is a question that might have triggered a myriad of reactions, ranging from a contemptuous scorn to the sort of pity reserved for twits, some seventy-five to eighty years ago, when it was used as the primary tool of resistance by the Indian National Congress against the British upon the insistence of Mahatma Gandhi. But I feel the question is pertinent in today's nuclear-powered, economically vibrant and jingoistic India.

When it was first used, people in authority dismissed satyagraha simply as a form of passive resistance—meant for those who can't resist actively. But they soon realized that it was far more potent than just passive resistance. The evolution of satyagraha as a tool of resistance against oppressive forces did not begin in Bardoli or Champaran but in distant Transvaal, South Africa, during the early 1900s, when Mahatma Gandhi was there. When the Black Act, which was highly discriminatory against Indians, was introduced by the local government, the large Indian community in Transvaal decided to protest against it.[3] The proposed Act did not recognize Hindu marriages as legal, besides forcing all Indians to register themselves and produce the certificate whenever demanded. A meeting that was held in Transvaal on 11 September 1906 to organize protests against the Black Act gave birth to a unique form of resistance, which later came to be known as satyagraha. One of the participants of the meeting, Sheth Haji Habib, a very old and experienced member of the Indian community in South Africa, urged those gathered at the meeting to never agree to the Act and take an oath in the name of God to never submit to the government. The idea of taking a public oath in the name of God appealed to Gandhi so much that he began to envision the various possibilities of a group of people taking an oath in the name of God and sticking to it, irrespective of its consequences.

---

[3] M.K. Gandhi, *Satyagraha in South Africa* (London: Forgotten Books, 2018), pp. 108–109.

A large number of the Indians gathered at the meeting took the oath against the Black Act and stuck to it. In time, their resilience against the South African government's pressure tactics got wide coverage and recognition. Back then, the peaceful protests against the Black Act were called 'passive resistance', but as the resistance movement progressed, other communities in South Africa began to take notice. Gandhi and his associates who were heading the movement felt that the term 'passive resistance' did not do justice to the struggle they were engaged in and searched for an Indian word or phrase for the same. The deeper meaning of the struggle taken up by the Indians in Transvaal was discussed in detail in the publication *Indian Opinion* and its readers were urged to suggest a new name for the movement.

In his book *Satyagraha in South Africa*, Gandhi described the genesis of the word satyagraha:[4]

> Shri Maganlal Gandhi was one of the competitors [to suggest a name for the movement] and he suggested the word 'Sadagraha' meaning 'firmness in a good cause'. I liked the word, but it did not fully represent the whole idea I wished it to connote. I therefore corrected it to Satyagraha. Truth (Satya) implies love, and firmness (agraha) engenders and therefore serves as a synonym for force. I thus began to call the Indian movement 'Satyagraha' that is to say, the Force which is born of Truth and Love or non-violence.

As the resistance movement progressed, Gandhi and his associates fine-tuned the principles of satyagraha. He later defined it in simple terms as a 'soul force', which was exactly the opposite of armed or brute force.

---

4 *Satyagraha in South Africa*, 'The Advent of Satyagraha', p. 109.

After his return to India, Gandhi was fully convinced that satyagraha was the most effective way to fight the massive British administrative machinery and began to groom his associates for minor satyagrahas to protest against the unjust policies of the British government. The protest against revised land settlement rates in Bardoli was the first major such protest that gave Indians confidence on the efficacy of Satyagraha.

The resolution to refrain from paying revised land settlement rates in Bardoli taluk and conduct a satyagraha campaign until the government accepted the old assessment amount was passed on 12 February 1928. Led by Sardar Vallabhbhai Patel, the satyagraha was meticulously planned, involving members of all communities in the taluk and even included a communications department to ensure that people in Gujarat and the rest of the country were updated on all developments. On the planned date, a small but committed group of people began their satyagraha protest. They resolved to gladly accept any form of torture for refusing to pay the taxes but never to succumb to the pressure; neither would they react physically or otherwise. The campaign, despite minor setbacks in the beginning, gained strength gradually as the days progressed.

The people's participation increased steadily, with more and more willing to subject themselves to torture and harassment at the hands of the British government for non-payment of the taxes but refusing to give up their protest. The participation of women in the campaign was near complete and turned out to be a major factor in its success. Although there were only a few women in the first few daily meetings of the satyagraha, after a few weeks their number increased steadily and sometimes they even had their own meetings. Several instances of women volunteering to send their husbands to prison as punishment for non-payment of taxes have also been reported and grabbed the attention of the nation back then. As the days passed, the no-tax movement gained more and more strength and news reports on the resolute satyagrahis spread across the country. Youth associations, farmers' groups and even pandits from Bombay and several other parts of the country collected funds and sent them to Bardoli to support the satyagrahis who faced every hardship thrust upon them by the government bravely.

Soon, the mill workers and those employed in other industries in neighbouring Surat and other cities, too, joined in and ensured that all production activity got stalled. When news of the Bardoli protests reached England, there was a section of the British who wanted an amicable settlement with the satyagrahis. Eventually, the British government accepted to form an inquiry committee to look into the revised rates and acceded to the satyagrahis' demands of paying only old tax rates until the committee completed its inquiry. The spectacular success of the Bardoli satyagraha resonated across India and the slogan 'Bardolize India' became the mantra for the country's freedom struggle. Satyagraha, as a weapon of resistance, spread everywhere following the triumph in Bardoli.

Why was Bardoli chosen for such a satyagraha?

Unlike other parts of Gujarat, Bardoli was blessed with certain salient features that made it most suitable for an experiment of that nature back in the early 1900s. One of the most important reasons was that a considerable number of Gandhi's satyagrahis in South Africa were from Bardoli and had given enough proof of their courage and determination there. It was Gandhi's familiarity with the satyagrahis of Bardoli that led him to approve the taluk as suitable for a mass civil disobedience campaign in 1921–22, according to Mahadev Desai.[5] Although the civil disobedience movement plan was dropped due to other developments, Gandhi's followers in the region undertook constructive activities observing strict discipline. Over the years, most villagers gave up alcohol, took up spinning khadi and lived an austere life, which eventually reflected in the low crime rate in the taluk, and the citizens of

---

5 Mahadev Desai, *The Story of Bardoli*, pp. 12–13.

Bardoli came to be known as the most law-abiding lot. All these factors made Bardoli most congenial for a satyagraha campaign. It was that spirit of satyagraha I had come looking for when I had boarded the MEMU train from Surat.

---

My hotel in Bardoli was a block away from Linear Bus Station, a large campus with adequate space and bus bays for long-distance buses to park, pick up passengers and proceed to the next destination. On the other side of the station was the bazar area cluttered with eateries that served pooris, chapatis, pav bhaji, vada pav and other lighter snacks. Sweet shops and cold drink stalls were also present in significant numbers. Though shops in the bazar area were small, crowded and packed together, I could spot quite a few clothing brand outlets, pizzerias, even swank cafeterias selling cappuccino, espresso, etc., alongside regular kirana stores filled with customers, especially during the evening hours.

Roaming around in the bazar area and chitchatting with random shopkeepers and their customers, I found that most residents did not make a big deal of the historic significance of their town; some of the youth weren't even aware of the satyagraha or their ancestors' role in the freedom movement. Overall, I found nothing unusual or interesting—yet another small town in India—but for large masts hosting the tricolour at important junctions. The Bardoli of the satyagrahis, sugar cane farmers and other peasants who had risen in protest against a mighty imperial power, women who had stood shoulder to shoulder with their men and fought for their rights, was nowhere to be seen. When I spoke about this to the manager of my hotel, he told me that I was searching in the wrong place. 'To see what happened to those peasants, you have to go to Baben. On the way, don't forget to drink sugar cane juice from Asia's largest sugar factory,' he advised.

So I took an auto rickshaw from Linear Bus Station next morning, after confirming the fare was the same as locals typically pay, and headed to Baben. We drove through the bazar, went past the Bardoli Sugar Factory, claimed to be one of Asia's largest, a few plush residential neighbourhoods and reached Baben in just under ten minutes or so. A grand signboard sprouting out of a well-maintained lawn by the roadside welcomed us. The signage and the vista behind it were so unlike the rest of Bardoli—sheer opulence lay ahead of me as the auto rickshaw turned into the wide multi-laned Bardoli–Mota Road towards Vidyabharti College. An advertisement billboard welcoming visitors to the newest and best mall in town, Callista The Mall, lay ahead as we drove. Along the road was a long line of posh villa communities interrupted by the occasional multi-storey apartment complex in between some of them. Apart from these buildings were acres and acres of sugar cane fields as far as the eye could see.

I got out of the auto rickshaw at Callista The Mall and walked in. Unlike the DMart in Godhra, Callista was indeed a mall but still under construction, with just one wing open, housing Pantaloons, Reliance Trends, at least three different pizza outlets, a coffee shop and a huge parking lot that was reasonably filled for a hot weekday afternoon. The sight to behold was, however, exactly on the other side of the road.

Greenish-brown sugar cane fields sated my view. Against its backdrop were beautiful row villas with off-white walls, sloped peach-coloured roofs topped with white chimneys protruding towards the sky. Despite the scorching sun that afternoon, the fields were full of labourers who chopped the fully grown brown canes from the root upwards with their sickles and bunched them together. Dozens of skinny men and women with brown-olive sunburnt skin tied these canes together and loaded them onto bullock carts. The carts were filled with these sugar cane piles to such an extent that they resembled giant porcupines from a distance, with the two bulls forming the face of the porcupine. The weight of the sugar cane dumped onto the cart was so much that the canes almost swept the road clean as the bulls marched towards the sugar factory. The men who rode the carts had to shout and scream at the bulls to make them climb the tar-topped road from the fields due to the unbearable weight they were carrying. As one cart left, the next got filled, while the workers shouted and screamed at the bulls and at one another, trying to get the bulls to climb up the road after which the ride became relatively smoother. And inside the mall, hundreds of construction workers were engaged in constructing its second wing, supervised by two men wearing yellow plastic helmets, probably the overseeing engineers.

Next to Callista The Mall was the sprawling Vidyabharti College campus, with its tall palm trees and lavish parking lots. As it was a Saturday, there were hardly any people on campus. Facing the college on the other side of the road and to my right was another swank mall called Empire Square, which was open and operational. But on that afternoon only about half a dozen of its outlets, mostly eateries, were open. Not a traditional mall that one finds in big cities, Empire Square had a long central courtyard, both sides of which were lined with shops ranging from travel agencies to cigarette sellers and tea/coffee outlets. The courtyard had a row of benches where groups of youngsters, both boys and girls, presumably from the campus, sat and chatted, sipping tea and smoking cigarettes. Even here, opulence was all around me.

I walked the length of the courtyard looking for a nice restaurant but couldn't find one. So I returned to an organic food supermarket at the entrance to the mall, which also had a bistro on the first floor. The supermarket, with plush, shiny, wooden interiors, had very few local vegetables, while the cold storage section was filled with avocados, kiwis, Washington apples, Australian oranges, etc. The regular racks were also filled with food and grains that were mostly imported. Hershey's Kisses, Toblerone and other expensive chocolates lined the billing counter of this supermarket, where I was the only customer. I walked upstairs to the empty bistro and ordered a Mexican pizza and a kiwi mojito (obviously the virgin version). From the first-floor glass panel of the bistro, I could see the off-white, grey and peach roofs of more villa communities of different shapes and sizes in between the vast sugar cane fields. Inside the bistro, the speakers blared the hit song '*Saami saami*' from the film *Pushpa*, while a group of boys and girls sat on stone benches below and chatted, sharing drags off a brown cigarette. The Baben I was in did not even remotely resemble the Bardoli where a satyagraha could have taken place. Baben had truly transformed into an international village or suburb right in the heart of Gandhi's Gujarat. A chat with one of the employees of the organic farm fresh store confirmed my suspicion. 'Baben has very few local residents. This region is full of NRI homes. All the villas that you see from here are empty for most of the year. The owners live in the US, the UK or some other country and come to their hometown once a year to spend some time with relatives. Until then, local caretakers like me maintain the homes and even use them if we need to,' the waiter, a tall man in his twenties, said. 'This region is home to the Patels of the world who want to replicate their worlds here,' he clarified.

The global Patels truly deserve such a haven in their hometown for their sheer entrepreneurial spirit, if not anything else. I know from personal experience! About twenty years ago, when my wife and I lived in Atlanta, US, we had gone on a late evening drive to Chattanooga at the Georgia–Tennessee border and got lost, thanks to a sudden thunderstorm that night. Worried about our safety in a remote, conservative part of the country, we stopped at a rustic motel on the Georgia–Tennessee border and approached the front office cautiously, as the region is known for its racist past. To our surprise, an Indian was at the reception even at that hour and introduced himself as a Patel—I don't recall his first name but I couldn't forget the last. He did not have rooms available for us, but he immediately called up his friends. A White couple living nearby arranged for our stay in their guest bedroom for the night, so we didn't have to go searching for a motel in the middle of a thunderstorm. The next morning when I went to thank him, he also offered a bit of advice: 'Get a green card soon and buy a motel instead of a home.'

---

While present-day Bardoli, with its chai-sutta bars, swank malls and gated villa communities, has certainly moved on from its satyagraha past, there are still isolated bubbles where that spirit of early-twentieth-century Bardoli continues to be barely alive. Sheer serendipity led me to one such bubble on a warm afternoon. Having completed my meandering in this historic town, I decided to pay a visit to the Swaraj Ashram, the former home of Sardar Vallabhbhai Patel that is now maintained as a tourist destination, on Station Road, just to take it off my to-do list as I was only expecting something similar to the Sabarmati Ashram but on a smaller scale.

For the most part, my hunch turned out to be right. At around 1 p.m. or so on that weekday afternoon, I was the first visitor of the day. The large campus was like a framed photograph from the past. But for a receptionist at the visitors' cabin in the entrance, there was not a soul present at that hour. After checking with the middle-aged male receptionist on the dos and don'ts (as there is no entry fee) at the ashram, I walked through an open central courtyard, where the tricolour was flying high atop a giant pole. To the right of the flag was a well-maintained nineteenth-century home with sloped roofing. The doors and windows of the house were painted with a fresh coat of sky-blue paint, while the brick wall was coated with red oxide. Behind a wooden bench at the front portico was a plaque that claimed the property was 'Sardar Patel's Country Resort'. 'Here lived Gujarat's great leader Vallabhbhai Patel, who in the year 1928 led the cultivators of Bardoli tehsil in a non-violent no-tax campaign on the issue of enhanced land—tax imposed to be levied by the British government. From here, under his leadership, the meek, unarmed peasantry of Bardoli challenged the might of the British Empire (on which the sun never set) and baffled them,' the first paragraph on the plaque read. It also mentioned Sardar's interest in gardening, which was amply evident in the tall trees, shrubs and flowering plants that surrounded the house even now.

After walking around the locked house photographing the deceased leader's belongings, including a horse cart, reclining chair and other well-preserved artefacts, I sat down on a bench under a neem tree and enjoyed a quiet siesta, wondering if the great leader also did the same on steamy summer afternoons. I sat for almost an hour outside Sardar Nivas and did not see a single visitor walk in. Bored out my wits, I went back to the front office to find out if this was the norm or if there were visitors only during weekends and other occasions, and if there was some freedom fighter with whom I could talk about the satyagraha. The man at the reception told me that people did come to the ashram during weekends, but weekday visitors were mostly from the Sardar Kanya Vidyalaya located within the campus. He also suggested that I visit the school campus to get a feel of what went on in the ashram. 'Ms Kalarthi would be glad to show you her school. She would also be the best person to talk to about the satyagraha,' the receptionist said, and directed me down a dirt road that led to the rear exit of the ashram's main campus. A wrought iron gate, also painted blue, welcomed visitors to the Sardar Kanya Vidyalaya.

If Sardar's home was a framed photograph from the past, Sardar Kanya Vidyalaya was truly an intimate postcard from an era that is gradually and systematically getting erased from Gujarat.

Looking back at the few endearing hours I spent at the institution, the most striking image that comes to mind is that of an empty corridor leading to a neatly arranged row of rubber slippers, with blue flaps and white soles, of slightly varying sizes in one of the open rooms of the school. The organized manner in which the slippers were arranged in a school where only teenage girls (students of classes nine and ten) studied spoke so much of the disciplined life they led. Taken on a tour by one of the administrative staff at the Sardar Kanya Vidyalaya, I was stunned by the neat and organized manner in which the girls maintained every part of the campus, be it the toilets or the kitchen, which were purposefully built next to each other, the library, classrooms or even the dormitory. I had walked in unannounced on a weekday afternoon just a couple of hours after lunch, but the kitchen and canteen had no semblance of any recent activity: The steel plates were washed, dried and neatly arranged. The cooking and serving utensils were clean and dry, with not a morsel of food to be found anywhere. The teachers, students and staff were so quiet on the campus that had it not been for the guided tour, I would have thought the school was still closed due to the pandemic.

After taking a tour of the various departments, including the library, students' handicrafts section and the computer room that was only recently set up, I walked into one of the classrooms, where a bunch of girls dressed neatly in white round-neck shirts and long blue skirts were seated cross-legged on the floor with a low stool serving as a table in front of them, engrossed in a lecture given by one of the teaching staff. When I walked in, the girls immediately wished me 'Namaste' and returned to their lessons, ignoring my presence. Only after a tour of the school could I even imagine the discipline and cleanliness that must have prevailed at the Gandhi ashrams during his time. In all of Bardoli, this school was the only place that reminded me of Gandhi and his principles so far.

Octogenarian Niranjanaben Mukulbhai Kalarthi, who has been running the Sardar Kanya Vidyalaya since 1966 with missionary zeal, was with a guest when I had reached there and had sent an associate who explained the work that went behind what I had seen. Education in this institution did not begin and end with books. The eighty-six students (fifty-one in class ten and thirty-five in class nine) were handpicked by Ms Kalarthi from the surrounding tribal villages and brought here to transform not just their lives but also their families and communities. A typical day at the school begins at 5 a.m. with prayers, followed by the students cleaning the campus. After this, the girls split into groups and prepare breakfast for all of them. After breakfast, the students clean the kitchen and canteen before heading to the classrooms. All three meals in the residential school are prepared by the students with the help of guardians. From making their beds in the morning and cleaning the toilets to making rotis for breakfast and learning computer science in the evening—the mission of the Sardar Kanya Vidyalaya is to provide all these life skills along with the academic proficiency necessary to lead a productive life.

'It is my life's mission,' Niranjanaben told me later that afternoon, her contagiously cheerful demeanour already energizing me that sultry afternoon although we had met just a few minutes ago. 'Gandhiji always said choose one problem and dedicate your life to solving it. I did just that. In 1966, I went on a tour of rural Gujarat and found the plight of women, especially tribal women, so deplorable that I decided to do something about it and started this school. If you can reverse one social problem, I think your life is worth it,' Niranjanaben reiterated that afternoon in her airy, modest and brick-walled quarters adjacent to the classrooms. Dressed in a milk-white saree and bubbling with energy, the lady spoke with a captivating smile that seemed to be a permanent fixture on her face. 'I've also decided to live here, as I can always keep an eye on the girls,' she said with a wink.

Since starting the school, Niranjanaben has successfully educated over 6,000 girls, mostly tribals. 'Six thousand girls and not one has failed yet. My school has 100 per cent results, always. My girls have become nurses, lawyers, teachers, lecturers, and are shining in so many other fields. Many have gone back to their villages, where they impart the knowledge they gained here and make a difference. This is my life's purpose,' the 2021 Nari Shakti Puraskar awardee asserted.

Niranjanaben's father, Uttamchand Shah, a close associate of Mahatma Gandhi and Sardar Vallabhbhai Patel, was pursuing his graduation at Wilson College in Mumbai when he heard Gandhi speak at his campus one day and decided to become his follower. Coming from a well-to-do family, Uttamchand bequeathed all his wealth and joined the Sabarmati Ashram as a full-timer to serve the country. The ashram was where Niranjanaben and her siblings were born and raised. 'Since we always grew up on the ashram premises, we never got in touch with the outside world and material comforts never mattered to us,' proudly recalled Niranjanaben, an alumna of Gujarat Vidyapith, founded by Gandhi. 'I had no money when I started the school, and after all these years I still have no money, but the school goes on.'

Having finished her MA and MEd, Niranjanaben had the choice to take up teaching in colleges as a professor but gave it up to begin her school. Soon, she fell in love with Mukulbhai Kalarthi, also an academic, who was twenty years older than her and a Dalit. The couple tied the knot despite the social pressure prevailing at the time and her mother and elder brother objecting to the union. 'I knew he was the right person who would help me pursue my passion. My passion was this school and I have been at it all my life.'

Despite her age, Niranjanaben's day begins at 5 a.m., when she wakes up along with the students. 'I know all the girls who are studying now, and the ones that have passed out of my school, personally. I interview them and their families before granting admission. Here admissions are not based on one's competence or qualification but their need. The neediest students get admitted to this school,' she reiterated. And her guidance doesn't end with the girls graduating from class ten. 'They can come to me any time. Even later in life, if they have marital trouble, family trouble or any kind of problem, the girls know that they can always trust me and have a home here. In all these years, not even one of my girls has died by suicide, a malaise common among tribal women,' she said, beaming with pride. 'The important thing is that all this happened without any kind of investment. Now my daughter helps me, my friends help me, and this goes on,' she triumphantly declared. The school, which is recognized by the Gujarat government, gets grants for teachers' salaries, besides a few other benefits from the state.

We chatted through the afternoon in Niranjanaben's living room, with her daughter, Pragnya, recalling various anecdotes from her mother's experience of running the school for three and a half decades and her grandfather's interactions with Gandhi and Sardar Vallabhbhai Patel.

In his book *The Story of Bardoli*, Mahadev Desai allocates significant space to highlight the role played by women in the success of the 1928 Satyagraha. While reading it, I had wished to meet at least one of the women he had written about, just to get a feel of that spirit. When I walked out of the Swaraj Ashram later that evening, I finally felt like I had experienced the essence of 1920s Bardoli and its brave men and women who made the satyagraha a success.

## Dandi Beach, Surat District

GOOGLE MAPS CALCULATED THE DISTANCE BETWEEN my hotel in Bardoli and Dandi Beach to be just about 55 kilometres. But I could not find any public transport to the historic beach, the final destination of Mahatma Gandhi's Salt March that began at the Sabarmati Ashram and ended with the breaking of the salt law in Dandi. Neither could I book any accommodation online, as no hotels or guest houses were listed anywhere on the web. Since I couldn't find other modes of public transport, I tried private taxis, but they refused to ply if I was travelling just one way and charged exorbitantly for a round trip. I was very confused at having to face so much difficulty in reaching a historic destination so close to where I already was. Eventually, I managed to convince an auto rickshaw driver, whom I had met at Chai Sutta Bar outside my hotel in Bardoli, to take me to Dandi Beach in his electric auto rickshaw, after sharing my frustration with him. If Gandhiji and his men had marched to Dandi, I figured I could at the very least travel by a non-polluting electric auto rickshaw just to keep up with the spirit of the journey.

Dumping my meagre luggage in the rear of the auto rickshaw on a windy Sunday afternoon, I proceeded towards Dandi, hoping to find accommodation close to the beach to spend the night, after which I could visit the memorial and beach at leisure. The eco-friendly, smooth ride along a largely desolate highway past acres and acres of sugar cane fields, mustard crops, rice paddy and other vegetable crops on both sides of the road, with warm wind lashing at my face, was indeed exulting. The vast stretches of agricultural land on both sides of the highway were interrupted briefly by cute, identical villages with a few dozen sloping low-roofed homes, a couple of tin-roofed bunk shops and defunct, discarded tractors and earthmovers lying by the roadside. We reached Navsari, the only major town on this route with bus service, in about thirty minutes or so. From there, a narrow, black-topped road led all the way to Dandi Beach. Along the way, large brown-and-yellow notice boards provided details of the various stops Gandhi and his marchers made during their historic march along the same route. When we neared the coast, the lush vegetation turned sparse, with tall palm, mango and other fruit trees replacing sugar cane and rice paddy. In some parts, the land just remained barren, but there was no sign of any kind of a salt marsh or salt pan that I had anticipated.

The long, winding road ended abruptly in front of a high wall. Beyond the wall was Dandi Beach, but the wall was so high that I couldn't see anything. Although we reached the beach by 1 p.m., tourists had already started arriving in cars, bikes and auto rickshaws, carrying large, colourful plastic baskets and steel tiffin carriers probably stocked with food and drinks for the beach. Except for a few sugar cane juice vendors near the parking lot and about half a dozen shacks to the right of the parking lot selling tea, short eats and cigarettes, there was no other commercial activity in the vicinity.

My plan to find some form of accommodation near the beach failed. Local vendors at the beach confirmed that the only guest house nearby was maintained by the Gandhi Ashram in Wardha and had just three cottages, which were booked months in advance. All other tourists had to book accommodation only in Navsari and travel to Dandi by private vehicles or cabs/auto rickshaws. Buses did operate to Dandi from Navsari, but they were highly irregular and very few in number. If you did not own or rent a private vehicle, Dandi was almost out of bounds, unless, of course, one decided to walk all the way like Gandhi did. A little probe online later revealed that Dandi Beach and its surrounding areas had been declared an eco-sensitive zone by the government, therefore no commercial activities were allowed or encouraged. With my auto rickshaw driver getting restless over his vehicle draining itself out of power soon, I decided to return to Navsari right away to find some suitable accommodation and then return to the beach later.

With this being my first experience of Dandi Beach, I wanted to revisit what Mahatma Gandhi and his seventy-nine marchers had experienced ninety-two years ago as they left Navsari for Dandi on 5 April 1930. One of the original marchers, Anand Hingorani, reminisced about the mood of the crowd as the marchers had neared Dandi nearly fifty years later to Australian author Thomas Weber, calling it gleeful:[1]

> They [the marchers] were more and more delighted. The murmur of the sea was loud and musical and could be heard from a distance. On the way, we came across salt deposits in the dried-up hollows. With almost childish glee, we picked up the salt from them and gazed at it in a manner as if we had found a treasure. There was salt all around. The high tides

[1] *On the Salt March*, p. 373.

> brought in sea water, it collected in hollows [pits] and left salt as it evaporated. It was there for the picking up.

By 7.30 p.m. that evening, Gandhi and his marchers had reached Dandi, described as a tiny village of about a dozen pukka houses belonging to middle-class cultivators and about a hundred kuccha houses of the Koli tribals. On his arrival, Gandhi took up residence at the bungalow of Seth Sirajuddin Vasi (now converted into a memorial) and gave a speech later that evening addressing mostly the locals who had gathered in large numbers to cheer him. In his speech, Gandhi described the coastal village as follows:[2]

> Dandi was chosen not by a man but by God. How otherwise could we have chosen for the battle-field of satyagraha such an out-of-the-way place—a place where no food grains are to be had, where there is scarcity of water, where thousands can assemble only with difficulty, walking ten miles from the railway station, and where if you are travelling on foot, you have to negotiate creeks full of slush and mud? The truth is that in this struggle we have to put up with suffering. You have made the road from Navsari to Dandi famous throughout the world by arranging for free drinking-water at frequent intervals all along it. If this struggle did not have your approval, your blessings, why would you be doing this? Dandi should be a sacred ground for us, where we should utter no untruth, commit no sin. Everyone coming here should come with this devout feeling in his heart.

By 4 a.m. on 6th April, everyone was up and ready. Prayers were offered; Sanskrit verses were recited. After the prayer meeting,

2 *The Collected Works of Mahatma Gandhi*, vol. 49, pp. 16–17.

Gandhi led his faithful marchers to the sea.[3] For two weeks, the locals had been organizing for the forthcoming historical event, preparing and arranging meals, water and other conveniences for the marchers. At the beach, Gandhi was asked if he was going to bathe. As 6th April was considered a day of penance and purification, he replied that such occasions must begin with a ritual bath. He removed his chaddar and dhoti and went into the shallow water at 6 a.m. Gandhi had to wade out quite a long way in order to reach a depth in which he could squat and immerse himself. The waves were big and threatened to knock the slight leader over, even as some of his assistants held on to him. In his wet loin cloth, Gandhi walked back over the dark, fine sand with its dusting of white salt crystals, towards the bungalow. The sky had gradually become brighter, as many eager would-be lawbreakers, too, bathed in the sea.

'Early in the morning, all of us bathed in the sea, and that over, all repaired to a salt-pit followed by several hundreds of people in a long stately procession. Almost all the people in the procession were dressed in snow white khadi and their Gandhi caps added to the picturesqueness of the scene which was at once grand and imposing ... in a few minutes we reached a hollow of salt and mud mixture. Amidst enthusiastic shouts of "Gandhiji Ki Jai" and "Vande Mataram", Bapuji entered the pit barefooted and brought out a handful of saline mud. No sooner had Gandhiji thus broken the Salt Law, all of us, including the crowd followed suit ... The atmosphere was thick with rumours that Mahatmaji would be arrested the moment that he actually violated the law of the land—but nothing of this sort happened,' recalled one of the marchers several decades later, reflecting on the actual events leading to the historic moment.[4]

---

3 *On the Salt March*, p. 388–89.

4 Ibid., p. 389–90.

Thus began a new phase in India's freedom struggle, amid the salt marshes of Dandi that have long gone dry.

After returning to Navsari, I paid off the auto rickshaw driver and booked a white Volkswagen driven by a tall and lean Parsi man with green eyes. His name was Mehrdad Patel—Mehrdad representing his Zoroastrian roots in Iran, from where his ancestors had migrated sometime in the twelfth century, and Patel showcasing his Gujarati heritage. As we drove from Navsari to Dandi yet again on the narrow, black-topped road, the loquacious Mehrdad gave me more updates on the present geography of the region and explained why the salt marshes described by Gandhi and his associates have vanished from Dandi. The incursion of sea water is no longer as rampant as it was in 1930, thanks to the embankments that have been built on the beach to prevent sea water from moving inland during high tide.[5] Incursions still take place in some pockets and can resemble a marsh, but they have mostly been curtailed now. When incursions take place, salt deposits still form, but salt extraction for commercial purposes has ended in the region. In late February, the month when I was in Dandi, there was no high tide and the land was bone dry, save for some mango, chikoo and other fruit-bearing trees throwing in a splash of greenery here and there.

By sunset, the crowd at Dandi Beach had multiplied drastically, with cars, vans and auto rickshaws parked at least half a kilometre away from the parking lot allotted to beach visitors. Mehrdad parked his car behind the other vehicles and we walked towards the tall wall and climbed the stairs past the wall, which led to the blackish-grey

---

5 Amarendra Jha, 'Salt production now history at Dandi', *The Times of India*, 31 March 2005, https://timesofindia.indiatimes.com/india/salt-production-now-history-at-dandi/articleshow/1066424.cms

sands of Dandi Beach, packed with people. For a south Indian from Chennai who was used to roaring deep blue waters and shining yellow-white sand, Dandi Beach appeared gloomy and depressing. The slushy beach sand stretched for at least a few 100 feet from the tall wall, beyond which dark grey waves rolled towards the flat shore in a quiet, subtle manner. The water at the shore was so shallow that I could spot people, even little children, at least 400–500 feet away, wading in just about waist-deep water.

The beach was packed with picnicking families: women, young and old, dressed in bright, colourful sarees, tops with jeans or skirts, or salwar kameez, gathered around the more soberly dressed male members of the family, munching snacks and sipping tea and soda. At least half a dozen camels with gigantic humps and twice as many horses awaited clients to go on a stroll along the shore. Blue-and-grey beach bikes criss-crossed the sands with screaming couples holding on to one another seated behind the driver. Vendors carried large vessels on their heads and sold steamed peanuts and chana with chopped vegetables, looking for customers, some of whom gobbled it down awkwardly.

The overall mood was joyous and people seemed to be having a good time, perhaps because the beaches had opened only recently after the long Covid-19 lockdowns. By around 6 p.m., the entire coast gleamed in the golden rays of the setting sun beyond the greyish-black sealine. After sunset, when the grey sky and sand turned black, I took off my shoes and waded past the gentle, warm waves just to get a feel of the sea in this part of the country. Weeds, bits of cloth and even a slipper brushed against my feet during their back-and-forth trips with the waves. I stood in knee-deep water for a few minutes before retreating to the shore.

To the right of Dandi Beach is the majestic National Salt Satyagraha Memorial, with its glowing lights brightening even the sky above. Like the beach, the memorial was also full of tourists, mostly from outside Gujarat, strolling past intricately detailed narrative sculptural murals depicting the various stages of the Dandi March. Young couples took selfies by the murals, groups of boys hooted and screamed at each other, families with little children dragged them along and tried to explain the significance of each event of the march as reproduced in the murals. Mehrdad and I just took a quick tour of the memorial and the home of Seth Sirajuddin Vasi, where Gandhiji had stayed after reaching Dandi. In front of the house was a glowing statue of Gandhi breaking the salt law, and an inscription announced that the statue was at the exact point where Gandhi had bent down and picked up a handful of salt and mud, thus breaking the law. Selfie-takers thronged that particular statue more than any other to record their moment with history. As we returned from the memorial, I recalled what Gandhi had said about Dandi, a sacred land where no untruth should be uttered, no sin should be committed and everyone was to visit with a devout feeling in the heart.

On our way back to Navsari, Mehrdad enlightened me on another fascinating piece of history of this region. Navsari in Gujarat is also the hometown of some of the most prominent members of the Parsi community. Some of the biggest names in the country, including members of the Tata family, Dadabhai Naoroji and so many other Parsi icons, trace their roots to Navsari. He also shared soft copies of magazines and newspaper articles highlighting the Parsi heritage in Navsari for my reference. But that's another story for another book.

## Dharampur, Valsad District

I REACHED DHARAMPUR, A QUAINT LITTLE TOWN IN Gujarat's Valsad district, around 7.30 p.m. on a cool, windy night, by which time the roads had become deserted, most shops and markets were closed, and the residents were back in their homes unwinding for the night. Unlike modern towns and cities, Dharampur still has a formal entry gate, an antique brick structure known as the Rajya Rohan Gate, with three passageways—a large one in the middle for the bulk of the traffic and two smaller ones on both sides of the main gate—reminiscent of its princely past. A little beyond the Rajya Rohan Gate, three young men waited for me in a Maruti Eeco to take me to their quarters, where I was to spend the night.

I liked Dharampur from the moment I passed through that gigantic gateway. The weather was pleasant, the vegetation was soothingly green and the town seemed to be surrounded by rolling hills—at least that's how it appeared from where I stayed. Dharampur was not in the original itinerary I had prepared, as no significant event related to the freedom movement or during the post-Independence period had taken place here. This town and its surrounding villages had been ruled by tribal kings for several centuries, after which it came under the control of the Sisodia Rajputs until Independence, when the territory was ceded to the union of India. I had come to Dharampur to meet Nilam Patel, a young Gandhian and an alumnus of Gujarat Vidyapith who worked extensively in the tribal villages of this part of Gujarat. Atul Pandya, director of the Sabarmati Ashram in Ahmedabad, had mentioned him during our conversation on Gandhi's dwindling relevance among the youth in India. Atul believed Gandhi's ideas remained relevant even today and that it was more obvious in rural Gujarat. 'You won't find any significance in Ahmedabad but visit the tribal areas in Gujarat and you will see Gandhism still at work. Close to 15 per cent of the state is populated by tribals, yet you won't find any extremist trouble in this tribal belt in Gujarat, unlike in other parts of the country. It is purely due to the work done by Gandhians in the area,' he had claimed. I was in Dharampur to see if that claim was true.

The three men who came to pick me up were all less than twenty-five year of age and worked for Nilam Patel's NGO, Lokmangalam Charitable Trust. They drove me to a posh, gated villa community in Dharampur where the NGO had rented a two-storey villa for the Lokmangalam staff to stay. I was offered a guest room on the ground floor, while the others, five of them, stayed on the first floor. The presence of a state-of-the-art villa community in a remote town with an ancient entry gate was indeed a pleasant surprise and an indication that the idea of suburbia, with its gated communities typically found on the outskirts of large cities, had reached deep inside Gujarat.

I couldn't meet Nilam that night or even the next morning. Daksheesh, one of the Lokmangalam volunteers, apprised me of this at a dark, dingy eatery, the only one open at that hour, where we ate rice rotis and green gram curry. Nilam was busy with an andolan organized by the residents of Dharampur and its surrounding villages against the Par-Tapti-Narmada Link the next morning. During the meal, Daksheesh explained in detail about the river linking project and the reason for the tribals' resistance. Like most Lokmangalam volunteers, he was an undergraduate student at a Dharampur college and volunteered with Nilam during his holidays.

The next morning, Daksheesh took me to the Lokmangalam office, where I was told by him and another young volunteer about the various projects taken up by the trust. The two explained their work, which ranged from running nurseries offering free saplings to villagers to building check dams, teaching children and even liaising with the state government on implementing their projects—all neatly printed in brochures and booklets. I was also asked to join the other staff of Lokmangalam for their weekly review meeting, which took place on the roofed terrace of the home of one of their colleagues, about fifteen minutes away from town.

Twelve youngsters, including four women, from the surrounding tribal villages sat in a circle facing each other and discussed the week's developments in their respective projects in colloquial Gujarati, with me haplessly studying their facial expressions and hand movements to decipher what they were saying. Almost all those present at the meeting were tribal men and women pursuing higher studies in various colleges, except for a few full-timers, including a civil engineering graduate. Besides the engineer, I found the group also had a full-time accountant, a lady with a BCom degree and a nurse. They had all taken time off from their work or studies to join Nilam and help him improve the situation in the villages surrounding Dharampur, and were earnest about it.

When the meeting was underway, an energetic young man came to me and introduced himself as Gulab. He was just about 5 feet tall and had a short army-style haircut. I had noticed him bounce around like a balloon filled with energy soon after I had arrived. Gulab sat next to me and started conversing with me in broken Hindi, which was very similar to mine and comforting. He told me he was from the Khoba village on the Gujarat–Maharashtra border, where Nilam runs his ashram. 'I am his first student,' Gulab announced proudly. When I told him I was from Tamil Nadu, he shared with me his love for Tamil films of late. 'I watched *Pushpa* many times on my mobile,' Gulab whispered assertively. Clarifying that *Pushpa* was a Telugu film, I asked him why he liked it so much. 'It is about our people. The cutting of trees and everything that happens in the movie takes place in our villages too,' he said with a giggle. 'I also love the film *Jai Bhim*. It is also about our people. I showed it to all my friends a day before my first andolan to motivate them,' he elaborated. But before I could probe further, Nilam Patel returned from the andolan and took over the meeting. Within those few minutes, Gulab had made an impression on me and I made a mental note to find out more about him and his andolan later.

Following the review meeting, all the volunteers were served an elaborate lunch comprising rice rotis, a staple in these parts, a green gram dish and different types of chutneys, along with rice and dal, which we ate sitting cross-legged on the floor. After lunch, Nilam, his associate Ajay Patel and I left for Khoba village, about 55 kilometres from Dharampur and along a winding and scenic ghat road, past several tribal hamlets surrounded by dense vegetation. The greenery in this part of Gujarat was so unlike the rest of the state I had travelled to. As we rode, Nilam shared anecdotes from his journey—from Gujarat Vidyapith to getting recognition as a 'Young Gandhian', a title that only seemed to make him more and more uncomfortable.

Until his graduation, Nilam was like most youngsters of his age: aspiring to find a good job and lead a cushy life either in Mumbai or in some other big city. At least, that was the plan when he applied for an MA in economics at Gujarat Vidyapith. Coming from a slightly affluent family—his mother is a former village sarpanch and his elder brother is the present sarpanch of his village—Nilam took off to Ahmedabad, dreaming of a bright future soon after his admission at Gujarat Vidyapith was finalized. 'But I got spoiled at the vidyapith,' he said, laughing, as we rode past the rolling hills. 'The strict discipline on campus, the systematic way of life, the prayers, the frequent references to Gandhiji's life and how he dealt with problems he faced—it all influenced me significantly and I began to look at people and places differently,' Nilam recalled, going back to his postgraduate years.

Though he did begin thinking about making a difference to society through his work instead of pursuing a corporate life, he wasn't yet convinced about fully committing to social work. It was only an external examiner's question during the viva voce in the final year of his MA that got him to think seriously about choosing his destiny. 'The examiner, a lady, asked me what issues people in my village, Gundalav, suffer from. Back then, there was no 108-ambulance service in our village, no good schools after class five, no government hospital, and even essentials like roads and access to drinking water were lacking. This was in 2007. I told her all the problems we faced. After patiently listening, she asked me who was expected to solve those problems. She went on to add that if all the youngsters fled to bigger towns, ignoring the problems of their village, like me, how would the villages ever improve? That conversation got me thinking about returning to my village and doing something about all its problems,' Nilam told me as we drove past one tribal hamlet after another on the way to Khoba. 'Gujarat Vidyapith should be held responsible for my present condition, if someone must be.' Nilam giggled again.

Back then, as is the case even now, everyone around him was heading to Ahmedabad, Mumbai or any other big city for a job, with the hope of migrating abroad someday. But Nilam decided not to follow that path. Returning home after his MA, he informed his parents about his decision to dedicate his life to improving the villages surrounding his hometown. 'They were in shock when they first heard about my plans and asked me if that was why I had gone to do an MA in economics,' Nilam recalled. However, upon realizing that Nilam was stubborn about his decision, the family agreed only on the condition that he was not to return home. 'I did not visit my home until five years later.'

Not knowing where to start his chosen path, Nilam sought help from Gujarat Vidyapith and got suggestions on how to go about rural developmental work. 'Then I left for Gundiya village, about 55 kilometres from Dharampur, with just a suitcase containing some books, clothes and a charkha.' Noticing my disbelief at what he had said, Nilam repeated, 'Yes, those days I used to carry a charkha wherever I went.'

After reaching Gundiya, he talked to the villagers about his wish to improve life in tribal villages and how he wanted to help them. But they were reluctant to believe him, as he neither knew their Konkani language nor was aware of their problems. Yet, they did host the young man for a few days. 'Those days, I had no proper place to stay or facilities to cook food. I ate what the locals gave me and stayed with the village postman, who was gracious enough to share his home. As I went about helping the villagers with their day-to-day issues, I came to know of other villages in the neighbourhood that were worse off. Since I had already decided to dedicate my life to this work, I thought I'd start with the most backward village in that region, which was Khoba, on the Gujarat–Maharashtra border. There was nothing to indicate progress in Khoba back then. So I just started walking every morning from the postman's house in Gundiya to Khoba and began interacting with the villagers. As was the case in Gundiya, the residents of Khoba were also reluctant to interact with me initially. The first question they asked me was which NGO I belonged to and which project I was working on. They were well aware of the NGO business, but I had no answer because I had neither an organization nor a plan back then,' Nilam reminisced, adding that the energy he had at that time to change at least some things in the world had begun dissipating then.

We were still driving on a narrow, winding road, with hardly any vehicles coming from the opposite direction. The villages we crossed on our way appeared impoverished and similar to one another when compared with other parts of Gujarat. Slouched in the center of the middle row behind Nilam and Ajay, I sat dazed as Nilam continued with his story.

In Khoba, Nilam realized that the simplest thing he could do was teach children at the only primary school in the village, as the government-appointed teachers rarely turned up. Every day, he went to the primary school and taught the children any subject for which the teachers were unavailable. It was there that he met Gulab, who was a little brat and his first student. 'As the weeks passed, the villagers started gaining more and more faith in me. One day, they asked me to stay in their community hall, so that I didn't have to walk every day from Gundiya. And so I shifted my residence. During this period, I also started writing to various government departments on the lack of facilities in the village, and slowly things started happening. Khoba got electricity, its school got new teachers appointed—the village began to change for the better. When I started getting responses from the government and things started changing, the local people began believing in me and became convinced that I was sincere about my intentions. I, too, began to feel something was happening,' Nilam remembered. Soon, the word spread among the tribals in other villages too, and, over the next decade and a half, Nilam became a household name in at least eighty tribal villages on the Gujarat–Maharashtra border. In this period, he has trained an army of volunteers, mostly tribal students, in various fields through his Lokmangalam Trust.

We had reached a narrow bridge atop a steep valley, when Nilam asked Ajay to stop the car and got down. I got down after him. Pointing at the valley, he said, 'This is the proposed venue of the new dam that we are fighting against and had protested this morning. All this land will be buried if the government goes ahead with the project. The proposed dam could lead to the displacement of tribals from their homeland, and we are trying to resist it in the Gandhian way, through non-violence. But politicians have entered the fray and are trying to mislead. We have to see now how long this battle is going to continue.'

We resumed our journey. The black-topped road ended about 15 kilometres before Khoba, and we were now on a bumpy dirt road, which kicked so much dust every time the wheels bounced off a pit that the side and rear windows of the car were completely covered in dry soil. We left behind a mud storm trail all the way to the Gujarat–Maharashtra border, where the Khoba Ashram, as Nilam had named it, sat perched on an elevated piece of land overlooking a stream that had gone dry by that time of the year. Smooth, oval-shaped boulders and pebbles of various sizes were the only indicators that water once flowed through that channel. On the other side of the dried-up stream was a hill populated with dense shrubs and short trees, which was officially in the state of Maharashtra. The main building of the ashram, a mud-walled hut with a cow-dung-plastered floor and a tiled roof, overlooked the stream. A few feet behind the main ashram building was the guest house, a slightly more modern construction with red-oxide flooring, plastered walls and a western toilet for visitors intending to stay at the ashram. The front courtyard was filled with beautiful flowering and non-flowering plants, neatly maintained by the ashram staff. In the centre of the courtyard was the giant trunk of a huge tree that towered above the ashram. The entire campus was maintained by Binod and his wife, Banita, whom I had met earlier that afternoon at the coordinators weekly meeting.

Due to the Covid-19 pandemic and the closure of schools, just about five or six children from Khoba and its surrounding villages were staying at the ashram when I was there. Behind the main building was a much larger hall, with tile flooring and a tin roof supported by strong concrete pillars. 'This has been recently inaugurated and can accommodate 150 children. I intend to provide shelter for as many children from the surrounding villages as possible. From here, they can go to government schools to study without any hindrance,' Nilam explained as he took me on a tour of the ashram.

As we sat in the ashram's garden, sipping black tea prepared by Binod and Banita, and looking at the long row of photographs of Nilam receiving various awards and citations for his work, I asked if he was proud of his achievements. 'It has actually become a burden,' he said. 'There is so much scrutiny now on what I do that I don't feel as free as before. Everything I do is seen with suspicion. I am the same ... nothing has changed about me, but everyone is watching me so closely. The State Intelligence, the Centre's IB—everyone wants to know what I will do next. I think it's because the villagers trust me and listen to me. And that has increased my responsibility tremendously,' Nilam clarified.

While many youngsters had joined Nilam, impressed by his enthusiasm and success, most left midway as they found it hard to continue developmental activism as a lifelong mission. Of the few who stuck with him, Ajay Patel was the one whom Nilam rested his hopes upon. 'He quit a government job to join me and has been with us for over five years. Like me, no one asked him to come and do this. He is here because he likes doing this work,' Nilam said.

Ajay was just twenty-seven years old and also from Valsad. He had heard of Nilam Patel and his work through various media reports, interviews, etc., and was keen on getting in touch. 'Then we met at the Jal, Jungle, Jameen protest in 2016 at Jantar Mantar in Delhi and I spent a week with Nilambhai. Upon our return, I quit my job and joined him full-time,' Ajay said, as if it were a trivial act that did not warrant any serious attention. 'Nilambhai was doing exactly what I wanted to do. So I joined him and have no regrets so far.'

After spending a couple of hours at the ashram, we got back into Nilam's car to return to Dharampur and were about to leave when a middle-aged couple—a short, stout man wearing a shirt, trousers and a white topi and his wife, who was taller than him, wearing a saree and with a large bindi adorning her forehead—walked towards us and asked Nilam if he could drop them off at Kaprada. Nilam gladly agreed and the couple got into the back seat of the car. A few 100 metres later, another woman, also in a saree, waved her hand, and Nilam offered her a ride too. The car was now full as we rumbled along the dirt road. The local man and two women chatted casually in their language, a mix of Warli and Konkani. Nilam, who had learned the same dialect, having spent so many years in their midst, conversed just as freely with them. When Ajay negotiated a sharp curve a little farther down the ghat road, we spotted another middle-aged, thickset man wearing a half-sleeve shirt and khaki half-pant who was carrying the lobbed-off branch of a tree on his shoulders and was walking uphill. He waved at Nilam with a big smile and both Nilam and Ajay waved back. 'Looks like you know everyone here,' I observed. 'Oh, no, that's our Gulab's father. He is one of the first few villagers who became friends with me,' Nilam pointed out.

When we reached the bottom of a valley and began the climb towards Dharampur, the rear wheels of the car got stuck in soft sand and the vehicle slid to one side. All of us got down and pushed the car forward, after placing some stones under the tyre. While I was pushing, the middle-aged villager turned to me and said in broken Hindi, 'Nilambhai has done many things for us. Now he has sent a proposal for a bus service to our village. Nilambhai should get that too!'

The rear wheels rolled out of the sand and we continued our journey. The villagers, who were on their way to a temple festival, got off at Kaprada to walk the rest of the journey. After they left, I pointed out to Nilam and Ajay how even the tribal women were so casual and friendly with them. 'They trust me; nothing has changed between us. But only down in Dharampur, things have changed,' Nilam said.

Since afternoon, Nilam had been bringing up the topic of 'change' time and again, so I probed him further. 'This "Young Gandhian" title has brought me so much trouble,' he confessed, aware of how awkward he sounded. 'I like to keep my Gandhi to myself. If I take up that label, people ask me so many questions. Why do I ride a car to the village? Why am I not wearing khadi? Why am I not looking impoverished? And I'm like, "Arre bhai, it was probably necessary for Gandhi to do all that back then but now it isn't." But people don't get it,' he emphasized. According to him, the only reason today's youth is so distant from Gandhi is because people (meaning Gandhians) are very rigid about what a Gandhian should be like. 'Gandhi himself wasn't that way. He experimented with his life all the time and made practical changes whenever necessary. However, his disciples are far more rigid, but that's not how I see the man and his teachings. I studied at Vidyapith, was inspired by the Mahatma and decided to work for the tribals. Now please let me do it my way, is what I tell those who try to find fault. I consciously stay away now from any Gandhi-related events, out of fear that I might not be able to conform to their rigid standards. I have a personalized vision of the Mahatma and that's good enough for me.'

As we neared Dharampur, Ajay stopped the car by a flat piece of land adjacent to a temple, where a group of young men were playing cricket. Even before the car halted, one of the players came running towards us. I recognized him from the morning meeting—he was one of the karyakartas. Nilam had a little chat with him for about a minute and then we resumed our journey. In the car, he turned towards me and said, 'This is what I mean. Now, if I tell him that Gandhi never played cricket, so he shouldn't play as well but spend his time in seva, he will run away from Lokmangalam this very moment. What is the harm in playing cricket during your free time? How is it against Gandhiji?'

---

Nilam's idea of a personalized version of Gandhi has evolved, perhaps due to one of his mentors and former vice chancellor of Gujarat Vidyapith, Dr Sudarshan Iyengar. As a professor of economics, Dr Iyengar taught the subject to Nilam during his postgraduation. He was also instrumental in putting together the Gramshilpi programme, a rural developmental initiative of Gujarat Vidyapith, of which Nilam is a beneficiary.

I met Dr Iyengar outside his modest residence in the wooded campus of the Action Research in Community Health and Development (ARCH), Dharampur, the day after I went to Khoba with Nilam. Dressed in traditional light-coloured khadi wear and Paragon chappals, for which he was once smirked at by a subordinate staffer when he was at Gujarat Vidyapith, the expert in Gandhian studies and I sat for a chat outside his house. Against the backdrop of delightful birdsong and a young girl reciting Gujarati lessons next door, Dr Iyengar tried to help me understand the 'old man', an affectionate term he used to refer to the Father of the Nation, and his message to us.

'People think wearing khadi is Gandhi, spinning the charkha is Gandhi, drinking goat milk is Gandhi. It's not. You [have to] decide if what you're doing will help the perspective [Gandhian] ultimately. If so, then do it. Please don't say that Gandhi did something, so I'm also doing it, for the old man would have never liked that. Gandhi wanted us to see his life and find out for ourselves if his way of living has potential to improve vyakthi, samashti and shrishti [individual, population and creation]. If you're convinced, then do it. Gandhians should have done that instead of simply spinning the charkha,' Dr Iyengar elaborated, as he spoke about Gandhi's relevance today.

Having roots in south India, Dr Iyengar grew up in Gujarat after his family moved to Kandla when his father got a job there during the construction of Kandla Port in 1951. The sixty-seven-year-old, who lives with his wife, Lakhsmi, however, still manages a 'vaango' and a 'pongo' in a tone as authentic as the filter coffee in Mylapore cafes. So, when and why was this south Indian attracted to Gandhi?

'I don't know. Back in those days, when I was in college, Gandhi was still fresh and a much-debated person. His ideals were spoken about and many of the leaders of the time, such as Jayaprakash Narayan, came from a similar school of thought,' he recalled. Going back to his schooldays, Dr Iyengar said that most Gandhian values, such as the abolition of untouchability, Hindu–Muslim brotherhood, etc., were ingrained in him even at school. 'We had excellent teachers who taught us the right values. At home, there was still some prejudice. "Don't touch this person, don't eat from that person ..." was still there. But we were very clear about the right value system and that clarity came from school,' he said. The country was still fresh from Independence and the spirit to do something good and contribute to nation-building was still a goal among the youth back in the 1960s, the economist recalled.

When Dr Iyengar was in college, he was attracted to Jayaprakash and his politics when the euphoria over independent governance was fading and several problems began surfacing across the country. Jayaprakash seemed to have the answer to those problems. Just like the other young people of that period, Dr Iyenger, too, actively participated in the Bihar Andolan and Chhatra Yuva Sangharsh Vahini when the call came, before returning to the campus to pursue his PhD in economics. Since completing his studies, Dr Iyenger has worked mostly in rural areas for upliftment of the vulnerable. He has had a long stint as an academic, including at the Centre of Gandhian Studies at IIT Mumbai and as the vice chancellor of Gujarat Vidyapith.

To the economist in Dr Iyengar, Gandhi was always about the decentralization of wealth and politics. Elaborating on the idea, he explained that if wealth generation and political decision-making are brought to the lowest level, i.e., to the villages, then accountability would be a given. 'And that is what Gandhi wanted. Anyone who is instrumental in decentralizing wealth and politics is a Gandhian. Any kind of decentralization that helps benefit the most vulnerable villages is a Gandhian thought and a Gandhian way of life. Instead of trying to fulfil that vision of Gandhi, most Gandhians today still spin the charkha, wear khadi and drink goat milk, which are totally irrelevant today. The ones who will save Gandhi today and for posterity are those who question Gandhism time and again so that it can be reinvented,' Dr Iyengar clarified. Referring to a top Tamil-Nadu based tech entrepreneur who runs a multi-billion-dollar software firm out of his native village, the economist said that to him, that entrepreneur was a Gandhian. 'Anyone who empowers the most backward villages and distributes wealth is a Gandhian. Simple.'

The Gramshilpi programme of Gujarat Vidyapith had been initiated and implemented by top academicians of the varsity, including Dr Iyengar, with the intent of empowering villagers economically and politically, as Gandhi had wished. The students are provided a monthly stipend to go and do developmental work in villages. While Nilam has been one of the earliest beneficiaries of the programme, several others have followed in his footsteps, including Nilam's junior Mohan Mahalla from Nandgaon, who has also dedicated his life to empowering the most backward villages in the region. Mohan is also an alumnus of the Gramshilpi programme and receives a monthly stipend to continue his work. 'Despite running the Gramshilpi programme for over fifteen years, having just a handful of youth to showcase the success of the project is not something to boast about. But I'm incredibly proud of these boys,' the former VC told me.

Speaking of Nilam, he said, 'Nilam has to be very careful. He is popular now and they will try to make a neta out of him. I often tell him, "Don't become a neta, yaar!" But he has to resist the temptation.'

---

On my last night in Dharampur, Gulab and his Lokmangalam colleagues took me to the local Maha Shivratri Mela, supposedly one of the largest public events in the region. 'You cannot be in Dharampur and miss it. It is a lot of fun,' one of the boys told me while driving the CNG-run van down dark, winding roads, surrounded by dozens and dozens of other cars, two-wheelers and vans, all heading to the mela. As we neared the mela, we saw that the narrow road leading to its venue was lit by thousands of colourful serial bulbs and packed with a huge crowd of men and women of all ages and sizes, even toddlers and nonagenarians, heading for the temple-related festivities. Parking our van in a cramped corner next to a bunk shop at least a few 100 metres away from the temple, we joined the crowd heading towards the mela grounds. I walked with Gulab and Daksheesh flanking me, while two of their other friends, not from Lokmangalam Trust, walked behind us.

I was told that every year on the night of Maha Shivratri, the last day of the three-day mela, at least a few lakh people from all the surrounding villages, dressed up in their best attire of the season—young men in skinny-fit jeans, sweatshirts, T-shirts, etc.; women in sarees or salwar suits, with red lipstick on; children clinging on to balloons, puppets, hoots and other toys they bought on the way to the mela—thronged the venue, where at least a thousand vendors, ranging from fashion jewellers and cloth merchants to pani puri sellers, from across Gujarat had put up stalls to sell their products to the visitors. Amusement rides, including a Ferris wheel, tora tora, rotating cups, roller-coasters and carousels of different sizes, abounded at the venue, beside which people waited impatiently in serpentine queues for a ticket to the ride. The food stalls, especially ones with Chinese food, and sugar cane and other fruit juice vendors made brisk sales as the largely window-shopping hordes that halted and inquired at every stall guzzled the freshly prepared dishes and juices. Every once in a while, groups of young boys, drunk perhaps, hooted and sprinted through the crowd like a train passing through a tunnel.

Walking next to me, Gulab noted that a huge number of people were expected that year, since the mela had been cancelled for the past two years due to the Covid-19 pandemic. It was then that I realized I was walking shoulder to shoulder with a sea of people, very few of whom wore masks or maintained any social distancing. The number of Covid-19 cases across the country was low, but the mela was a complete violation of any Covid-19 protocol. When I brought it up with the boys, they apprised me that Covid-19 hadn't affected their villages as much as the towns. 'Very few people fell ill and none died, as far as we know,' Gulab said, as we finally reached the Shiva temple past the mela grounds.

The boys went in, prayed and came out. We then went to a relatively less crowded fast-food outlet and had fried rice with raita. By around 11 p.m., the crowd had cleared a little and we strolled back to the entrance—we could finally walk at a leisurely pace, without rubbing the sweaty shoulders and arms of other visitors.

'Have you seen *Jai Bhim*?' Gulab asked me for the second time in as many days, while walking back to the van.

I told him I had.

'I have seen it several times. I also showed it to all my friends the night before our andolan to motivate them,' he said.

I told him he had mentioned this before and asked about the andolan that he kept bringing up.

By then one of his friends had started the van, and we were on our way to the guest house. Gulab sat next to me and shared the story of the first andolan of his life—a four-day sit-in protest inside his college campus.

While the actual indefinite sit-in protest by the students of Vanseva Mahavidhyalaya College (where Gulab was pursing his bachelor's degree) in Bilpudi, near Dharampur, commenced on 8 February 2022, three weeks before my visit, Gulab and his associates had begun their preparations at least two weeks ahead, even as their semester exams were taking place. The demands were discussed in detail among the students and clearly identified. The main demand was a change of trustees of the college management, as there was overall apathy on their part. One of the hostel buildings was in very bad shape and the women's toilets did not have a proper roof, as a result of which men from nearby villages often peeped in. The students did not even have access to proper drinking water.

Since the hostels were mostly occupied by Adivasi students like Gulab, a total of 120 Adivasi students of the college decided to organize a peaceful protest against the management. But they faced stiff resistance. The students couldn't print posters and pamphlets because private printing presses in the area refused to cooperate. The protest was against the powerful trustees of the college management, who were influential in and around Dharampur. When the management heard the students were planning for a stir, they threatened the few teachers who were supporting the students with strict action. Defying the odds, Gulab and his associates, all clad in white kurta-pajamas with disposable masks covering their nose and mouth, began their protest on the cold morning of 8th February by rallying across Dharampur, carrying placards with their demands printed on them and raising slogans against the management with practically no outside support.

The students marched through most of Dharampur town before heading to the district revenue office, where they handed out a copy of their demands to senior revenue officials. The marchers later went to the police station and sought police protection for the sit-in protest that was to follow. After marching all morning, all 120 students assembled outside their hostel building in the afternoon, braving the cold weather, for an indefinite strike. As night fell, blankets were brought out and the students spent the night out in the open, despite requests from the college management to give up their stir and return to the hostels.

The first night passed with hardly any reaction from the management. All 120 students, of whom quite a few were Adivasi girls, still clad in white kurta-pajamas with masks around their nose and mouths, slept out in the open while clinging to their blankets. The following day, the local media took notice of the Gandhian style protest organized by the students inside the campus and began coverage. A few locals who got to know about the stir gathered at the venue to observe the protest and support in their own way. Soon, media channels from bigger cities rushed in and began livestreaming the protest along with the demands put forth by Gulab and his associates. Since the students refused to budge until their demands were met, the media coverage gathered momentum by the third and fourth days. The college trustees, who were stubborn in not interacting with the protestors until then, eventually turned up at the venue and agreed to renovate the hostel building, along with most of the other demands.

'It was only after we got an assurance from the top management that we decided to end our peaceful andolan that was executed in the Gandhian way,' Gulab recounted with an infectious energy as we reached the guest house in Dharampur. 'The protest was not for us. We were all graduating that year; it was mainly for the Adivasi students who would be coming to the hostel next year and the year after. We did not want them to suffer like we had, and the management had done nothing about the building since 1987,' he said. Although the change of trustees, which was the main demand of the protestors, did not materialize, all other demands were met. And Gulab still keeps track of their progress.

Later, upon watching YouTube videos of their protest, I was stunned. The students were so disciplined and organized; none raised their voices more than what was necessary to be heard. No stones were hurled, no verbal abuse or physical indiscipline could be observed. During my undergraduate years at an arts and sciences college in Chennai, I had also participated in several protests. Most of those were for trivial reasons, like protesting against an increase in canteen rates, or the principal's action against a group of unruly students, or some other such development. On most occasions, my friends and I had never even bothered to find out why the protests were being held or if they were really necessary, but we had readily joined the sloganeering crowd. The first act by the protesting students in our college back in the early '90s was to get to the Poonamallee High Road and stop all vehicular traffic, especially government buses. Stones were hurled and a few windowpanes were broken before the police and college management forced us to disperse. Not once had we participated in a peaceful protest such as the one in Dharampur. Our demands were mostly trivial, the approach, even more so.

About four months after meeting him, I had made a phone call to Gulab from Chennai, seeking clarification on some material I had gathered during my visit, when he updated me that he was now in Ahmedabad. 'I have got a seat for a master's in social work at Gujarat Vidyapith,' he said. I was so happy for him. I had met his father, who is still chopping wood and doing odd jobs in Khoba, like his ancestors had done for generations. But his son now has a seat in a postgraduate degree course in a reputed university.

To me, with Gulab joining the vidyapith, a cycle had been completed. Dr Iyengar and his colleagues had introduced the Gramshilpi programme to improve the life of tribals in the Gandhian way. Their efforts had helped Nilam end up in Khoba. But Nilam had not gone alone; he had taken the 'old man', as Dr Iyengar said, with him to Khoba. And Gulab, who was Nilam's first student, had borrowed the 'old man' and his ways from Nilam and made good use of these philosophies back in Dharampur.

With the success of his first andolan, Gulab had proved yet again that satyagraha and Gandhi remain relevant even today. Had Nilam not gone to Khoba, Gulab, whose ancestors had suffered all the injustice meted out to them and fought using force in futility, would have resorted to the same. But Gulab had now found a tool that his ancestors had never had.

'So, looks like the next successful Gramshilpi has already been found, Gulab?' I asked him before ending the call. The young man laughed hard, despite getting interrupted by a cough. 'I don't know, sir. If that is what I'm destined to do, I will,' he said.

[illegible] the old man and he was once more [illegible] [illegible] philosopher [illegible]

[illegible]

[illegible]

# TWO

# Jhansi, Jhansi District

IF YOU GREW UP IN POST-INDEPENDENCE INDIA AND ARE educated, you ought to have read or at least heard about Jhansi. It's one of those cities like Agra or Delhi that have become an integral part of our consciousness as Indians. How can an Indian not be familiar with Agra's Taj Mahal or Jhansi's Rani Lakshmibai? One remains a symbol of Indian grandeur and the other, Indian valour.

My earliest memory of Jhansi goes back to my English prose textbook in class five or six. A short lesson titled 'The Brave Rani of Jhansi'—accompanied by a colourful illustration of an attractive young woman reining an equally striking horse with one hand, while wielding a huge sword in the other, with a baby tied to her back—introduced me to Jhansi and its beloved queen. I do not recall the contents of the lesson, except that the people of Jhansi loved their queen and that she jumped off a fort with her infant son and escaped the British Army. A few years later, a more banal version of Rani Lakshmibai's life and Jhansi graced the pages of my history textbooks, as part of India's freedom struggle narrative.

Jhansi, to me, has since then been just an ancient town trapped in its glorious past. But is it?

On my first evening in Jhansi, I was out for a casual stroll in the Civil Lines area towards Panchatantra Park, when I had to shelve that perception. It was early March but the city was yet to shed its winter weather. As I walked past narrow, winding lanes that led to the main road ahead of the railway station, I noticed at least half a dozen young women donning stretch pants and sleeveless tops zoom past me on flashy scooters, the offices of three DJ music artistes, and two state-of-the-art fitness centres advertising aerobic sessions for men and women, besides the usual supermarkets, kirana stores and chai-cigarette-paan bunk shops that appeared to have percolated everywhere in the neighbourhood. Bearded young men wearing branded leather jackets and roaming around on fancy motorcycles with modified silencers weren't missing either. Residents of this heritage town—from auto rickshaw drivers to sales executives and college students—obviously lived like they did anywhere else in India, with their loud wedding parties, live DJ music sessions and flashy cafes serving cappuccinos and Americanos, and yet Jhansi's fixation with its past also remains intact. It is obvious from the moment one lands at the recently renamed Virangana Lakshmibai Railway Station, formerly Jhansi Railway Station. It's not just the railway station—more than 150 years after her demise, Rani Lakshmibai continues to adorn hoardings all over Jhansi and remains the most prominent personality of this ancient town soaked in history. Jhansi today boasts a Maharani Laxmi Bai Medical College, Rani Lakshmi Bai Central Agricultural University, Maharani Laxmi Bai Balika Inter College, Veerangana Maharani Laxmibai Rajakiy Mahila Mahavidyalay and Maharani Laxmi Bai Rajkiya Paramedical Training College, besides countless other institutions named after the warrior queen. She is also present on almost every government flex board across the city, sometimes wielding a sword in military fatigues, sometimes atop a horse with her child strapped to her and occasionally just as a bust. A distant second is hockey legend Major Dhyan Chand, who also belonged to this historic city and has a few institutions, mostly related to sports, named after him.

Jhansi is also one of those cities where you are likely to bump into a historic monument left uncared for in a dilapidated corner of a bustling street or end up in a sprawling palace right at the heart of a congested market area. Most writers will relate to those random flashes of insight that appear out of nowhere during their travels and nail the destination for them. One such moment of clarity flashed to me when I visited Rani Mahal, one of the palaces where Rani Lakshmibai lived, on a steamy weekday afternoon. As the only tourist in the mahal at the time, I had the palace to myself for a paltry entrance fee of Rs 25 and meandered aimlessly from one section to another.

In the Durbar Hall on the first floor of Rani Mahal, a 6-by-3-foot window opened out to a bright billboard on the other side of the dusty, narrow road. The billboard read: '*Chutney nahi, Rocket hai, Rocket! Ching's Secret*', with some Chinese-like alphabets and the black-and-white logo of the company that makes those Chinese sauces. Beneath that billboard was another board that read: 'Arun Kirana and Ration Store'. The kirana was teeming with customers busily bargaining with the shop owner. The congested road between the shop and palace was dusty, with litter strewn pretty much everywhere. Two-wheelers, green-and-yellow auto rickshaws and luxury cars occupied the curbs as well as a good portion of the road, leaving little space for motorists to manoeuvre. Next to the kirana store was an open parking lot, where dozens of white cars with yellow registration plates were parked. The sprawling palace has at least a dozen other windows of different sizes on all its sides, and the views were no different from any of them: More shops, parked vehicles, brown dust rising off the road whenever an auto rickshaw or car passed and lots of people going about their daily life—quite depressing a view from the palace windows of a powerful queen.

According to the Lucknow Circle of the Archaeological Survey of India (ASI), the palace, built by Raghunath Rao II of the Newalkar family (1769–1796), was a flat-roofed, double-storey structure on all three sides, except the western. The palace has several rooms, six halls and parallel corridors with multi-foiled arches. The walls of the Durbar Hall on the first floor are decorated with brilliant paintings in floral and faunal designs; even the inside portions of the building arches are embellished with peacock and floral designs. The Durbar Hall is accompanied by small galleries that continue to house paintings. The interiors of the long and opulent hall next to the queen's quarters have also retained some of their past glory in the form of beautiful Bundelkhandi-style paintings of birds, animals, flowers, etc. However, all four corridors surrounding the courtyard have been filled with idols, mostly broken and deteriorated over the years, providing little space for visitors to find their way around them. Most other rooms in the palace have also been filled with similar damaged stone idols.

Rani Lakshmibai spent one of the most despondent phases of her short life at Rani Mahal after the death of her husband, Maharaj Gangadhar Rao, on 21 November 1853.[1] A series of events following the death of Gangadhar Rao that led to the British annexation of Jhansi in 1854 and takeover of the majestic Jhansi Fort forced Rani Lakshmibai to shift from her quarters in Jhansi Fort to the city palace, as Rani Mahal was known back then. Having lost her kingdom and much of the wealth, she shifted to this palace with her son, Damodar Rao, and just a few trusted associates. In her book, author Pratibha Ranade describes Lakshmibai's life in Rani Mahal as one filled with challenges. 'The Rani struggled with negative forces. She nurtured the hope of recovering her kingdom and lived in the manner of the widow of a Hindu Brahmin. Her

---

1 Pratibha Ranade, *Rani Laxmibai: Warrior-Queen of Jhansi*, trans. Sanjay Ranade (Noida: HarperCollins India, 2019), p. 45.

days were occupied in worship and prayers, fasting and rituals, and in the rearing and education of Damodar Rao,' the author, putting together several books and other pieces of evidence, concludes.[2]

The young widow was adept at horse riding, sword fighting and mallakhamba, a kind of pole exercise prevalent during the period, but stopped regular practice after moving to Rani Mahal because there was not enough space. As the British had removed all soldiers and courtiers from service, only a handful of soldiers were left to guard the mahal and a few servants to serve the queen. The stables in front of the palace, which have now been replaced by a dirty road with haphazardly parked vehicles and petty shops, had hundreds of horses during the good days. But after the Rani shifted here, only fifty were left. Describing what Rani Lakshmibai must have seen from those windows of the palace, Pratibha writes, 'The empty stables and the fort [Jhansi Fort] were visible to Rani Laxmibai. She must have felt distressed, humiliated and helpless at losing her kingdom unfairly. One can imagine the anger and irritation tearing at her heart as the days passed by.'[3]

In a way, the palace appears to have remained trapped in that despondency even a century and half after her demise. And that's exactly how I felt while walking out of the palace that evening and into the bustling streets of Jhansi. Ironically, most locals haven't even bothered to check out the palace in their neighbourhood, even out of curiosity. That's Jhansi: there is so much history everywhere that it's no longer taken seriously, unless it suits one's view of the world.

---

2 *Rani Laxmibai*, p. 56.

3 Ibid., p. 57.

In stark contrast to the palace is the breathtakingly magnificent Jhansi Fort. Located just about 700 metres from Rani Mahal, it can be seen from the palace windows, especially at night, when it glows against the backdrop of a dark sky. The fort is easily Jhansi's most attractive tourist destination and has a steady stream of awestruck visitors walking in and out of the various corridors and entrances/exits in the 15-acre structure. For locals, it is a symbol of their heritage and makes hearts swell with pride.

At least that is the case with Mahesh Rai, an auto rickshaw driver who operates out of the auto stand at the fort. In the mornings, Mahesh waits at the railway station to pick up train passengers and drop them to their destinations, and later in the day, as the tourist flow picks up, he waits outside the fort for visitors. That was where I caught up with him for a little chat.

'I have been seeing this fort and hearing stories about the battles that took place here since childhood. At night, when it is lit up with the tiranga, the fort looks so magical. Its grandeur reminds us of our glorious past,' Mahesh said. On days he doesn't have much work or feels down, Mahesh confessed he smuggles in a quarter bottle of whisky and settles down outside the fort in his auto rickshaw to have a few quiet drinks. 'And I feel good and strong. If our ancestors could build something like this, we can do things too,' he said.

Mahesh's great-grandfather and grandfather lived and worked on the land they inherited from their ancestors in Jhansi. With the changing economy and urbanization, his father sought employment in the Uttar Pradesh Animal Husbandry Department, as he did not own enough land to pursue agriculture full time. Mahesh, who is now forty-two, did not even have such an option as they hardly owned any land by the time he reached adulthood, and began his career as an insurance agent. He worked in the industry for several years before choosing to drive an auto rickshaw to make a living.

Despite witnessing the family's fortunes turn around, Mahesh has never thought about leaving Jhansi to move to a bigger city. 'It's just not something we do here; we belong to Jhansi and will only live and die here,' he said when I asked him if he could have found private-sector employment in a bigger city. To Mahesh, not moving out of one's native land is the right way to live. 'My forefathers fought the British and so many others to protect their land. Why would I leave it and go now?' It's a sentiment, I've noticed, many native residents of Jhansi share. They are too proud of their land to leave and go. Jhansi Fort also contributes its share in retaining loyalists, irrespective of whether they know its long and complicated history or not.

In the long legacy of the fortress, Rani Lakshmibai played a small but significant role. The original fortification was done by Raja Bir Singh Deo of Orchha in 1613 on the hill known as Bangara. According to historians from the region, the fort came into the possession of Maratha rulers in 1731, and Naru Shankar, a Maratha chief, made further alterations and additions to the fort, which later came to be known as Shankargarh due to the construction of a Shiva temple. After that, the fort underwent constant renovation and destruction in various wars, including Lakshmibai's wars with the British, when parts of the massive structure were completely ravaged. The queen and her son, Damodar Rao, are believed to have escaped from the fort when the British Army captured the city of Jhansi in April 1858.

The entire fortified area of Jhansi Fort stretches up to 49 acres and is one of the best-maintained forts in the country. When I visited on a Saturday afternoon along with hundreds of other tourists from across the country, I was also simply awestruck by its size and its intricate design. Every wall in every direction had openings of different sizes for rifles, guns, spears and other weapons to be slid through, with watch-windows that offered a great view of the area surrounding the hillock on which the fort was built. The giant cannons at the entrance displayed the military might of its rulers who had mixed fortunes despite their possessions.

As mentioned earlier, Rani Lakshmibai was forced to spend several years at the city palace, following the death of her husband, Gangadhar Rao. But she returned to the fort in 1857, following the Sepoy Mutiny or Revolt (depending on one's interpretation), when the deserting Indian soldiers had killed most of the British citizens in Jhansi, including those who had taken refuge in the fort, and had handed over the control of Jhansi and the fort back to their Rani. During her second tenure at the fort, Lakshmibai, who had learned from her previous mistakes, decided not to surrender meekly to the British as she had done earlier and braced for battle when the time came.

After the Sepoy Mutiny failed and the British began to regain one territory after another, the battle for Jhansi became inevitable, and Lakshmibai began preparations for it in a big way. In March 1858, a huge British Army led by Sir Hugh Rose marched towards Jhansi to capture the kingdom yet again.[4] A pitched battle ensued; the Rani's positions could not be breached for the first three days, and during this period she regularly visited the frontlines to motivate and reward for their bravery. While there are several versions of what happened during the next few days of the battle, the general consensus is that some traitors in Lakshmibai's army had ill-advised her, which led to the fall of Jhansi Fort and the queen's escape from the fort with her son.

While Lakshmibai did leave Jhansi with her trusted lieutenants, the battle continued on the streets of Jhansi, as the British and Indian soldiers of the Company faced stiff resistance even from the common public. Several accounts mention how the streets of Jhansi were filled with the corpses of men, women and even cattle. Thousands of women were reported to have jumped into wells and drowned after their male family members succumbed in battle. Rani Lakshmibai, however, reached the neighbouring Kalpi, where she

---

[4] *Rani Laxmibai*, pp. 112–15.

again joined hands with like-minded forces and fought the invading British soldiers unsuccessfully. From there, she was forced to retreat to Gwalior, where the British, who were on her trail, continued their brutal attack, leading to her death.

Tourist guides at Jhansi Fort give various interpretations of this story to unsuspecting tourists day after day. Depending on a tourist's knowledge of history and the state they belong to, I suspect the story is altered to suit their interests. One such guide showed me a narrow opening towards the rear of the fort and said that the Rani had jumped down from there with her son and rode her horse waiting below. A peep through the opening made me wonder if it was possible for any human to jump safely from that height (perhaps, with some CGI help, one could in a movie).

After spending close to two hours soaking in the history and legacy of such a monumental structure, I could relate to what Mahesh Rai had told me earlier. For a region with history dating back to thousands of years, the past seven and a half decades of a democratic government can only be seen as just another passing phase in the long saga of the good, the bad and the ugly rulers and governments this land has endured.

When I asked Mahesh his opinion on seventy-five years of independent India, he began to hurl abuses at most of the major political parties that came to power in his state during this period. 'But the last few years have been good,' he said, before declaring that he was a diehard BJP man. To him, the pride of chasing out the British in 1947 and electing a right-wing government several decades later seemed part of some grand, expansive plan of regaining the past glory of his hometown.

---

Having immersed myself in the Hindu history of Jhansi till now, I ventured next afternoon in search of the less popular Jhansi

Cantonment Cemetery, where British citizens and Anglo Indians killed in the 1857 mutiny were buried. As I had expected, very few in the city even knew about its existence as it was clearly not in the tourist circuit. After roaming around Jhansi city for almost an hour, asking around and stumbling upon all sorts of ASI-protected monuments in and around the city, which included a well where Hindu women had allegedly jumped in and died by mass suicide to protect themselves from British Army sepoys, we finally reached the cemetery in a quiet corner of the Army Cantonment area. Only those visiting Jhansi from the UK and other parts of the world came to this cemetery to pay homage to their deceased family members. A young couple living in a hut outside the cemetery were the caretakers when I visited, after the Anglo-Indian lady who had been the caretaker for several decades had passed away recently.

Walking inside the deathly quiet cemetery after receiving keys from the caretaker couple, I was taken back by the sheer number of tombstones, large and small, all painted white. The cemetery was empty, the sun was on its way down and the green grass, not too overgrown but just enough to please the eye, was inviting. As the caretaker couple had left after handing over the keys to me, I slowly walked from one tomb to another, trying to make sense of what might have exactly happened. While the lower-rung officers, their staff and their families were buried in an open area stretching at least a few acres behind the main area, the senior officials were provided a kind of chamber with a tablet pasted on the wall with details of the people murdered during the revolt and of their family members who had the tombstones and memorials built. I walked past one tablet after another, taking down details of the deceased and their kin, until I stumbled upon the one in memory of William Samuel Carshore and his family. The tablet read:

> To the Memory of Willian Samuel Carshore aged 35 years and Mary Jane Franklin, his wife aged 28 years, and their four

> children Arthur aged four years, Clara aged three, Violet aged two and Herbert, aged eight months, who were massacred on this spot by the rebels and mutinous *native soliders* on the 14th of June 1857. This memorial is placed here by the sorrowing parents of the above, named Mary J F Carshore and her affectionate friend Mary Amelia Vansittart.

The information in the tablet froze me. To think that on that very spot where I stood, four little children, including an eight-month-old infant, were massacred along with their young parents over 150 years ago by my countrymen was chilling. After reading the contents of that tablet, I could not proceed further. Several other tombstones listed out more such sordid deaths, but I skipped them.

The bloody revolt began on 11 May 1857.[5] A band of sepoys from Meerut who had killed their European officers the day before crossed the Yamuna river, captured Red Fort and declared Bahadur Shah Zafar, the Mughal emperor who had become a British pensioner, their 'Shahenshah-e-Hindustan'. This event triggered a series of revolts across the country in which hundreds of British and other European citizens, including several in Jhansi, were killed. During that period, Lakshmibai was living in Rani Mahal after handing over her throne and the fort to the British. On 5 June 1857, the revolting Indian sepoys of the British Army began their battle against their officers in Jhansi.[6] Over the next few days, dozens of British and Anglo-Indian men, women and children were butchered in broad daylight by the revolting sepoys. The deceased included some top-ranking British officials and their families, such as the superintendent of Jhansi, Captain Alexander Skene, his wife and two children, whose names appear first in a long list on

---

5 Bipin Chandra, et al., *India's Struggle for Independence: 1857–1947* (New Delhi: Penguin Books, 2000), p. 31.

6 *Rani Laxmibai*, p. 72.

a tablet at the Cantonment Cemetery listing the Europeans and Anglo-Indians murdered in Jhansi. Most of them, including women and children, were made to stand in a line and their heads were chopped off, according to some accounts.

What could have triggered this brutality among the revolting Indian sepoys? While historians have put forth several reasons for the pent-up anger against the British despite receiving training from their officers, the most immediate cause was that the Indian sepoys were asked to use cartridges greased with cow and pig fat. The cartridge casing had to be ripped off by biting, but neither the Hindu nor the Muslim soldiers could do so because it was against their religion. Despite widespread discontent against British rule, people were somehow tolerant of all the injustice meted out to them until it went against their religion.

During my travels across India in 2015–16 and now again in 2022, I found that not much has changed in people's approach to their religion in several parts, especially in the northern and central belts. On several occasions during this trip as well as the earlier one, I faced that difficult and unsettling question: '*Aapka dharam kya hai*?' What is your religion?

And I have found that people are comfortable if you belong to their dharam; belonging to a different dharam is not very comforting but still fine, especially among Hindu and Muslim leaders. But when you say you are an atheist and don't believe in any dharam, the looks and treatment you get are completely different.

I often ask myself this question: Does one's staunch belief in his or her religion justify an act of brutality even when the belief is only superficially threatened? In a region full of people like Mahesh Rai, who have never really moved out of their native villages and towns for generations and have been fed on stories of grandeur and courage associated with their religion, merely seventy-five years of imposed secularism are, perhaps, hardly sufficient to erase over 1,000 years of religious devotion, as I could see first-hand. I don't know if I can ever agree with it, but I have come to conclude that I should at least try to understand their point of view.

---

My quest to find out more about the British and Anglo-Indian families massacred during the 1857 Mutiny led me to St. Jude's Shrine in the same Cantonment area. The caretaker couple, who neither had any clue about the history of the Cantonment Cemetery, nor had retained any contact with the family members of those buried there, directed me to the then parish priest of St. Jude's Shrine, Fr. Frederick Mendonca. A native of Mangalore, Fr. Freddy (as he's known to the patrons of this church) has been with the Jhansi Diocese for the past fifty-five years, including six at this shrine. I was told he has been associated with the Christian community of around 3,000 families in Jhansi, including Catholic and other sects, for several decades now and has observed the change within the community over the years.

St. Jude's Shrine in Jhansi is among the few churches anywhere in the world to be dedicated to St. Jude Thaddaeus, one of the disciples of Jesus who was misunderstood and not accepted due to his association with Judas, betrayer of Jesus. A Maltese priest brought this devotion to St. Jude to India, and this church is among the first churches for St. Jude in India, an imposing white structure built in 1966. When I reached the church around 4 p.m. or so on a Saturday, the choir was practising devotional hymns in Hindi to the beat of a pair of jingles, while four or five devotees knelt down and prayed. The spacious, air-conditioned office of Fr. Freddy was right behind the chapel, where he offered me a seat and reluctantly agreed to speak.

Fr. Freddy had no knowledge of the mutiny victims, but he had observed the Christian community in the Bundelkhand region closely for the past five decades. 'The Catholic community in Jhansi and the northern states in general has been small when compared with the south, as the British were not keen on promoting Catholicism here. A few churches were there but they were not really encouraged. The Catholic community began to grow only post-Independence in Jhansi,' he surmised. 'During those days, most of our church members had been from other states, railway staff, telephone company employees and other government officials. A large population of Christians were Anglo-Indians and Goans, but they have all left now. Though new families have moved in due to job transfers and other reasons, very few remain. The community must be only around 3,000 families or so, and our church has 100 members as of now.'

The priest, who has also served as the principal of a higher secondary school associated with the church for several years, felt that as a minority, some of their rights had been threatened of late. 'Now, we are being questioned. Our loyalty and honesty are being questioned, especially over the past twenty years. The local politics has worsened the situation over the past ten years or so. Some years back, we had lots of problems with fringe groups attacking churches, minority-run schools and other institutions.[7, 8] Now, they have been streamlined by and large. As such we don't have any problem, but we still feel we are being watched all the time,' he explained.

---

7 Ziya Us Salam, 'Churches under attack: Uttar Pradesh reports most cases of anti-Christian violence across India', Frontline, 17 November 2021, https://frontline.thehindu.com/the-nation/communalism/churches-under-attack-uttar-pradesh-reports-most-cases-of-anti-christian-violence-across-india/article37474505.ece

8 Tejaswi Ravinder, 'Anti-Christian violence in India's Uttar Pradesh "part of the state machinery"', World Watch Monitor, 20 July 2018, https://www.worldwatchmonitor.org/2018/07/anti-christian-violence-in-indias-uttar-pradesh-part-of-the-state-machinery/

When I asked him to clarify in detail the fear of being watched, he elaborated on a recent case. 'Earlier this week, a Punjabi family of three had come to the church seeking baptism of the father. The mother is a Christian and the child is also baptized, but the father is a Sikh. He came to the church seeking baptism, but we were reluctant and refused to baptize him. The truth is we are all afraid as the anti-conversion law has been implemented in all BJP states. If someone wants to create a problem, this would be enough,' Fr. Freddy said. 'It has never been the case in the past.'

Quickly clarifying that a majority of the people were generally not bothered about such matters, he added that only certain groups were watching out for any such activity. 'We can't even teach moral science to children; we are being watched that closely.'

After a little pause, the parish priest once again clarified that Jhansi was much better when compared to the rest of the state and that people were a lot more cosmopolitan and accommodative. 'It's a nice town, you know?' he said.

Asked if he would like to go back to the south some day, since he is from there, and is now past retirement age. Fr. Freddy, who was seventy-three then, responded with an emphatic 'No'. 'The south is too developed and people there have no values anymore. It's too cosmopolitan and nobody has time for anyone. The south has gone to the dogs ... in north India, people still take care of their parents, joint families are prevalent. There is at least some humanity left here!'

---

The instruction given to my middle-aged auto rickshaw driver Rajan—auto rickshaws are the easiest and most Covid-19-friendly commute, with no Ola or Uber cab services available in Jhansi yet—was to take me to those villages that have not changed since Independence and where I could see the authentic Bundelkhandi way of living. During my interaction with Fr. Freddy, he had pointed out that most people in Jhansi were non-natives who had migrated from across the country seeking employment and weren't aware of the city's past; the few who knew its past were often too politicized to give an unbiased version. He asked me to go to the surrounding villages and talk to the simple Bundelkhandi folk to get a grasp on the region. I conveyed the same to Rajan the next morning.

'I know exactly the place you should visit. Let's go to Pali Pahari,' Rajan said. He was one of those rare auto drivers who didn't look like one. Dressed in an ocean-blue long-sleeved shirt, fully buttoned up, and neatly pressed cotton trousers with the shirt tucked in, Rajan conversed in refined Hindi and was even good with English.

Soon, we set off on the Jhansi–Shivpuri highway. After travelling about 10 kilometres, Rajan took a detour to the left into a single-lane black-topped road. Surprised at the neatly laid road, he updated me that the roads had been in very bad shape when he had come here two years ago. A few kilometres down the road, he found out why it had been neatly laid as we passed the sprawling campus of the Shemford Futuristic School on our left. With no classes due to Covid-19, the campus was deserted. A little farther away was an even bigger school building with a huge pink compound wall, on which the words 'RNS World School' were painted in a bold font. Behind the compound wall was a palatial building with dozens of rooms looking truly international. 'This belongs to Ram Narayan Sharma, whose family produces Baidyanath Chyawanprash,' Rajan said, and claimed that the roads were laid only for them and not the villagers. As he had predicted, barely a few 100 metres away from the RNS World School, the tar road ended abruptly. An uneven dirt track continued, on which the auto rickshaw struggled to move ahead without jolts even for a few feet. 'This is the road I am used to,' Rajan said, as we continued on the desolate track. About half a kilometre away, we spotted a solitary home with its front wall built of mud bricks and stopped our vehicle.

*'Koi hai?'* Rajan got out and screamed; I stood behind him. There was no response. From the entrance, we could see the living area was quite far from the outer compound wall. Rajan screamed again and waited. After a few minutes, a slim teenage boy wearing just khaki shorts and an older woman with sunburnt skin and draped in a red saree came out. Rajan looked at the boy and asked him for directions to the village pradhan's house. The woman responded instead, and gave some directions. But Rajan ignored her and asked the boy—who behaved like a mute—again. Even as the woman gave directions to the pradhan's house once more, Rajan screamed again, louder this time, *'Koi haiiii?'* He pretended not to have noticed the presence of the woman at all.

A few minutes later, a one-legged man hopped outside with the support of a thick stick and gave Rajan directions. 'Go a little farther and ask for Bahadur Singh. He is not the pradhan but he will talk to you about the village. You can find him in his petty shop,' the man said, as the older woman, who stood next to him, observed the two in silence.

Rajan thanked the man and we left. After we got back into the auto rickshaw to go to Bahadur Singh's petty shop, I asked Rajan why he refused to interact with the woman. 'It's not like in the city. In villages, women aren't supposed to talk to strangers. They are only allowed to talk to men in the family,' he clarified.

Rajan has a master's in economics and a bachelor's in library science—I should have guessed from his clothes—and yet chose to drive an auto rickshaw because he could not find any other decent employment in the city. His father had been an Indian Railways employee who had retired as a head signalman, while both his elder brothers were also employed by the railways. Even Rajan had cleared the written exam for railway recruitment in 2002 but had failed to clear the interview round. The next year, he had gone to Lucknow and stayed there for several months, trying to 'fix' a railway job, but even that had not materialized. 'You have to be in government service, otherwise there are no jobs here. You can find so many postgraduates like me driving auto rickshaws, selling insurance and even running petty shops,' he told me, as we reached Pali Pahadi.

The auto rickshaw bumped and bounced on the dirt track with Rajan deftly swerving it to the right and left depending on the position of the potholes and dirt mounds, and reached a tiny bunk shop where a few packets of paan masala, Haldiram's chaat items and colourful sachets of shampoos and other essentials were hung vertically. An old man wearing a loose white vest confirmed we were in Pali Pahadi and that the shop belonged to his son Bahadur Singh.

The entire village overlooked a rocky hillock that probably gave Pali Pahadi its name. The scene in front of me was so typical of all the UP villages I had seen in films. Dry, yellow-brown dirt roads that appeared to lead to nowhere; old, unplastered brick homes with tall compound walls mostly painted white and decrepit wooden gates. Large mounds of cow and buffalo dung lay on both sides of the road, with a cement drain passing by the roadside choked with plastic waste, rotten vegetables and plain muck. At least half a dozen large buffaloes, tied to wooden posts beyond the dung mounds, chewed on dry grass lethargically. At the entrance to the village, a little ahead of Bahadur's petty shop, a couple of young women, their faces covered by their sarees' pallus, stood next to a hand pump collecting water in plastic pots.

The old man seemed friendly. He put out a couple of chairs at the entrance for us to sit on and turned on his stove to boil water for tea. 'You have come from so far away to our village,' he said, justifying his reason for making us tea without us asking for it. A former railway staffer, Bahadur's father had even visited Chennai for an Indian Railways employees' union conference once and started chatting instantly when he heard I was from there. 'It's a nice place ... Chennai. I was surprised by how much rice you south Indians eat. We can't eat so much rice, so I had to make rotis for all of us for the ten days we stayed there. Otherwise, it's a nice place.'

I told him about the purpose of my visit and sought his help in finding Bahadur Singh. By then a group of elderly villagers, who were probably the only ones present in the village that afternoon, had surrounded us. They were all clothed in dirty white kurta-pajamas and colourful turbans. The oldest among them, who looked like he was ninety or so, had a sweater on and walked with the help of a walking stick, while another man, slightly younger than him, with a thick, bushy moustache, wore sleek black leather slip-on chappals that had almost turned brown in the dust. Otherwise, they were all dressed the same. Upon finding out that I had come from Chennai to know more about their lives, the men ranted non-stop. 'We have a school but no teachers ... no primary health centre is available ... there is just one hand pump for the entire village of around 150 families ...' they went on one after another. 'With no proper roads, no public transport is available, and even sick people are taken on motorcycles to the main road and then transported to a bigger vehicle,' said another old man, while yet another complained that children walk at least 3 kilometres to the main road to go to middle school, as the village school is only up to class five. 'But they have laid a tar road so that the children coming to the big private schools don't have any difficulty,' he pointed out as others continued to nod grimly. Apparently, the entire village had just about fifteen graduates and only two or three people with stable government jobs. The rest of the villagers depended on buffaloes and their milk for their sustenance, as agriculture was no longer feasible due to flooding from a nearby reservoir. Their dependence on buffaloes explained the heaps of dung all over the village.

Even as I tried to soak in the environment, a character so unlike the surroundings I was in walked towards us. He was in his early thirties, fair, with shiny, glowing skin that obviously hadn't seen much sun ever. Slightly stout and with a jet-black handlebar moustache, the man was wearing a printed shirt and skinny trousers and sporting brown sunglasses. 'That's my son Bahadur Singh,' announced the old man at the shop.

Bahadur Singh sulked even as he came and sat down on a bench next to me. It was as if he was already annoyed by my presence. When I told him that I had come to interview people in his village, he sulked even more. 'What is there to say? Can't you see for yourself? Everything is rotting here; nothing has changed in this village in the past seventy-five years. We have no roads, no drinking water, nor any form of sanitation. Where are the free toilets? Where are the schemes the government had announced? We have got nothing,' Bahadur Singh lamented. Removing his coolers and placing them in his shirt pocket, Singh asked me if I was representing the government. When I clarified that I wasn't, he decided he had sulked enough and left. His father, who was a lot more tolerant of the plight of the village, took over the conversation as he served us tea with some salty biscuits.

As we talked, at least half a dozen women walked past us carrying pots of water on their heads, despite the scorching heat of the afternoon. While some of the women, curious, peeked out from under the tips of their pallus draped over their heads, their presence was again deliberately unacknowledged by all the men gathered around me. Even my postgraduate auto rickshaw driver tried not to look at them or acknowledge their presence.

---

From Pali Pahadi, we drove to another village off the Shivpuri highway, where a twenty-eight-year-old man had just become the village pradhan eight months ago, after contesting independently. Jai Singh from the Punawali village, 17 kilometres from Jhansi, was educated and progressive, I was told. It was also obvious from the condition of his village of around 800 families, where roads were decent and smooth and drinking water was available on every street. Confessing that he did not play a big role in bringing all this development to the village, Jai Singh boldly proclaimed that he had brought about one change in the region: He had built a new office for the pradhan, where he could sit with the villagers and address their issues. 'Whoever comes to meet me here will sit on the chair you're sitting on now and discuss with me their problems on equal terms. I cannot do it in my home (allow people of all castes to sit on par with him) and neither does any other pradhan around here. If a lower-caste man comes with a problem, he has to squat on the floor and talk. But in this office, all are equal,' Jai Singh emphasized. I asked him about women who might have any issues and whether they would also receive the same treatment. 'Why would they have to come to my office at all? The men in their house will come with their problems. But there are at least a dozen graduate women in this village,' he pointed out.

---

From Punawali we continued along the same road towards the state border, halting at one village after another full of bad roads, worse sanitation, men who do all the talking and women who do most of the work. The last village in this stretch was the picturesque Simrah, located beyond soothing water channels, lush green wheat and mustard fields bounded by bamboo and other tall shrubs.

As we parked the auto rickshaw and began walking, Simrah appeared quite similar to Pali Pahadi, except there weren't as many heaps of cow dung everywhere. Otherwise, the roads were unpaved and bumpy, open sewers criss-crossed everywhere, women in ghoonghats sat outside homes and peeped out from under their saree pallus, while the male folk, mostly in kurta-pajamas, sat in their front porticos, chewed paan and relaxed. Upon reaching a large sewer that cut across the road, Rajan stopped and asked a young man stepping out of his home for directions to the village pradhan's house. When the man wanted to know who I was, Rajan delivered the discourse with which he was by now so familiar—about me and the book I was writing. He had been introducing me to villagers since morning, his pride evident in the increasingly raised pitch of his voice with every repetition. When he repeated the same with this young man, pat came a retort: '*Hindu-jan to hoga*?' Must be a Hindu?

'Just ignore him and come,' Rajan told me, and we continued walking. In about 100 metres, we reached an ancient home with walls made of limestone surkhi. It was the pradhan's house, but we were told that he had gone out for some other work. When I phoned him and asked if he could come and speak to us, he asked me to get an appointment and return later. I was surprised, for usually village pradhans rush to come and talk to any visitor in the village, especially ones from the media. Since this man wanted me to take an appointment, I told him that anyone who knew the village well would do, if he was busy. 'In that case, you can talk to my younger brother, Shankar,' he said.

Shankar came out soon and agreed to speak to me. Since he looked very young, I asked for his age. 'Thirty-two,' he replied.

'And you are the pradhan's younger brother?'

'Yes.'

'What is the name of the pradhan?'

'Pallavi.'

'What?'

'Pallavi. This is a reserved ward. My bhabhi is the pradhan,' he clarified.

'Can I meet her then? Is she home?'

Rajan intervened. 'No, no, women don't talk to strangers here. It's not like your city.'

'My brother Rohit Yadav takes care of everything. Of course, Bhabhi is with him,' Shankar clarified again.

'Why is that?'

'Being a pradhan, one has to move around, ride a vehicle and, you know, get things done. Now, how can Bhabhi do all that?' he said, sitting on a wooden bench in the front portico of his home in Simrah village, just about 20 kilometres from Jhansi Fort, where a woman had led an army of soldiers and fought the British more than 150 years ago.

# Unnao, Unnao District

Unnao has the capacity to shock visitors from the moment one gets out of the railway station. Here, taxi and auto rickshaw drivers do not solicit passengers who walk out of the railway station lugging their baggage; if you want transportation, you go to them. Even as the city resembles a nineteenth-century shanty town, sleek electric auto rickshaws in blue, green and other bright shades can be found everywhere, instead of the ugly, fuel-guzzling black-and-yellow diesel auto rickshaws. When smart, young IT engineers come home to Unnao, they stop wearing seat belts while driving their cars even at a speed of 80 to 100 kilometres per hour, almost running into vehicles dashing at similar speeds in the opposite direction; and if the side mirror of his or her car accidentally hits the hand of an on-duty police constable while driving through a congested market area, neither the driver nor the police personnel bothers about it. Pharmacy shop owners with DPharm degrees put up hoardings claiming to be qualified doctors with the prefix 'Dr', and patients queue up morning and evening to seek treatment from them. Dozens of engineering, science and humanities colleges exist only for the purpose of selling degrees, as classes are rarely held, and while everyone knows about it, none bother to complain. If you are a postgraduate student unable to appear for a semester exam due to other pressing work, the question paper and answer sheets are sent to your home so that you can take the exam at leisure and return the paper to the college. Young boys who have completed their postgraduation in arts and sciences often take up diploma courses at an industrial training institute (ITI) to learn a trade to make a living. Primary schools in some villages have sturdy new gates and compound walls, but the classrooms do not have walls or even a roof. A tablet pasted at the memorial of a famous freedom fighter in a village close to Unnao city proclaims to be the birthplace of the revolutionary, although the man was born in neighbouring Madhya Pradesh; most people here know about it, and yet, none question the blatant lie embossed at the memorial. In most villages, every home has an LPG cylinder provided by the government, but very few have been refilled, as most of the families have no money to do so. Farmers who possess documents for their agricultural land often have to work as casual labourers on their own land for Rs 250 a day, as the land is in possession of upper-caste people. The Central and state governments have built toilets under the Swachh Bharat Mission in every village, but these are mostly used to stack hay or other produce, although these toilets are put to use if there is a differently abled person at home. Girls in villages barely 20 kilometres away from the city still get molested when they go out to relieve themselves, often by their classmates or seniors at school, and yet, no one files a complaint with the police. Nobody has any faith in the police or law and order, and yet, everyone claims that the situation is much better now. Village pradhans openly admit that there are so many problems in their village but that they have no clue what to do about them. People in some remote villages—adults and children—continue to live like their forefathers did hundreds of years ago, with no semblance of progress whatsoever and absolutely no hope of a better future, and yet, they welcome any visitor with a warm and hospitable smile as if nothing is missing from their lives. And if you need proof for any of these, just spend a few days here or check with friends who've lived in this region.

Sandwiched between Kanpur and Lucknow, Unnao district in Lucknow division of Uttar Pradesh is described as the land of kalam (pen) and talwar (sword) by Wikipedia for the number of intellectuals and freedom fighters this backward district has produced. Noted Hindi writer Suryakant Tripathi 'Nirala', Urdu poet and freedom fighter Maulana Hasrat Mohani, who coined the slogan 'Inquilab Zindabad', actor Sarvadaman Banerjee, and even celebrated freedom fighter Chandrashekhar Azad's maternal family hail from Unnao district. Graced by the Ganga, the district is largely fertile, with lush fields stretching along the banks of the river for most part of the year. Unnao and its surrounding areas are also soaked in history. According to the official district portal, Hiuen Tsang, the famous Chinese pilgrim who stayed in neighbouring Kannauj for three months in 636 CE, had journeyed a distance of about 26 kilometres and reached the city of the Na-fo-ti-po-ku-lo (Navadevakula), which stood on the eastern bank of the Ganga.[1] The city, known for a magnificent temple, several Buddhist monasteries and stupas back then, was situated about 3 kilometres north-west of Bangarmau in Safipur tehsil of Unnao district. Some scholars claim the site to be an important ancient city that was upturned in the thirteenth century by the curse of a saint, and is still known as Aundha Khera or Lauta Shahr—both meaning an upturned city. The dargah of the Muslim saint, whose curse is said to have befallen the city, is arguably the oldest Muslim monument in Bangarmau or perhaps all of Unnao district.

---

1 District of Unnao, Government of Uttar Pradesh, https://unnao.nic.in/history/

But Unnao hasn't become a part of this book or my itinerary for any of the reasons mentioned above. This nondescript town and district grabbed my attention as well as that of the entire nation back in 2017 in connection with the sensational rape case of a minor girl, for which then BJP MLA Kuldeep Singh Sengar was accused and later convicted. The horrific details of the alleged rape as well as the subsequent twists and turns in the case, with one after another in the victim's family getting killed or seriously hurt by various means, took the country by storm and put Unnao on the national crime map. Since then, rape cases in Unnao began to get noticed and were reported vigorously. In 2019, Unnao was called the rape capital of Uttar Pradesh, with over eighty-six rape cases reported in that year.[2] One would think that Uttar Pradesh had replaced New Delhi as the rape capital of India.

During that period when Unnao became synonymous with rapes and abuse of women, a casual chat with a former colleague, a young woman from a village near Unnao who had since shifted to Chennai, exposed me to disturbing new insights into the lives of women in the rural villages of the district. The colleague recalled how kitchen discussions among women in the household revolved around who was sexually abused by men in the family and when it happened; about male neighbours and acquaintances, both young and old, sexually exploiting young women who go out at night to relieve themselves, as if it were their right; and even friends who grew up together sharing details of the abuse they suffered, mostly at the hands of family members, treating such abuse as a way of life. Ironically, none of these incidents were reported to the police, and even if they were, no action of any kind was taken. Growing up in

---

2 'With 86 reported rapes in 2019, Unnao emerges as Uttar Pradesh's "rape capital"', *The New Indian Express,* 7 December 2019, https://www.newindianexpress.com/nation/2019/Dec/06/with-86-reported-rapes-in-2019-unnao-emerges-as-uttar-pradeshs-rape-capital-2072469.html

Unnao meant putting up with sexual and physical abuse, especially for women from poorer sections of society.[3] Those discussions eventually led to my colleague writing a report that was well-received but kept her away from her hometown for at least a few months.

Since then, I had wanted to visit Unnao just to see if all that I had heard and read was true. Ironically, the few days that I spent wandering in and around the district exposed me to a world that I wasn't even aware of until then.

---

We began our foray into the dark recesses of Unnao district from Nandulan Khera, a predominantly Dalit village in Belhadyal Ganj, Bighapur block, approximately 32 kilometres from Unnao city. The brief I had given to my local contacts while finalizing my travel plan for the next few days was to show me all that they had spoken about in their hometown. I mention 'we' here because unlike my other travels across the country, where I had travelled alone or, at best, had been escorted by a driver, in Unnao I was accompanied by a full convoy comprising a local journalist, a politician and a few others everywhere I went. Only later did I realize that it was a way of life in this part of the country—people rarely ventured out alone. My convoy included a schoolmate of my former colleague, who happened to be in Unnao because he was still working remotely for a Bengaluru-based IT firm. He brought along his relative, a local activist with political connections, who in turn brought along his friend for reasons unknown to me—although I suspect the man came along simply because we were travelling in a big car and there was extra space for more bodies. Since none of them knew journalism,

3 Shweta Tripathi, 'This used to be my playground…', *DT Next*, 18 December 2019, https://www.dtnext.in/national/2019/12/15/this-used-to-be-my-playground

they took me to the office of a local pharmacist-cum-journalist, who also agreed to join us for the next few days. The five of us were the permanent members of this convoy, which the local journalist had named 'Ground Zero Survey' team, again, for reasons best known to him. Apart from us, at the entrance to every village, a local also decided to tag along so that the villagers didn't feel threatened by us marching past their homes and making small talk. And that increased the final convoy size to six!

When we, the Ground Zero Survey team, left for Nandulan Khera on a Tuesday evening in March—just days before the 2022 UP assembly election results were to be announced—the sun was about to begin its descent for the day. After picking up the local journalist, we took off on NH 31, a dusty highway under expansion for the past two years, to Lal Kuan, from where we continued on a narrow, 6-foot-wide concrete road surrounded by wheat fields and vegetable patches that ended approximately 50 metres before the village. A middle-aged man, wearing a long-sleeved shirt and khaki pants who was waiting for us at the entrance to the village, also joined our GZS team. After parking the car at the end of the concrete road, we walked on a narrow, uneven dirt road, full of mounds and pits, towards a mud hut that resembled the prehistoric dwellings of early humans I had seen on the Discovery Channel as a child and had wondered where, in this day and age, they might belong.

Even as we entered the village, the pungent stench of cattle dung that penetrated the nostrils was hard enough to cause a mild irritation in the nasal passage until we got used to the odour. Heaps of buffalo dung were piled together in little mounds, and buffaloes, cows and even a few goats lazed around everywhere, chewing hay strewn next to the mounds of dung. The hut, measuring about 20 by 10 feet, had mud-plastered walls and a sloping thatched roof. The doors and windows were just holes in the walls with dirty pieces of cloth hanging from iron nails and the thatched roof was supported using the chopped bark of hardwood trees. Right next to the hut was a smaller hut, where three buffaloes were tied to a pole in the centre that held the roof together. Outside the main hut, a bare-bodied and frail old man with a prominent jaw and stained teeth, fully decayed and caved in due to years of chewing tobacco, welcomed us with a bright smile. His strong, curved shoulders suggested he must have been a robust young man engaged in hard labour during his prime. As he seemed short on hearing, the local journalist took the initiative of talking to the old man in his native dialect and later translated for me.

The man's name was Rampathal. He was one of the oldest members of the village and belonged to the Dalit community, which accounted for over 75 per cent of the population of this impoverished village—the rest were members of the Yadav community, who lived in concrete homes in slightly more affluent settlements. Rampathal did not remember exactly how old he was but he remembered the ages of his two sons, Phoolchand and Chandan, as forty-eight and forty-six. Since these villagers married young, I suspected Rampathal to be around seventy. He had never been to any school and had lived in that mud home all his life—the thatched sheets were replaced once every few years and the walls were repaired occasionally, whenever they threatened to crumble. Some years ago, electricity cables and posts were laid in the village, after which he managed an illegal hook-up connection to light a 40-watt bulb inside his home. By and large, that was the biggest technological advancement Rampathal's home had seen.

When he was old enough to go and work, Rampathal began to do casual labour in other people's farms. He remembers his first wage vividly. '*Ek rupiya*,' he said emphatically, for a day's labour. The rates remained in single and double digits for much of his adult life, until the Mahatma Gandhi National Rural Employment Guarantee Act (MGNREGA) scheme came and the landlords, whom these Dalit villagers refer to as 'lambardar', were forced to match the government's wage to get the labourers to work for them. 'Now, I get paid Rs 250 a day for working in the fields,' Rampathal told us.

His sons are slightly better off and live in separate huts nearby in the same colony, again doing odd jobs. While Rampathal has never been to school, he sent both his sons to the government school nearby. However, they discontinued their studies before hitting their teens and can't read or write either—they can't even sign their names. 'My grandchildren are now going to private school,' Rampathal proudly declared to the journalist. 'We pay a fee of Rs 300 per month to the school and they will become policemen one day.' When the journalist asked him why he wanted his grandchildren to join the police, Rampathal said he had some relatives who had become policemen by paying bribes and that he, too, will make his grandsons police personnel with their help.

Like most people of his generation in the village, the old man has rarely travelled beyond his native village. He claimed to have gone to Unnao city about five or six times and to Varanasi once as a young man. Besides those outings, Rampathal's life had been spent within a radius of a few 100 metres from his hut, which is as impoverished and otherworldly as him. But when we asked him if he was happy about his life and his country, the old man broke into a bright smile yet again and said that he had no complaints!

The journalist rephrased his question and asked if there had been any change in his life over the past sixty years. 'Nothing!' the activist who had accompanied us intervened. 'Rampathal was born as a casual labourer's son, has spent most of his life doing hard labour in others' farms and lived his entire life in a hut slightly bigger than a cowshed without electricity or any other amenity. His two sons are also daily wagers with nothing to show as their own and make a living getting paid under the MGNREGA scheme or casual labour. His grandchildren are also likely to follow in their footsteps, as even now just about eight or ten youths have cleared intermediate or plus-two exams in this village of about 150 families,' he said, and began walking past Rampathal's home, as the dirt road inclined towards the rest of the colony. More mounds of cow dung, haystacks, goats, hens, and shacks similar to Rampathal's home welcomed us. Most of the huts were so alike that I couldn't differentiate one from another. A metal hand pump at the centre of the colony indicated the presence of some civic body activity in the village. Power supply had been brought through cement poles all the way to the entrance of the village, but none of the residents had a legal connection as they claimed to have no money to apply for one or pay power bills. The locals hooked the power lines to individual homes from the closest lamppost instead.

As we walked towards the more populated part of the village, the road got narrower but the huts were now made of bricks. Some of them even had concrete roofs, but I couldn't find a single plastered wall in any home in Nandulan Khera. A majority of the homes in this street had 40-watt bulbs, small television sets and LPG cylinders dumped in the porticos. Open sewers overflowed and cattle dung was scattered all over the mud roads, so one had to be careful with every step. As we walked past a few brick-walled homes, the journalist stopped me and pointed at a cluster of small 4-foot-high rooms built next to each other. 'Do you recognize them?' he asked me.

I did not.

'These are the famed Swachh Bharat toilets built by the Central government to end open defecation,' he explained.

I asked one of the men to open them for me, as the toilets or their front doors were in such a bad state that I couldn't even touch and open them. Ironically, the one we opened was stacked fully with hay. 'This is what Swachh Bharat toilets are used for here. Even if people want to use them, how can anyone get inside this small structure?' the journalist argued.

Asking around, we came to know that more than 90 per cent of the toilets were used as storerooms for stacking hay and other non-essentials—the only people who used the Swachh Bharat toilets were those who had differently abled family members or extremely old folks who couldn't walk to the fields to relieve themselves. The toilets had another major problem: none of them were attached to a septic tank, and an open 3-inch-wide pipe was all that had been provided to drain excreta and water. The few residents who had built septic tanks on their own also could not use the toilets, as once they got filled, the waste could not be pumped out because no lorries or other vehicles could be brought inside the village due to a lack of proper roads. In such a state, almost the entire adult and child population of Nandulan Khera has returned to open defecation.

As we continued walking past more decrepit homes and Swachh Bharat toilets converted into hay storerooms, a small crowd of bare-bodied boys started to follow us. The women, who were all outside their homes by now, pretended to mind their tasks, only occasionally glancing as discreetly as possible, but the male folk—very few had returned home by now—stood outside their homes and lamented about their condition. The narratives were all similar: Almost all the men and women in the village had been to school but had discontinued halfway due to either illness, or deaths in the family, or just poverty, as they had to work in farmlands to support their families. Some of the villagers owned small patches of land but did not cultivate anything on them as they had no money to buy seeds and fertilizer or employ workers to make productive use of the land. Out of the approximately 150 ration card holders, none had a job with the state government. When I asked my survey team and the villagers about the reservation quota for Dalits and members of economically weaker sections, they laughed.

In all these years, only one youth from Nandulan Khera had managed to land a government job with the air force recently. The proud father was Shivlal; his son Sachin Kumar had landed the job and was away for training. His home was also among the better ones in the village, with plywood chairs and a bamboo-strewn coffee table at the entrance. I stopped by at their home and asked him why their village was in such a bad situation when one of them—even if it was just one youngster—could land a decent job and get out of the mess. 'The government and country are only partly to be blamed; the rest of the blame remains with us. We don't have a TV or a fridge or any other gadget, but every youngster has a smartphone, which they use to share videos or watch movies. Nobody uses them to learn anything or expose the condition of our village,' he said to me. My convoy, which had by now halted outside Shivlal's home, nodded in agreement and urged the children who were following us to listen to the wise man and do as he was suggesting. The children, too, nodded as if they understood everything.

We continued our walk into the darkening alleys of Nandulan Khera, stumbling upon a picture tube television set in one home and worn-out microwave ovens or refrigerators in some of the other homes, which people had managed to sneak in from various sources. Towards the end of the colony was a slightly larger brick home, whose construction seemed to have been abruptly stopped midway several years ago. The double brick wall of the living room remained only half complete; wooden frames for the doors and windows were fixed but were covered by cloth screens. A frail old woman with wrinkled skin and thick silver-white hair sat outside the house, patiently combing her tresses. We found out that the woman, Shanti Devi, was eighty and had spent all her life in Nandulan Khera. She had two sons, both working as gas delivery boys in New Delhi, while the daughters-in-law and grandchildren were with her in the village. The journalist in the convoy, who had been doing most of the talking, asked her if she was happy with her life and her country. The woman remained silent for a few seconds and returned just a blank stare. 'How has your life been?' he screamed.

'*Kharab hai*,' she responded.

'What is wrong?'

The woman thought for a while and said that her life was actually quite good. 'Both my sons are away and my daughters-in-law are very sick. But my grandchildren are doing fine ... I have four of them,' she said. By then, a bright-looking teenage girl with large eyes and shiny, pale skin ran towards her grandmother from inside the home. 'This one is the eldest, Renuka.' Shanti Devi continued, 'We are getting free rations nowadays, so the children are no longer hungry!' She resumed combing her hair.

The activist came closer to me and said that this was what I could expect in most impoverished villages in the region. 'People have been reduced to mere cattle. They have been provided free rations for quite a while now, and no one is hungry anymore. So they naturally believe they are content and do not even feel their lives lack any quality. This policy of political parties to provide free food has reduced people to lose the urge to better the quality of their lives. As long as they don't have to work and get free food, these people are happy even if there is no electricity in their homes, no proper schools in their village or no [access to] healthcare,' he summarized.

The young girl, Renuka, looked at us and nodded as if she understood every word, but the old woman seemed disinterested in his discourse. By then, another young woman, a neighbour, came to us and shared her woes. Soon, a crowd gathered around us and more tales of maladies and misfortune poured out.

By the time we left, Nandulan Khera was blanketed in darkness. One or two streetlights did burn at that hour but were too dim to provide any significant illumination. Even inside the homes, there was hardly any light except in the kitchen area. As we got into our car to return to Unnao, I couldn't help but think of the bright, beautiful face of Renuka and all that she was likely to encounter on such dark nights when she stepped out into the caliginous fields surrounding her village to relieve herself or even just wander a few feet away from the shack she called home. At that precise moment, while driving on that desolate road, all the stories my former colleague had shared with me about the rapes and assaults that women suffered under the shroud of darkness seemed so real.

The next morning, by around 11, the Ground Zero Survey convoy was ready for me at Lal Kuan for day two of our tour of the impoverished villages in Unnao district. Now that I was aware of the ever-expanding size of our convoy, I had booked a seven-seater SUV for the day. As my local contact, the IT engineer who refused to wear a seat belt while driving in his hometown, had some urgent work, the convoy replaced him with a village pradhan from the Dalit community who tried to explain the backstory behind the plight of the villagers we interacted with.

We travelled several kilometres on the dusty under-renovation highway towards Raebareli, halting at one nondescript village after another, taking pictures of more mud homes, mounds of cow dung, unusable Swachh Bharat toilets, decrepit school buildings with broken walls and giant holes in the place of roofs, all the while talking to hapless women and children—the able-bodied men were all out at work—most of whom had no electricity in their homes, no televisions and no decent clothing. Several of the women we met went for work under the MGNREGA scheme when eligible and made a little money for themselves, while the rest depended on their husbands and other relatives to get by in life. We halted at half a dozen villages and interacted with people who were deprived of almost all government schemes and benefits for the poor—some of them did not even have ration cards, nor knew how to read or write. Ironically, wherever we went, everyone above eighteen had a voter identity card. Even those without ration cards were issued voter identity card and taken to vote for the most recent elections.

After just two days of traversing through these impoverished lands, I was already despairing over the pathetic living conditions of people I had interviewed or come across. In less than forty-eight hours, I felt like I had seen enough deprivation and poverty. When I shared this thought with the convoy, the village pradhan asked the cab driver to take me to the villages bordering the Ganga. But we couldn't reach there and, instead, landed up in Khutaha village in

Sikandarpur Karan block by late afternoon, as there was a roadblock preventing us from travelling any farther.

Unlike the other villages that I had been to since arriving in Unnao, Khutaha had good roads, brick-walled homes with concrete roofing, electricity and most of the amenities that provide a decent quality of life. Our SUV and convoy had been attracting attention wherever we went, and this village was no exception. A small crowd of young and old surrounded us as soon as we got out of the vehicle, wanting to know what we were doing in their village. The pradhan got out with me and walked towards the crowd. 'You can get a real sense of how things are from these villages,' he said as we went and sat on a low parapet outside a modest home. As the crowd grew large within minutes, the local journalist took charge of the situation with his usual questionnaire, while I stepped aside to a tea shop nearby to buy a soft drink because I was pretty certain the tales would be the same. When I returned, most of the men and women in the crowd were screaming at the top of their voices while the pradhan and the journalist patiently listened to them. The villagers thought we had come from the state government for a survey and were pouring out their woes. I pulled aside a young man who was particularly vocal and tried to find out what his problem was.

His name was Vimal Kumar; he was just twenty-five but a father of two. Like most of the young men and women in his village, Vimal was barely literate, having studied up to class five, and was a casual labourer working in the fields of the lambardar folk in the surrounding villages, earning around Rs 300 a day. On days when there was no farm labour, he took up work under the MGNREGA scheme for about Rs 200 a day. Both his children went to a private school nearby and his family had a decent home when compared to the plight of those in the villages I had just been to. However, he appeared more disgusted and angrier than anyone I had met in the past two days. 'It's not just me. You talk to anyone here and they will tell you why all those people, including women, are screaming like that,' he said, pointing at the crowd. 'Do you know I own two bighas of land by the Ganga and still work as a casual labourer, sometimes on the land I own, because some influential people have taken custody of my property illegally? The lambardar folk are growing wheat and other crops on the land for which I have pucca documentation in my name and have given me two bighas of wasteland instead,' he screamed.

Vimal belonged to the Scheduled Caste community, like most of his neighbours. In this village of around 600 families, at least one-third of the families belonged to the SC community and suffered the same fate as Vimal. 'All of us own fertile lands by the Ganga, some families up to even twelve bighas, but none of us can cultivate on our lands. Sometimes we are even taken to work as labourers on lands we own. Such is the plight here,' he lamented. The villagers had complained to the local police, tehsildars and even local politicians, but nothing changed. One of the biggest problems those farmers faced was that the officials they approached often belonged to more affluent communities, and trying to help the Dalits would mean putting their own lives in danger. After several failed attempts, the villagers were finally able to elect a village pradhan from their own community last year. Their only hope now was that he would use his political clout and retrieve their lands.

After listening to Vimal, I joined the crowd with whom the other men were still interacting and heard more horror stories of Dalits' lands being usurped as if it were a right. The people gathered around us claimed that the practice had been going on for generations, and until about twenty or thirty years ago, none from their communities could even read or write, which kept them at the mercy of the educated lot. 'Now, we can file a complaint with the police or magistrate and actually know what is happening. But still we find it so difficult to take possession of the lands we own,' said a young woman who was among the few literate women in the village.

After interacting with the villagers, we went to their pradhan's home to find out if their grievances were genuine. Unlike Vimal, the pradhan was a much older man, whose calm demeanour was reassuring. 'I have just completed a year. They should give me some time and we will do our best. If I can't get the officials to do it, we will have to go to court. What else can we do?' he said.

As we walked back to our car, I asked the local journalist why no media outlet had shown interest in this story, especially since it was election season in UP and it was a great story by any measure. 'Why would any journalist put it out? All the journalists in this region belong to the lambardar community. Why would they write against their own people? Even if there are some good people who might want to do it, do you think there won't be consequences? They would suffer the consequences and it would be bad,' he said.

---

On my last day in Unnao, a day before the 2022 UP assembly election results were to be announced, I went after the news story that had brought me here: The ex-BJP MLA Kuldeep Singh Sengar rape and murder case. Mankhi village, where both the former MLA Sengar and the minor victim are from, was about 17 kilometres from my hotel in Unnao. Even as we were driving, I noticed the difference between Mankhi and all the other villages I had been to. The road leading to Mankhi was black-topped, smooth and wide, with no potholes; dust storms did not erupt whenever a vehicle sped on the road, and I couldn't even spot any noticeable encroachment. Tall, shady trees on both sides of the road, behind which lay acres and acres of wheat fields, made driving a pleasure even on that sunny afternoon. As we reached the village, I also noticed the buildings were newer, stronger and imposing. A little chitchat with the locals in the surrounding areas also revealed that the people still had a lot of respect for their former MLA for bringing so much development to his constituency. Many of them do not even believe he raped the minor girl, despite a trial court convicting him of the offence, which was also widely reported. As of August 2023, an appeal challenging the trial court verdict is pending before the High Court.

As we entered Mankhi, the shut-down campus of the multi-storey international school that we passed on our way vindicated the villagers' belief in their MLA: This was no impoverished village. To the left of the school was a temple and a sprawling bungalow, behind which were about a dozen modest homes. Spotting the home of the victim wasn't difficult, as a Central Reserve Police Force (CRPF) section was permanently stationed outside the house following a court directive. The section, comprising three constables overseen by a superior, was present although the family had all moved out of their ancestral home since the chain of events that followed the minor girl's rape.

The horrid story began on 4 June 2017, when the minor girl went missing from her home in Mankhi at around 8 p.m. one weekday. Six days later, she was sexually assaulted at the residence of the BJP MLA and was later found in a different village on 20th June and brought back home. With the police extremely hesitant to take any action on the abduction-and-rape complaint for months, the victim's family tried to escalate the issue at various levels. That was when the victim's father was brutally attacked, allegedly by those close to Kuldeep Sengar, on 3 April 2018. Ironically, the father was arrested by the police a day later in connection with a twelve-year-old complaint and was lodged in prison. As tensions heightened, the victim attempted immolation outside the UP chief minister's office on 8 April 2018, and a day later her father was reported dead in police custody.[4]

---

4 'Unnao rape case: A timeline', *India Today*, 1 August 2019, https://www.indiatoday.in/india/story/unnao-rape-case-a-timeline-1576186-2019-08-01

The chain of horrific events grabbed public attention with the death of the victim's father and support began to pour in for the victim's family. As a consequence, the case got transferred out of the hands of the local police. Yet, no concrete action was taken and the victim's family continued to be harassed. One more year of twists and turns continued with the rape-accused MLA Sengar still controlling the show. On 28 July 2019, when the victim, her lawyer and two of their relatives, while travelling in a car, were hit by a speeding truck whose number plates were blackened, the alleged influence wielded by those close to the ex-MLA and his family came out in the open. The victim and her lawyer sustained life-threatening injuries, while the other two passengers were killed. The heinous nature of the escalating crimes, even amidst national outrage, shocked the nation. After the Supreme Court's intervention, a speedy trial ended with the conviction of Kuldeep Singh Sengar for life and a hefty fine in December 2019. Later, he was also convicted for culpable homicide not amounting to murder in connection with the death of the victim's father.

More than two years had passed since the conviction of Sengar, but the victim's family still stayed away from their ancestral home in Mankhi out of fear. The CRPF personnel told us that one of the younger siblings of the victim was present at their modest home to take care of some errands and that we could speak to her. The rest of the family was now residing at a rented accommodation in the city. I also came to know that the victim's mother was a Congress candidate for Unnao in the 2022 assembly polls.

After getting details about the family's residence, we asked the CRPF personnel for directions to ex-MLA Sengar's house. Pointing at the sprawling temple and school compound, one of them said the bungalow behind the temple was his home. The school, the temple and all the property surrounding it belonged to the family of the ex-MLA, who was now in jail. Hoping to meet some of his family members, we walked to the giant gate at the entrance and knocked. Since the compound wall was at least 12 feet tall, we could barely spot the entrance to the house. As we yelled to get someone's attention, a cyclist who was passing by stopped and told us that nobody lived there anymore. 'The family has moved to Lucknow, and they come here only for Diwali and Holi ever since he went to jail,' he said. He asked us to get in touch with the residents of another big house adjacent to the CRPF tent, where a saffron flag with the lotus symbol fluttered atop a tall lamppost. 'They are close relatives of Sengar,' he said before leaving.

However, we chose to meet the victim's mother instead, and returned to Unnao. A few phone calls and a little bit of asking around for directions was all that was necessary to find the residence of the Congress candidate for the Unnao constituency, who stayed put in a modest two-storey home in a residential colony just a few streets behind the hotel I was staying at. The home had been rented by the Congress party for her and her family during their campaign. Though the counting of votes for the 2022 polls was less than twenty-four hours away, there was no indicator that a prominent party candidate stayed at the home—no cadre, no supporters, nothing—but for the presence of gun-wielding CRPF personnel.

After screening us for weapons and noting our contact details, a young CRPF personnel escorted my local contact and me inside the house. We noticed a little boy, aged around ten, playing in the sparsely furnished living room on the ground floor and asked the child for the Congress candidate. The boy immediately turned around and ran upstairs, giggling. Unable to find anyone else, I debated whether to go upstairs or not, when a fair, middle-aged woman hurried down the stairs wearing a faded floral-print white-and-pink polyester saree and an apologetic half-smile. Observing the woman's slumped shoulders and submissive body language, my first thought was that she must be the personal assistant or a helper of the candidate, coming down to take me to her. Upon climbing down the stairs, the lady immediately covered her face and head with the flowing end of her saree and said namaste with folded hands. She was Asha Singh, Congress candidate for the Unnao assembly seat.

My acquaintance and I were taken to a room behind the living room, where she dragged over two plastic chairs and asked us to sit. After we sat down, Ms Singh chose to sit cross-legged on the floor. Embarrassed, we got up immediately and offered the chair to her. 'No, no, I am comfortable sitting like this,' she said, and became even more apologetic. But we were so uncomfortable that after some persuasion, the lady agreed to sit on the chair and a third chair was brought out for us by a young woman. That woman, wearing a bright pink salwar kameez, looked a lot more confident and sophisticated. 'What do you want to talk to her about?' she asked us.

My acquaintance spoke to the younger woman in the local dialect and explained that I had come to interview her mother about women's safety in the villages surrounding Unnao and how she felt about it, besides discussing what had happened to their family.

'But so many people have interviewed us and it is all there on YouTube. What more do you want?' the young woman asked my acquaintance. By then, Ms Singh intervened and asked if we were from a TV channel. When I told her that I was writing a book and that our interview would not appear on any TV channel or newspaper the next day, both the women appeared more comfortable and allowed me to record our conversation. With the counting of votes barely twelve hours away, the Congress candidate showed no signs of tension or excitement; she seemed more worried about my presence. However, as we spoke, the forty-five-year-old mother of four calmed down and, without any prompting, narrated the entire sequence of events that had happened to her loved ones, starting from the abduction of her daughter. She had probably repeated the story several times in the past to umpteen media houses and it must have been so refined by now that I chose to ignore that part of the conversation.

I asked about her transformation from a rustic housewife to becoming the candidate for a major political party in a state where a woman's presence is not even acknowledged in public places. 'I have to thank Didi [Priyanka Gandhi] for everything she did for me. I am a village woman with no education. I don't know how to speak in public. Until that incident, I had never interacted with men outside my family. I know how to run a house but nothing else, as I have always been confined to my home. Didi gave me confidence and told me to tell the people what had happened to me and my family and promise to them to never let it happen to another family. And that's all I did,' Asha Singh explained. 'I don't know politics ... whether I will win or lose. But it doesn't matter.'

I asked her if anything had changed in the five years since her daughter had been raped.

'Nothing has changed at all.' She was fervent now. 'It's still the same. Women are not at all safe out here. How many more rapes have been reported in Mankhi and the surrounding villages since my daughter's case and how many families have got justice? Has anything changed?' she asked me.

She was right. The number of horrific rape cases reported in rural UP has never changed. Even during my stay in Unnao, yet another young woman from a neighbouring village had been raped and it had made headlines. 'At least in our case, the perpetrator of the crime and we [the victims] belonged to the same caste, and because of that whatever happened to my family became news, even if it was after a struggle. If it had been a Dalit woman or a woman belonging to some other caste, there would have been no case at all,' she said. 'Even in our case, my daughter still worries about her safety. We get veiled threats from people even now. I am not educated and don't understand politics. I am standing in this election for the sake of other women so that no one faces what my family did,' she reiterated.

There was no questioning the intent of the lady: She was earnest and wanted to make a difference. But as I could clearly see, this simple housewife was no match for the seasoned politicians of this region who had until now kept their women confined only to their kitchens. Only a brutal rape and several suspected murders and blatant attempts to thwart investigation by central agencies could catapult this woman to the poll front, and that too after a lot of cajoling. But a few years in New Delhi and some tutoring in politics can hardly make anyone a successful politician. UP has indeed produced a Mayawati and several other successful politicians from the fairer sex, but the condition of the ordinary woman remains the same: They simply remain invisible in the large scheme of things.

I got to know later that the confident young woman who had asked us the purpose of our visit was the victim. She was definitely smart; perhaps in a decade or so she would be ready for the polls and Unnao might then have a serious contender from the fairer sex. For now, there appeared no hope in sight, and the election results that were out the next morning were the proof.

# Chauri Chaura, Gorakhpur District

LAKSHMI MOBILE CARE, A TINY CELL PHONE REPAIR SHOP run by Mahant Prajapaty in the Futahawa Inar complex near Mundera Bazar, is right on the busy Gorakhpur–Deoria highway, close to Chauri Chaura Railway Station. Mahant is dusky, sports a neatly trimmed beard and is thirty-three but has the energy and boyish looks of a twenty-five-year-old. During the day, he usually sits behind a large worktable in his shop, amid damaged chargers and scattered mobile phone parts, and fixes broken mobile phones. For the past few years now, besides repairing broken mobiles, the youngster has also taken up the responsibility of representing the dwindling voice of the families of freedom fighters from Chauri Chaura, who feel they are yet to get the recognition and respect due to them for sacrifices made by their grandfathers and great-grandfathers. The thick set of files on a corner of his worktable containing details of the freedom fighters' families and their demands, neatly printed in colourful pamphlets, ready for anyone who would care to take a look, aptly showcases his commitment to the cause.

An active office-bearer of the Swatantrata Sangram Senani Evam Uttaradhikari (Aashith) Jan Kalyan Parishad, Gorakhpur, Mahant has of late been travelling across UP and the rest of the country with the demands of the 200-odd freedom fighters' kin in the Chauri Chaura area, which include family pension for descendants of freedom fighters, permanent recognition as Senani families and preference for government jobs, among others. His grandfather Viswambar Jhuri was among those imprisoned for the killing of several policemen as well as for setting Chauri Chaura police station on fire in February 1922—a sacrifice he claims has gone unnoticed.

On a sultry Saturday afternoon in April 2022, when the midday sun roasted Mundera Bazar and the surrounding areas, I went to Lakshmi Mobile Care. Mahant, his father, Bandan, and their neighbours, Kamala Prasad Gupta and Paras Bhod, were waiting for me. I had contacted Mahant over the phone earlier that morning to inquire about his role in the Swatantrata Sangram Senani Parishad and had asked him to gather as many Senani family members as he could.

All the four men Mahant could assemble in that short notice belonged to the Dumri Khurd village—home to a majority of the freedom fighters who participated in the Chauri Chaura violence, many of whom have even paid the price for it with their lives. The men were keen on explaining their demands and also describing the condition of the Senani families a hundred years after the incident. While most of the direct descendants of those freedom fighters have died, Kamala Prasad, Paras and just a handful of others are still alive and receiving pension. They were now keen on securing something for their families before their time came.

Before getting to their present-day woes, I insisted they narrate those stories to me first. While Paras and Bandan do not recall any first-person accounts of that period from their fathers—as their parents had died young, soon after their release from jail—seventy-seven-year-old Kamala Prasad vividly recalls his father narrating tales of the villagers' role in the Chauri Chaura violence and their suffering under the police and British officers.

He, however, clarified that all that he was about to tell me was what he had heard from his father, and he had no proof or documents to prove anything. 'We were little children then. My father, who worked as a daily wager, would come home late at night and tell us [Kamala and his brother, Jainath] bedtime stories, mostly revolving around what had happened here in 1922 and its aftermath. It was the only story people in Dumri Khurd told their children and grandchildren back then; it is still our favourite story,' recalled Kamala Prasad, who wore a kurta-pajama and white cap.

The narrative began on 8 February 1920, when Mahatma Gandhi visited the Balamiyan grounds in Gorakhpur to spread his non-cooperation movement among the masses. 'My father, a young man at the time, went to Gorakhpur to listen to Gandhiji along with his friends. He was so impressed with the crowd and Gandhiji's speech that when they came back to the village, he immediately joined the Congress party and started paying the membership fees. In those days, the village had its own local Congress committee and its members used to keep each other updated regularly on the developments across the country. Since the police were always suspicious of Congress members, my father and his associates used to exchange little notes and used code words to spread messages,' Kamala Prasad said, as we settled down comfortably and listened. Although this has been the oldest and most repeated story of Chauri Chaura, Paras, Bandan and Mahant were as attentive as I was. My cab driver, who had appeared disinterested in what I was doing until then, also pulled a stool out from under Mahant's worktable and sat near Kamala Prasad, crowding the little mobile repair shop.

'On the day of the incident, thousands of people gathered in Dumri Khurd. They wanted to seek answers from the police for what they had done to Bhagawan baba, a local leader who was allegedly attacked by the police, and marched towards the police station—that was when things got out of control. Violence broke out and both sides lost a number of people. After the incident, all the men in the village went into hiding. Most of the stories my father told us were from that period, when he shifted from one hideout in the forest to another within the region to escape the police. All the men in the village hid in different places as a large battalion of police and military arrived by train at Chauri Chaura Railway Station to track down the freedom fighters. But there was none in Dumri Khurd. My father, Chinagi, initially stayed at a relative's place out in the jungle when the search was on. Meanwhile, the police and military picked up every man in the village and beat them up to get information about the freedom fighters. The families of the freedom fighters were tortured, and their lands and cattle were taken away. They were subjected to all kinds of torture to give away the hideouts of their men,' he reminisced with an excitement that betrayed his age.

One day, a cousin of Chinagi who had harboured him for a few days was caught by the police. He was taken to the Chauri Chaura station and tortured to reveal his hideout, but the cousin, like most of the villagers, remained tight-lipped. When the torture became regular and unbearable for the cousin, Chinagi came out of hiding and surrendered to the police, according to Kamala Prasad. He was immediately shifted to the Cellular Jail in the Andamans, where he spent several years before returning home. Kamala and his brother were born upon his father's return, by which time he had lost his ancestral property and all other wealth and had to take up hard labour even to make a modest living.

'Some years after Independence, the government actually recognized the sacrifices of the Chauri Chaura freedom fighters and offered us land in Nainital, Meerut and a few other places, besides a home and a tractor. But my father refused to take any of it. He was still suspicious of the government, and used to tell us that he had surrendered and fallen for their trap once but that he would never go to government officers again. He was always afraid and never trusted them until his death in 1964,' Kamala said.

After their father's death, Kamala and his brother, who were educated only up to class six or seven, took up casual labour to support their families. 'Like my father, we also did not finish school and spent our lives working on farms. After the family members of Chauri Chaura freedom fighters repeatedly pressed for recognition, the state government started giving us family pension in 1993. Now, we get around Rs 20,000 every month as pension, but that will end with me. I have four sons who are still struggling to get a foothold in life, but they will not be entitled to the pension or any formal recognition as a freedom fighter's family,' he pointed out, as Paras and the others nodded.

Kamala Prasad has four sons who are all educated but mostly do odd jobs or run small businesses. Using his contacts in the state government, he recently managed to secure a job in the police department for his second son. 'But the others are without steady employment. Like most freedom fighters' families in this region, we are also struggling to make ends meet. Governments keep coming and going but nothing much is offered to our children or the other dependants' families,' Kamala rued.

Mahant, who had also been patiently listening to Kamala Prasad, intervened and said that most other states have extended the pension to the grandchildren and even great-grandchildren of freedom fighters, but theirs is yet to. 'Our association is making every possible effort to get that recognition. Also, after this generation of whom just four or five elders like Kamalaji are still alive, nobody will know who we are or what our ancestors sacrificed for this country. Even so many years later, their sacrifices and contribution to the freedom struggle have been considered secondary to that of freedom fighters who participated in other movements elsewhere,' reiterated Mahant. He also took photocopies of all the files he had with him and handed them over for my reference, and suggested I visit the villages where freedom fighters' families live to understand their plight first-hand.

---

Less than 500 metres from Lakshmi Mobile Care, on the highway towards Deoria, a tar-topped road turned towards the left, narrowed farther into a 6-foot-wide RCC road and continued past wheat fields, towards a modest temple painted pink with a tall dome on its left. On the right side of the road was a vacant piece of land with a huge tree, bereft of any leaves. A little ahead of the tree lay an empty volleyball court with flood lights hanging from a tall pole. The gigantic trunk of the tree was surrounded by a raised platform of about 5 feet, on which sat about a dozen men, young and old, chatting the evening away. Beyond the temple was a congested residential colony with narrow lanes mostly filled with shabby, decaying houses built wall-to-wall. The temple, the vacant piece of land with the leafless tree, the volleyball court, the modest houses built on narrow lanes and the surrounding farmland completed Dumari Khurd, popularly known as the village of freedom fighters.

Paras Ghor, whom I had met earlier at the mobile repair shop, lived two buildings away from the temple facing the vacant plot of land and had accompanied me to the village; he had even offered a tour of the freedom fighters' homes. Ghor's grandfather Pachuputra Chotu, who was imprisoned in connection with the arson of Chauri Chaura police station and the killing of nineteen police personnel, had been lodged at the Varanasi prison, where he had died before his release. His father, Bandhan, had also died young, when Paras was just three or four years old. 'We did not get any assistance from the government for my grandfather's sacrifice for the nation. Whatever I have built today is through hard work since the age of twelve,' he asserted as we stepped out of his house.

Like Kamala Prasad, Paras also has four sons, none of whom have a stable job. He worries that the prestige and tag of a freedom fighter's family, which were bestowed upon him and his elders, will disappear with him, and his children will not be able to get any benefits for the sacrifices of his grandfather. 'It's good that the government has built a state-of-the-art memorial, spending several crores for the 100th anniversary of the event in our village, but they could divert their attention to our families too. We have lost a lot,' he lamented as we proceeded towards the home of Shaheed Nazar Ali, one of the leaders of the huge crowd that had marched towards the Chauri Chaura police station on 4 February 1922. He had succumbed to the police fire.

As we walked from Paras's home and through one dingy lane after another, he pointed at every second or third home and recalled the name of a freedom fighter who had either been hanged or jailed in connection with the incident. Most of the houses were shabby and decaying, and had barely seen any renovation for the past several decades. The paint had worn off the walls, the wooden doors and windows had bloated and the cement plaster had peeled off the roofs and sunshades, making them appear like they could collapse any time. Little children screamed at each other and ran across the streets between the homes, while elderly men stretched their backs and feet, lounging on plastic chairs outside their homes, enjoying the evening sun. Even as we were walking, at least half a dozen men approached Paras and asked him if I had come from the government and if their families would get anything. Among the few heartwarming sights in the village was the presence of Hindu and Muslim homes next to each other and children of both communities playing together, something I had not witnessed in most of the other towns I had been to while travelling through UP for this book.

Paras halted in front of one of the very few better-looking houses on the street and told me that it was Nazar Ali's family home. The freedom fighter's name, neatly engraved in gold letters on a black granite tablet, was pasted at the entrance along with the dates of the incident and Ali's hanging. Above the tablet, two national flags crossing each other were also stuck to the wall. 'You see that name plate, that was put up by the family and not by the government. We want the government to give recognition to freedom fighters' homes,' Paras pointed out. As the front gate was locked from the inside, we knocked and waited but got no response. Stuck on the wall opposite Nazar Ali's home were large posters of several other freedom fighters and their current family members. We waited for a while outside Ali's home before knocking again. When there was still no response, we continued walking. Along the way, some more men in various stages of impoverishment were introduced to me as grandchildren, grandnephews, etc., of the famous Senanis of Dumri Khurd. As far as I could see, none of the progenies I met had the stamina or the pride that probably drove their ancestors to protest against the mighty British.

After returning to his home, I asked Paras if there was any memorial in the village commemorating the event. He laughed. 'You saw that ground outside and those men sitting under the peepal tree? That's the memorial; that's where all the Senanis from different villages gathered around 4 p.m. on 4 February 1922 and decided to march towards the Chauri Chaura police station. Thousands of people assembled there and went out to create history. Only a few of us know all this; our children have no interest in any of these stories because times have changed and they don't take any pride in what their grandfathers did. In that way, after we die, there will be none to highlight the importance of that ground or this village,' Paras said, a tinge of sadness lacing his otherwise coarse, emotionless voice.

---

Understanding and interpreting the Chauri Chaura violence and its aftermath have been some of the most challenging exercises for those interested in the history of our freedom struggle, since the very idea of right and wrong begins to blur the moment one begins to discuss the violence, the build up to it and its aftermath. With so many strong opinions and explanations still floating around, I have consciously decided to get my version of the Chauri Chaura violence mostly from a century-old document obtained from the Chauri Chaura police station, which I believe gives a fairly neutral account of the mood that prevailed in this part of the country at the time, since the objective of this book is not historical research but to provide a glimpse of the past to portray an honest perspective of the present.

As I mentioned before, while the violence broke out on 4 February 1922, the seeds for the same were sown when Gandhi announced the non-cooperation movement in 1920 and a large number of people across the country heeded the call. The nationwide unrest also triggered a longing for Swaraj, self-rule, among a largely docile peasantry population in and around Gorakhpur. People here began to soak in the idea that Independence was not too far away and Mahatma Gandhi was going to lead them towards that goal. It was evident when Gandhi visited Gorakhpur and addressed a huge crowd of around 1,50,000 people[1] who flocked to the meeting venue from almost all the villages surrounding Gorakhpur. Many of the men and women who listened to Gandhi's speech were enthused by his vigour and were pitted against the British Government. Among them were enthusiastic young men from Dumri Khurd, Chauri Chaura and surrounding villages.

The hope that Independence was just a year or so away gave birth to several Indian National Congress committees across various zillas. Sub-committees were formed under these committees at the village level, and volunteers for Congress

---

1 *The Collected Works of Mahatma Gandhi*, vol. 22, p. 329.

Volunteer Corps, similar to the underground Bengal Volunteer Corps, were recruited from every village for a modest fee of merely four annas for every bigha of land they owned. Among those who rushed to join this volunteer army of sorts were anti-socials and former prisoners, besides patriotic youngsters who formed a sizeable number as they were promised due recognition for their service upon the nation attaining freedom and assured that their past records would be erased. With the number of Congress Volunteer Corps soaring in each village, people gradually grew emboldened and spoke openly against the British government, the police and other government officials in the hope that the present government would be replaced soon. Congress leaders across the country were also prepping these volunteers for a revolution and to take over the reins of the government from the British. As a part of these preparations, small units of foot soldiers were professionally trained as an alternative law enforcement force through drills, parades, etc.

According to police records, after the Ahmedabad Congress Session in January 1922, Lal Mohammed Fakir and Uprothak Shikari from Dumri Khurd and Bhagauti from Mundera Bazar were appointed as officers or leaders of these volunteer law enforcement units in the Chaura region. Soon, recruiting, training and equipping of the volunteers began in a full-fledged manner in these villages, and the leaders began to engage them in drills and military-style parades. Nazar Ali, vice president of the local Congress committee, approached his superiors in Gorakhpur for formal permission to train volunteer corps as a disciplinary force but was denied, as they felt the villagers of the Chaura region were too rustic and unprepared for disciplinary training and action. However, Nazar Ali wasn't convinced that his villagers couldn't be trained, and so he appointed Bhagwan Ahir from Chaura village, a government pensioner who had relevant experience, as the leader of the unit and began providing training to and conducting parades of the volunteer corps near the Chauri Chaura police station. Along with the training, the volunteers also organized frequent meetings in which they openly criticized the British government.

As the number of participants in these meetings grew, the volunteer forces grew bolder and began to force the closure of shops at Mundera Bazar and shut down liquor shops, often looting them instead, as part of their larger plan to throw out the British and attain freedom. Ahead of one such forced closure of Mundera Bazar, the Chauri Chaura police station in-charge, Gupteshwar Singh, met Bhagwan Ahir and warned him that as a government pensioner, he should not engage in anti-government activities. Bhagwan responded fiercely to that warning and the police official is alleged to have physically assaulted him. The insulted man rushed to inform his leaders, Lal Mohammed, Nazar Ali and Uprothak Shikari, and a meeting was held by the senior leaders of the Congress before a decision was taken to organize a march to the Chauri Chaura police station, with a large number of volunteers seeking an explanation for the assault on Bhagwan Ahir.

On 4 February 1922, the Congress volunteers began to swell from the surrounding villages and almost filled the ground opposite Paras Ghor's ancestral home by around 4 p.m. that evening. Nazar Ali, Uprothak Shikari and Lal Mohammed led the crowd, raising slogans against the British government and police, towards the police station. When the marchers reached Bopa Bazar, the crowd was estimated to be at least 5,000 strong. As the Chauri Chaura station in-charge received information that a huge crowd marching through the bazar was headed towards the police station, he sought additional reserve police and patrol vehicles, and the procession was forced to halt at the bazar. However, upon seeing the police, the crowd became more agitated and did not disperse. In an attempt to mediate, a local zamindar, Sardar Haricharan Singh, and four of his staffers intervened and spoke to the agitators. After the interaction with the marchers, the sardar allegedly asked the police inspector to allow the procession to continue to the police station. Following this, the inspector pulled back his constables.

The marchers reached the Chauri Chaura police station and some of the leaders went and asked the station in-charge why Bhagwan Ahir had been assaulted. An argument ensued, and when the marchers got wind of the situation, they grew wild and unmanageable. The station head ordered the marchers to calm down and disperse, but the volunteers assembled in a single file, took out wooden logs and rained blows on the police. The police reportedly fired in the air, forcing the volunteers to disperse. When the firing took place, the crowd became even more agitated and rushed towards the police station, screaming that they were willing to even take bullets for Mahatma Gandhi.

When the situation began to get out of hand, the police started firing at the protestors. To escape the bullets, several marchers rushed towards the police station, which forced all the police personnel to run inside the station and lock themselves in to escape the rampaging mob. It was then that the crowd set the police station on fire with kerosene brought from the bazar. When police personnel tried to escape the fire and rushed out, they were allegedly beaten and thrown back into the fire. All the inflammable materials in the station were razed and, but for one constable, all the staffers died. Two sub-inspectors, one head constable, fourteen constables and five chowkidars were killed in the violence, according to police records. Among the protestors, Nazar Ali, Jolaha and Bardolia from Chaura village and Bhagvan Teli from Mundera Bazar were shot down by the police, according to the FIR. The only constable who escaped was Mohammed Siddiqui, who alerted other stations of the violence and sought their help.

On 12 February 1922, the Congress Working Committee led by Gandhi resolved that the mass non-cooperation movement would be suspended following the Chauri Chaura mass killings and other violent incidents that had unfolded in Bombay and Madras around the same time.[2]

---

About 2 kilometres from Chauri Chaura Railway Station is Mehiyan village, where Ram Narayan Tripathi lives with his children and grandchildren in their modest one-storey home with cement flooring, plastered but unpainted walls and windows with broken, stained-glass panes. He is eighty-two, mostly bedridden and dependant on his walking stick and grandson Suryansh, even to go to the toilet behind their living room. Ram Narayan's grandfather Lal Behari, a.k.a. Meghu Tiwari, was hanged by the British government in 1923 for his role in the Chauri Chaura violence when he was just thirty-seven. Hailing from an influential family with substantial wealth at the time of the riots, Ram Narayan's parents and grandparents suffered the brunt of the British brutality and were stripped of all their wealth in the years following the Chauri Chaura violence. More than a hundred years later, Ram Narayan, his children and his grandchildren barely manage a middle-class life. Until health began to fail him, Mr Tripathi had been the voice of the Senani families of Chauri Chaura for several decades, a role that Mahant of Lakshmi Mobile Care has now taken over from him. When I called Ram Narayan and asked if I could meet him at his residence, he immediately agreed and provided directions through his son, Ravi Narayan Tripathi. 'I will also try to bring other families of freedom fighters,' he suggested.

Upon reaching his home, I found two other men, also grandchildren of freedom fighters, sitting around Ram Narayan's cot in the living room, where he was lying on his back. His son, Ravi Narayan, and eldest grandson, Suryansh, were also present in the living room with us, listening to him speak about the legacy they

---

2 *The Collected Works of Mahatma Gandhi*, vol. 26, p. 138.

had inherited. After sitting upright with the help of Suryansh, Ram Narayan introduced the other Senani kin, whose grandfathers hadn't been hanged but had served prison time and later died of natural causes. While most of the Senani kin remain largely illiterate and spent their lives working on their farms or as casual labourers, Ram Narayan began his career as a teacher, and later got a law degree and practised as an advocate for most of his adult life. 'Even now, I do go to the court rarely,' he uttered in clear English when I asked about his occupation. Due to his qualification and family background, he became the unofficial spokesperson of the freedom fighters' families in his younger years, a role he performed well. 'Basically, there is only one thing to say about our freedom fighter families,' he declared. 'Except one or two, most of us are living hand to mouth. This is the truth of the Chauri Chaura freedom fighters' families.'

While his grandfather had died much before Ram Narayan was born, he had heard from his parents that Meghu Tiwari was one of the prominent residents of Mehiyan and owned farmlands both in Mehiyan as well as in Pahalganj. The family also owned a textile business at Mundera Bazar until the police station attack took place. 'After the incident, they took away everything. My grandfather and his relatives were harassed and looted of all their wealth. We all know what would happen to those who set fire to a police station and kill nineteen policemen now in 2022. Imagine how brutal the British reaction to the incident was when someone killed their officers and men in 1922! None of the families of those involved in the riots were spared of anything; even our cattle weren't spared,' he explained, as the other men around him nodded in agreement with every detail. 'My father, Rambali Tiwari, had to literally start from scratch again, and what you see now is what we built since then. Everything we had until that point was wiped out.'

While the family had been relieved of its wealth, the adulation and respect they received from the villagers and even the government has never been in short supply. When Ram Narayan was an active lawyer, he got an opportunity in 1978 to be a part of the inner security personnel of the late Prime Minister Indira Gandhi during her visit to Gorakhpur. 'When I got an opportunity, I told her about my grandfather and the Chauri Chaura incident and how there is not even a memorial to commemorate their sacrifice, while the dead policemen have a memorial. Ms Gandhi had come to campaign for a bypoll and assured me that she'll do something about it if they win. The Congress won and sure enough, money was sanctioned for a memorial,' he recalled. Since then, Ram Narayan has stayed in constant touch with the bureaucracy and Congress leaders in New Delhi. To prove his proximity to top national leaders, Ram Narayan also pulled out black-and-white photographs with some of the leaders and showed them to me.

While getting a memorial in Chauri Chaura turned out to be relatively easy, getting recognition as freedom fighters' families, who were thus eligible for pension, turned out to be a more cumbersome affair and took some more years. Only in 1993 were the families of those who were hanged for the Chauri Chaura violence entitled to freedom fighters' family pension. 'The P.V. Narasimha Rao government finally recognized our families as freedom fighters' descendants and granted the direct descendants family pension. What started as a modest sum of around Rs 800 or so has now increased to Rs 20,000, but we still face discrimination when compared with other freedom fighter families and I wonder why,' he said.

Ram Narayan had two sons, one of whom passed away some time ago. His surviving son, Ravi Narayan Tripathi, now works at the Chauri Chaura Memorial Library for a salary of Rs 8,000 per month, which he receives from the Mundera Bazar (Town Area) local body, his employer. The family also owns some agricultural land, from which he gets some additional income.

While Ram Narayan sounded hopeless and dejected, his forty-three-year-old son intervened and said that they were proud of their inheritance. 'We might not have a lot of money and the government might not recognize what my great-grandfather sacrificed. But we are proud of what they did and the villagers respect us for it. The recognition we get from society is enough. If we go about seeking alms, our ancestors' sacrifices will become meaningless,' he asserted.

Later that afternoon, I visited the Chauri Chaura police station. The present police station—a heritage building designed like a miniature fortress with arched entrances, diamond-cut iron grills protecting the windows, painted yellow with red borders, and a structure resembling a watchtower—was built in the year 1923, after the old police station was completely destroyed in the fire. Within the station premises, the British government had also built a memorial at the location of the original police thana, right behind the present station.

As the heritage police station frequently gets visitors not interested in policing work, the guards at the entrance immediately took me to an officer, who assigned a constable to take me to the memorial next door. Diwan Yashwant Kumar took me around the empty compound, explaining the various events of the past as they had unfolded, while I shared with him details of my interactions with the residents of Dumri Khurd and its surrounding villages.

At the centre of the memorial was a minaret of sorts built on a raised platform. The structure was painted white, which I suspect was done to conceal the original inscriptions engraved on the minaret, perhaps narrating the police version of the incident. I tried to read them but couldn't; the painters had ensured they were indecipherable. Behind the minaret were the individual tombs of all the police personnel who died in the incident, with their names painted on each. The names of the Muslim police personnel were printed in Urdu, along with the date of their death. In most of the Hindu tombs, used mud lamps with wicks soiled in oil were left behind by relatives of the deceased after they had paid their respects. Incense sticks were also found on some tombs. Each of these structures was called a Shaheed Smarak.

Diwan Yashwant Kumar, who had been hesitantly describing the sequence of events, pointing at various corners of the memorial compound, suddenly became quiet when we reached the central minaret. He folded his hands, straightened his back and just stood still. From the time I had arrived, I noticed a discomfort among the police personnel as I probed further into the violence that had taken place a hundred years ago. According to the villagers in the surrounding areas, the predecessors of these policemen and women are those responsible for their plight even today, and they considered the memorial built for the slain policemen a scar on the freedom movement. The local policemen were well aware of that sentiment and my visit to the police station after stopping by at Dumri Khurd and other villages probably made Yashwant suspicious of my motives. Noticing his discomfort, I shared a little personal history with him about my maternal grandfather, who had been a staffer at the Madras Central Jail at the time of Independence. 'He had also worked under the British government and was just doing a job to make a decent living, like these policemen who died,' I told him.

The policeman nodded and began to read out the names of the murdered personnel from their tombs for my records. He also pointed out that during those days, except for British officers and top Indian government officials, most police personnel were hired from local villages and that all the dead must have also been from surrounding areas. 'Their family members are also receiving a pension from the government,' Yashwant said. Eager to find out what had happened to the families of those policemen a hundred years later, I asked him if he could get me their contact details.

For the next hour or so, Yashwant and a few other police personnel, both men and women, desperately opened old hardbound files in the station and sifted through unevenly scribbled and typed pages that were several decades old for the addresses or phone numbers of family members of those who had died in the fire. But there was nothing beyond a narration of the incident from the old FIR and names of the victims, which he took a copy of and handed to me. 'Some of their relatives do come even now during Diwali and other occasions to light a lamp at the memorial of their loved ones,' Yashwant disclosed. 'We also know that they still receive their pension. If you check with the pension office, you can get their addresses.'

As I was about to leave the station, Yashwant's superior officer, who had been approached for his permission to hand me the records, called us back and informed me that while the police station did not maintain their records, all the names and addresses of the police personnel who died that night were in a booklet published on the incident, which was available at the Chauri Chaura Shaheed Smarak library, and that I could get it from there.

I immediately called Ravi Narayan Tripathi and asked him to come to the Shaheed Smarak right behind Chauri Chaura Railway Station. Unlike other heritage monuments I had visited recently, the Chauri Chaura Shaheed Smarak was anything but impressive —just another badly maintained city park. I couldn't see any greenery, except sparse patches of grass surrounding the circular memorial; the grass was also pale and almost yellow. A pond and a fountain were present but without a drop of water in them. Dried leaves, used packets of chips, pieces of beedis and other waste materials were strewn around in the central courtyard, where about a dozen benches had been laid. The inner walls of the compound were printed with the names and birth and death dates of freedom fighters from across the country, along with their portraits. The centrepiece, which looked like a mustard-brown PSLV rocket from a distance, stood out from its shabby surroundings. Upon getting closer, I noticed that the monument had three wings, on which the names of those freedom fighters who were hanged for the 4th February incident were carved in gold letters.

With the late evening sun still blazing, a dozen or so senior citizens occupied the benches and chatted with each other about how their 'Buldozer Baba' swept the Vidhan Sabha elections recently, among other topics. A young man and his wife tried to take a selfie in front of the memorial, trying different angles to bring the entire height of the structure within the frame of the picture, while a handful of local children ran around the PSLV structure, chasing each other over a ball. When I walked into the library building to the left of the compound, a middle-aged man approached me and introduced himself as Lal Babu, also a descendant of the Chauri Chaura freedom fighters, and said Ravi Narayan had asked him to help me out. 'You want to know about the family members of the dead policemen?' he asked. 'Are you sure? They were the enemy ... *Angrez ke naukar the* (workers of the English). Do you want to meet their families?'

When I replied in the affirmative, Lal Babu clarified that it might be difficult to get those details immediately, suggesting that it could take a few days, and asked me to come back later.

---

While passing Lakshmi Mobile Care on my way back, I suggested to my cab driver, who had enthusiastically joined me wherever I went, that we stop there and ask Mahant if he had the details. 'No, sir, why would he? *Woh Angrez ke naukar the!*'

It made sense, so we drove straight to Gorakhpur instead. My cab driver, a jovial middle-aged man who seemed to enjoy a good, hearty laugh every now and then, made another interesting observation. 'What a funny country we are living in! A hundred years after the Chauri Chaura police station was attacked, the government is still paying pension to the families of the freedom fighters who attacked the station. As if that is not enough, the same government is also still paying pension to the families of the policemen who were killed by these people—for a hundred years! Is there a better example of wastage of public money?' he asked, and laughed one of his laughs that appeared to come straight from his heart. Nevertheless, another good point!

Sitting in the passenger seat, I couldn't take my mind off the '*Angrez ke naukar*' phrase that Lal Babu and my driver had uttered with such disgust. As I mentioned before, my maternal grandfather was also one of them: *Angrez ke naukar*. Born into a lower-middle-class agricultural family in northern Kerala, he lost both his parents as a child and was raised by relatives. Fleeing to Madras (now Chennai) like most young men who had no land of their own, or family, or good education, he got a job at the Madras Central Jail when it was under British control and continued working there until 1975. His elder brother was also a police official in old Madras. Did they deserve to be referred to with such disgust? After all, what's wrong with a young man with no support system taking up a government job and doing well in life? At least some of the nineteen police personnel who worked at the Chauri Chaura police station could have been like my grandfather, who had to take up a job to simply survive and make a decent life. Do they deserve this contempt even after so many years for having done their job?

Growing up under my grandfather's care during his later years, I recall him being a Congress man and a staunch supporter of Indira Gandhi until his death. Perhaps he did not have the luxury of taking a political stand like Ram Narayan Tripathi's grandfather, since he was a young man coming from a remote village so far away from everything and with no possessions of his own. As I get older, I am more and more convinced that poverty and deprivation, more often than not, are the best determinants of what is right or who is wrong.

Nevertheless, I chose not to respond to the driver's question about wastage of public money and turned my gaze outside. Despite the evening traffic, we cruised into Gorakhpur in less than forty-five minutes. The city's transformation over the last six years, since my last visit there, had been nothing short of shocking. I could spot at least three swank malls and two multiplexes, besides half a dozen cinemas, as we drove into the city. Stylish sedans filled the roads, malls overflowed with young men and women in skinny jeans, colourful T-shirts and tops, and fast-food joints appeared on virtually every street corner. However, upon reaching within half a kilometre of my hotel, we were stuck in traffic for another thirty minutes before I could reach my room because the roads remained choked that evening, as they had been every other weekend of late, the driver informed me.

# Motihari, East Champaran District

ABOUT 9 KILOMETRES FROM MOTIHARI, ON NH 28, towards Muzaffarpur, a narrow road exits to the right towards a manned railway crossing; it winds past fecund fields brimming with wheat, black grain, baby corn and sugar cane crops, leading to Chandrahiya village, where the Champaran Satyagraha Memorial, built to commemorate the peaceful civil disobedience movement headed by Gandhi in the summer of 1917, is located. A half-buried plaque inside the memorial claims:

> Mahatma Gandhi, Father of the Nation, on his way to Jasauli Patti village, was crossing this village through this place on 16th April 1917. As soon as he reached this village, a sub–inspector served upon him a notice of the then collector, Champaran, Mr. WB Heycock. By this notice Gandhiji was required to leave Champaran with immediate effect. In the opinion of the collector, Gandhiji's presence would endanger public peace and tranquillity ...

The remainder of the inscription describing the event, which triggered one of the most important phases of India's freedom struggle, remains buried under a pavement inside the memorial.

Though the notice served to Mahatma Gandhi on 16 April 1917 prompted the Champaran Satyagraha, the story of Champaran's farmers' struggle actually began in the early nineteenth century, when European planters forced Indian farmers in this region to cultivate indigo on three-twentieth of their land holdings (known as the tinkathia system).[1] Indigo was used to prepare dyes meant for the textile industry and considered more lucrative than even sugar cane and other cash crops.

However, with the arrival of the German synthetic dyes in the market towards the end of the nineteenth century, Indigo went out of demand, and the European planters of Champaran, eager to release local farmers from the mandate of cultivating indigo on three-twentieth of all their land, tried to turn this lack of demand into an advantage by increasing their rents, besides pressing other illegal dues as the price for their release from cultivating indigo. While resistance against this system surfaced as early as 1908, the exploitation continued and the farmers suffered. A local farmer, Raj Kumar Shukla, appalled by the unfair taxes and charges levied by planters in the region, sought Gandhi's help in investigating the problem and putting an end to the practice.

Back then, East and West Champaran were united as a revenue district and Raj Kumar Shukla, keen on bringing the plight of indigo farmers of his region to Gandhi, followed him across the country. Shukla met Gandhi at the Lucknow Congress Session in 1916 and urged him to visit Champaran to see the distressed state of the

1 *India's Struggle for Independence*, p. 178.

farmers in person.[2] He also managed to get a resolution passed at the session, expressing sympathy for the farmers of Champaran. Later, Shukla followed Gandhi to Kanpur and even Ahmedabad, seeking his attention on the plight of the indigo farmers.

Eventually, Gandhi heeded the plea and visited Champaran in early 1917 to study the plight of the farmers. Accompanied by Shukla and a few lawyers, Gandhi went to Muzaffarpur and then Motihari to understand the situation in detail. As news spread of Gandhi's arrival in Bihar, crowds began thronging the venues where he was present. Alarmed by the increasing popularity of Gandhi in the region, the British government sought to pre-empt him. On 16 April 1917, Gandhi was issued the district collector's notice to leave Champaran with immediate effect, as had been embossed in the half-buried tablet at the memorial. When Gandhi was asked to either leave or face court arrest, he chose the latter, which stunned the British government. Recalling the incident in a letter to Maganlal Gandhi written on the same day, Gandhi stated:[3]

> They arrested me when I was on my way to a village for carrying on the inquiry. They then put me in a bullock cart and were taking me away. A senior police officer met us on the way and served the order upon me. At first, he only said, 'The collector wants you.' I turned back saying nothing. I have refused to leave the district. The penalty for this crime is six months imprisonment and a fine of Rs. 1,000.

When Gandhi was presented before the district magistrate in Motihari on 18th April, he even pleaded guilty, to the surprise of

---

2 M.K. Gandhi, *The Story of My Experiments with Truth* (New Delhi: Fingerprint Publishing, 2019), p. 360.

3 *The Collected Works of Mahatma Gandhi*, vol. 15, p. 335.

those present at the court. The magistrate, however, did not award him any punishment but postponed judgement after an assurance was obtained from Gandhi that he would not go out to the villages, pending instructions from the government.

On 21st April, in what was arguably a first under the British administration, the court decided to withdraw all proceedings against Gandhi, under instructions from the government.[4] Instead, the local administration was asked to assist him during the conduct of his inquiry with the indigo farmers regarding their woes. This was his first victory in Champaran, and his supporters were overwhelmed by the British government's retreat in allowing Gandhi's inquiry into the plight of the Champaran farmers.

Following the district administration's assurance of support for his inquiry, Gandhi and his associates made elaborate arrangements in Motihari to meet and interview the farmers from surrounding villages to understand and document their woes. He also approached the secretary of the Planters' Association, the organization that the farmers held responsible for their plight, and the divisional commissioner to get their versions. A detailed questionnaire was prepared and handed out to all his associates. The inquiry began, and as the days went by, crowds of peasants gathered to give their statements, followed by an army of companions who filled the venue where Gandhi and his associates were interviewing them. Between five and seven volunteers were required to take down statements, and even then some people were sent away in the evening without recording their statements due to the crowds. Those who took down the statements also had to observe strict rules. Each peasant had to be closely cross-examined, and whoever failed to satisfy the test was rejected. An officer of the CID was always present when the statements were recorded.

---

4 *The Collected Works of Mahatma Gandhi*, vol. 15, p. 349.

As Gandhi's work in Champaran kept getting extended due to the detailed nature of the process of gathering information, several of his associates were also summoned to Motihari and urged to take up social welfare activities to improve the lives of the villagers. After studying the lives of the peasants of this region from close quarters, Gandhi became convinced that providing quality education to children was the permanent benefit he could provide the people, and opened primary schools with help from his associates in six villages. The villagers were expected to provide boarding and lodging for the teachers, while Gandhi and his associates would take care of the teachers' expenses. As finding good teachers turned out to be a difficult task, Gandhi sought volunteers to pitch in and got a favourable response. Soon, the children of Champaran, who were otherwise simply roaming around and wasting away their childhood or assisting their parents on indigo plantations from morning to night, were now sent to these schools. The teachers came from across India and imparted basic reading and writing skills, besides good hygiene and sanitary practices.

Along with education, Gandhi and his followers turned their attention to sanitation, as they found the hygiene standard observed there to be far from acceptable in most villages. Even in this area, he needed external help, and doctors from the Servants of India Society volunteered to help. Clinics were set up in the villages and volunteers were trained to provide basic first aid and treatment to the ill. Doctors were summoned when the cases were slightly complicated and needed professional intervention.

All these activities went alongside the inquiry of farmers, which had reached several thousand recorded statements by then. The crowds continued to swell in Motihari, and the increasing popularity of the inquiry incurred the wrath of the influential planters, who tried everything in their power to stall the process. One day, Gandhi received a communiqué from the Bihar government that his inquiry was 'sufficiently prolonged' and that he should bring it to an end and leave Bihar.[5] In response, Gandhi wrote back that he had no intention of leaving Bihar until the tinkathia issue was addressed and would continue his work with or without government support. However, he also suggested that the government could end the inquiry by recognizing the grievance of farmers as genuine and address them or at least initiate an official inquiry into the practice.

The latter suggestion was accepted, and the province's lieutenant governor, Sir Edward Gait, formed the inquiry committee and invited Gandhi to be a member of it. The committee reported in favour of the farmers and recommended that the planters refund a portion of the exactions back to the farmers as well. The committee also ruled that the tinkathia system had to be abolished by law within a specific timeframe. With this, a century-old unfair practice came to an end and Gandhi's Champaran Satyagraha became an indelible part of the narrative of India's freedom struggle.

---

More than 105 years later, on a sultry weekday afternoon in the summer of 2022, when I tried to keep my date with history by visiting the precise spot where Gandhi had been served a notice, I found the gates to the memorial built to commemorate the event chained and locked. Probing around a bit, I found the mobile number of the caretaker of the memorial written on the compound wall next to the gate and called him. The blazing sun bleached the yellow memorial to white. To the right of the gate, a dark, fat man sat on a rock while taking a bath, wearing just an off-white langot. On the other side of the road, three little children, almost naked, their olive-black skin burnt dry in the sun, ran after each other taking turns; behind them were half a dozen cylindrical huts with thatched roofs and bamboo sticks tethered together for a wall.

---

5 *The Story of My Experiments with Truth*, p. 377.

For a moment, I wondered if the scene would have been any different when Gandhi was on his way to Jasauli Patti a century ago. Perhaps the man and the children would have been skinnier then, considering the economic conditions prevailing at the time, and the memorial would also have been farmland. Otherwise, I felt like I was watching footage from a pre-Independence era film while waiting for the caretaker.

Fifteen minutes later, a stunted, frail man in his mid-forties with sunburnt, reddish-yellow skin came riding a bicycle and introduced himself as Krishna Rai, caretaker of the Champaran Gandhi Satyagraha Memorial for the past seventeen years. Even as he opened the gates and walked me through the beautiful campus lined with neatly trimmed ficus trees, moderate-sized palm trees and other varieties of shrubs, passing yellow-painted halls with thatched roofs and tiled pathways, Krishna Rai began lamenting the state's lack of interest in maintaining the memorial. 'For the past several years, I have been the only government staff on this entire campus. I am the caretaker, gardener and watchman, all-in-one. Nobody else has been appointed and none [government official] even bother to visit. They don't even bother finding out if the works have been completed or not. This is the condition of one of the most important memorials of the freedom movement,' Krishna rued as he took me to a large, air-conditioned hall, where plastic chairs were strewn around haphazardly and a huge pile of dirty clothes was dumped on one of the chairs. A mattress and some blankets were dumped in another corner of the room. 'This is the visitors' centre of the memorial, but look at its condition. I use it as my bedroom now,' Rai said, quickly supplementing that he wasn't afraid of telling the truth about the condition of the memorial, as he had done several times in the past to various YouTube channels.

After ranting about his plight and the condition of the memorial for a while, Rai took me on a tour of the campus. Despite its incomplete status, the memorial was stunning from the outside. The compound wall at the entrance was shaped like Gandhi's signature spectacles with egg-shaped lenses; inside the sprawling campus, various halls and buildings, including the library and museum, were aesthetically designed and built. The pavements leading to the various buildings were wide, with sufficient provision for lighting too, but no staff had been appointed for their maintenance yet.

The original memorial, constructed decades ago, was much smaller. As part of the 100th anniversary celebrations of the Champaran Satyagraha, a proposal to renovate the memorial was approved and work began. The ambitious renovation project of the Chandrahiya memorial began sometime in 2018 and lost track midway, according to Rai. The state-of-the-art library building is yet to be fully furnished and the floor remains unpolished. The construction of restrooms for men and women has also been stalled midway, and even the water fountain where a statue of Mahatma Gandhi is present remains incomplete. The proposed building for the museum, a sprawling hall lined with beautiful glass cases to showcase documents and artefacts from the Satyagraha period, was in total disarray. Dust and cobwebs had completely covered the glass cases; many of the doors were broken and cracks were present in some. The tiled floors were so dirty and full of debris that I wasn't comfortable walking even with my shoes on.

The last government official to visit the memorial was a district revenue officer in October 2021. 'Since then, no state official has even come to check if the works that were supposedly in progress have been completed or not. The buildings have been practically left to decay, with me toiling alone to at least maintain the garden and other external artefacts. How much can one man do?' he lamented as we walked from one building to another. When Rai started working as the caretaker of the memorial as a young man, he had lived in Chandrahiya with his wife, Swarki Devi, and their four children, and would return home for the night. After his wife died in 2009 and their children moved out, the widower decided to shift to the memorial and was staying there on most days, and the clothes and bedding dumped at the visitors' centre belonged to him. Even though Rai locks the gates and keeps the keys tucked into his trousers, locals still come and go freely and use it for all the purposes for which badly maintained memorials are used anywhere in the country. Even when I was there, four or five boys in their early teens managed to sneak in and take selfies near the statues.

I spent about an hour at the memorial, taking in the caretaker's non-stop rant. On my way out, he handed me the visitors' book to record my visit. A casual glance revealed that despite the pitiable condition of the campus, the memorial did attract regular visitors from across the country who came in search of the venue of Gandhi's first satyagraha. The visitors' book had an entry just two days ago from a certain Satish Tiwari of Patna, who warned the authorities to at least fill up the gallery and library before his next visit. The entry before that belonged to a family from Andhra Pradesh, who also lamented the condition of the memorial. Most visitors had also written in detail about the lack of maintenance—the toilets are built but dysfunctional, RO water units are set up but inoperative, while the museum and library work have been abandoned halfway—and urged officials to honour Bapu and finish the memorial. To my surprise, the latest entry was registered just a few hours before my arrival. For my part, I, too, wrote a detailed note condemning the condition of the memorial before leaving.

In a way, the Chandrahiya memorial is an indicator of nothing having really changed in this part of the country in a hundred years. The most important tablet of the memorial, which described the event that had triggered the Champaran Satygraha, remained half-buried under the pavement; the construction workers who built the pavement had not bothered taking care while placing tiles around it; the contractor who was probably paid crores of rupees for the job had not cared to ensure that at least the written text should be fully visible when the pavement was laid; the government officials whose job was to supervise the work and ensure such blatant blunders didn't occur had not even turned up to inspect the work even after so many months; and the lone caretaker, who kept lamenting about the state of things to every visitor who came his way, wasn't even heard!

---

With the Champaran Satyagraha memorial turning out to be a symbol of the local administration's ineptitude, I proceeded to the interiors of Chandrahiya village to find out if the farmers' lives had changed for the better in the hundred years since the indigo protests.

Located amid lush plains just south of the Himalayas, Chandrahiya was certainly not as impoverished as some of the other villages I had visited over the past few weeks. The roads were wider and better maintained, although often coated with a layer of cow dung in populated areas; homes were solid, concrete structures, though modest and bereft of most amenities. Besides these, this village even had a State Bank of India branch, which operated out of a portion of the home of Ram Babu Prasad Yadav, former mukhiyan of the village.

A stout, bearded man, Ram Babu was about sixty and had three sons, three daughters and several grandchildren, most of whom lived in his two-storey ancestral home surrounded by the 10-acre farmland he owned. When he came to know I had come all the way from Chennai to find out about the plight of farmers in his village, I was immediately offered a seat in the large veranda of his home, where a handful of villagers, mostly from the surrounding homes, were summoned by him to gather and discuss the condition of Chandrahiya farmers in 2022.

In November 2020, farmers from Punjab, Haryana and Uttar Pradesh were actively involved in arguably the longest and most potent people's protests since Independence against the Farmers'

Produce Trade and Commerce (Promotion and Facilitation) Act, 2020; Farmers (Empowerment and Protection) Agreement on Price Assurance and Farm Services Act, 2020; and Essential Commodities (Amendment) Bill, 2020, popularly known as the 'Farm Laws'. At the time, Ram Babu and around 500 other farmers from Chandrahiya had also organized local protests against those laws and even marched from Chandrahiya to Varanasi over a period of two weeks for their repeal. I began my interaction with that context. Why had the farmers in Chandrahiya joined the protest? Were these laws as brutal as those laid by European planters for indigo cultivation a hundred years ago?

'The farmers' associations protesting outside Delhi approached us for support as our village is well known for the indigo protests a hundred years ago, and we immediately agreed to participate. Farmers from Odisha, West Bengal and other states assembled here to join the Punjab farmers. Unfortunately, due to logistical issues, we could not prolong it beyond a few weeks as the Punjabi farmers did outside Delhi,' Ram Babu said, while others gathered around him nodded in agreement.

For the next hour or so, we discussed several issues concerning farmers in the region, including the controversial farm laws and how these farmers saw them. According to the Chandrahiya farmers, one of the most contentious issues in this region as well as the rest of the country was the plan to gradually remove Minimum Support Price (MSP) on crops and leave price determination to market forces. Ram Babu and the others gathered around me tried to explain the same in as simplified a manner as possible. Ram Babu owned about 10 acres of land—a majority of his fellow villagers own even less than that, sometimes just an acre of arable land—on which he raised several crops, wheat and select grains being the primary ones. 'Now if I work hard for several months and grow wheat, I can sell it for around Rs 1,200 per quintal to the warehouse owner, who is the middleman and buys our crops. However, let's assume the state government fixes an MSP of Rs 1,800 per quintal as the most reasonable price for that year. Despite that, the middleman decides on a lower price and we are forced to sell to him as he takes up the responsibility of storing the produce in his godown and selling to the state or private agencies depending on the demand,' Ram Babu explained.

Despite the losses due to selling below the MSP, this practice has become so established that both farmer and vendor are comfortable with it. In the absence of the government fixing the MSP, we will be at the mercy of market forces. As far as the Farmers (Empowerment and Protection) Agreement on Price Assurance and Farm Services Act, 2020 was concerned, farmers could enter into pre-arranged contracts with buyers within a legal framework, and the Chandrahiya farmers feared that it would mean big companies could get into contracts with big farmers owning 50 acres or more for a good price, while the smaller farmers who usually sell their produce to warehouse owners and middlemen would be left out. With no government role in fixing prices or facilitating direct contracts, the farmers feared that eventually the situation would return to the indigo plantation days, when big corporations decided what crops had to be grown and sold at what rates. The farmers were also uncomfortable with the idea of doing away with the traditional middlemen and local markets from the supply chain cycle, as proposed by the Farmers' Produce Trade and Commerce (Promotion and Facilitation) Act, 2020, another contentious law.

Now that the government has repealed these laws, I asked Ram Babu and his neighbours if their lives would get better now. 'We sell our wheat for Rs 1,200 per quintal, which is, in turn, sold by agents for a higher price to their vendors. The saddest part is that the same wheat goes to the government PDS system and I will be forced to buy the wheat I produce for Rs 50 per kg from the open market. How does that make my life any better?' Ram Babu wondered out loud.

While all the farmers agreed that there was some profit with growing vegetables, they claimed food grains were a different game and that if the government did not fix the MSP, they feared they would be totally at the mercy of the middlemen who own godowns and stock their products. 'We can't hoard our produce and have to dispose of it as soon as possible for whatever price we get. At the end of the day, the farmer hardly makes any profit,' Ram Babu's neighbour Chandra Rai said, looking at the others for affirmation.

These were some of the practical problems. Besides, farmers here and everywhere else are at the mercy of unseasonal rainfall, hot weather, government policies, etc. 'The kisan hardly makes any profit for all his hard work. In our village, less than 1 per cent of the population depend on farming alone to make a living. I drive a taxi when I don't have work in the farm,' said Rajan Rai, another small farmer who owned a Mahindra Scorpio and worked as a driver during his free time. 'Some people raise cows and buffaloes to sell milk, others work in private office, while a few own businesses. Just being a farmer doesn't help meet our expenses.'

All the others nodded in agreement. 'What's the joy in becoming a farmer when you know that even if you work hard all your life, you will still remain poor and always in need of cash. Why would anyone be in such a profession?' asked another.

Over the next hour or so of interaction with a bunch of loquacious farmers, I reasonably surmised that the plight of farmers today is just about as bad as it was a hundred years ago. I wasn't exactly sure if I could understand the farmers' problems with the farm laws or if they were aware of what they needed to improve their profession, but one thing was clear: These people had a lot of woes and were, in a way, trapped in a constant cycle of needs and more needs that could never be fulfilled. Yes, a lot of development has happened in the last hundred years in their village as well as their lives—there was no doubt about that and none disagreed—but farming as a profession remains just as unattractive today as it was back then, when laws and rules were laid down by foreign rulers. And that, to me, is the most worrisome. 'We can grow any food we want and would never go hungry doing farming. But if you want money to get your daughter married or send your boys to study in good institutions or even to treat an illness, you have to do something else to make that money. If you're just a farmer, there will never be enough money for anything,' Ram Babu concluded. His neighbours Rajan Rai and Chandra Rai and the others nodded in agreement.

After the discussion with the small- and medium-landholding farmers in Chandrahiya, I left for Surajpur village on the other side of the Motihari–Muzaffarpur highway to meet Shankar Singh, one of the more affluent farmers in the region, with over 50 acres of land on which he grew several crops, including firewood and bamboo. As was the case with the road to Chandrahiya, the route to Surajpur was also filled with soul-soothing greenery in every direction I turned. Even in late March, the ponds and tanks were full, the canals flowed with crystal-clear water and the wheat crop was fully grown in most of the fields, ready for harvest in a month. Besides wheat and sugar cane, I also passed several mango orchards, lychee plantations and quite a few bamboo groves.

After cruising past one wheat field after another, the vehicle in which I was travelling had to halt suddenly on a desolate road as a large animal that looked like a cow but with a much longer neck and smaller head crossed the road and ran into the fields. At first, I suspected it to be a sambar deer and urged my cab driver to stop the vehicle so that I could take some pictures. The animal quietly observed me framing the pictures for a little while and then galloped farther into the wheat fields and disappeared. Later, my driver enlightened me that the animal we spotted was not a large sambar deer or a cow but a nilgai, one of Asia's largest antelopes, abundant in the region. The unusual and attractive animal is considered a pest in this region for destroying crops, mostly at night, and adds to the woes of farmers here.

Shankar Singh's home was at the far end of Surajpur, right next to his wheat fields, beyond which lay his mango orchard. To the right of the wide-open, large iron gate leading to his house was a work shed with a thatched roof where three Royal Enfield Bullets were parked—two of them dismantled completely. The front portion of a much-used tractor also adorned the front courtyard of this two-storey bungalow. About 30 feet or so away from the home was another open hut with a thatched roof, where an old man sat on an easy chair, resting his feet on a worn-out stool that looked as old as him. A dog, much younger than the old man and his stool, rested beneath his feet and gave him company. After waiting outside the front gate to the house for a while, my driver and I walked to the house and pressed the calling bell. A little child, aged about five or six, ran outside with a toy giraffe and stood before us. When we asked for Shankar Singh, the child pointed at the old man in the hut and ran back inside. By then the old man had also seen us; he waved and invited us to the hut.

Shankar Singh was eighty-two, but if one were to go by his physical appearance alone, he could easily pass for around seventy or so. But his pale brown eyes appeared old and fatigued and a mild stammer could be detected, too, when he talked.

When I told him about my interaction with Chandrahiya's farmers and sought his perspective on his profession as one of the larger farmers in the region, Shankar Singh, like most men of his age, grew autobiographical and recounted the past eighty years of his life as a farmer to illustrate his point. Born in a village bordering Nepal a few years before Independence, Shankar studied up to intermediate at a school near his hometown. 'My father was also an established farmer. After finishing my studies, I was assisting my father with his farm work, when he brought me to Surajpur for some work. I liked this place and its people and decided to live here. So I went back to my village, took some money and came here,' the octogenarian recalled.

Shankar was in his early twenties then. After setting up a small farm, he got married and spent the next six decades of his life as a full-time farmer in Surajpur. His wife gave birth to five sons and three daughters, most of whom are past middle age now. 'I have built all this due to sheer hard labour and have practised no other profession. Not a single day have I stayed off my farm. There is some work or another either in the wheat field or the mango orchard or vegetable patches; sometimes the motor pump stops working or the channels get broken, and on the days when none of these happen, a herd of nilgais or wild boar try to destroy the crops. There has never been a day without work. But do I have anything to show for it after all these years? Nothing ... that's the life of a farmer here,' Mr Singh said, staring at the ceiling of his hut purposefully. 'There's one thing, though. You can always find food in the house of a farmer any time you go,' he confessed. Just about then, a middle-aged man, probably his servant, brought two tall glasses of milky tea and a plateful of milk pedas and biscuits. 'Also, fresh milk and peda; this tea has been prepared with fresh milk and the pedas from homemade ghee. We don't use any other,' he emphasized.

While it was obvious to anyone that Shankar Singh and his family were no example of farmers in distress or those who lived frugally, there was truth in what he had said about farming no longer being lucrative as a career option. And the best validation of that was that while Shankar had five sons, none of them had taken up full-time farming. Two of his sons were employed in the Indian Railways; of the remaining three, one was a college lecturer-cum-politician, while another dabbled in real estate as well as in farming, splitting his time between both the professions. Shankar's youngest was a photographer who had recently opened a studio in Motihari. The sons choosing different professions wasn't completely out of passion, as the old man admitted that he did not, and would not, recommend farming as a full-time profession to any young man. 'When I was younger, the situation was slightly better. Back in the late '70s and early '80s, I would easily make around Rs 1 lakh or Rs 2 lakh as profit every year. It was a big deal back then. But now, I hardly make any money. Most of the money is spent on taking our produce to godowns or mills. Every other year, there are either floods or drought or something else. If none of those happen and somehow we have a good crop, wild animals raid and destroy everything. And if that doesn't happen, the prices of grains come down, or the middlemen don't buy the produce for a good price, or the godowns shift too far, thus reducing our profits. With so many uncertainties, why would I recommend farming to any of my children?' he pondered, stammering and taking deep breaths as he spoke.

Just about then, a slightly stouter and darker man arrived on a better maintained Royal Enfield motorcycle than the ones I'd seen outside, and parked it near the hut. 'Here comes the neta; he will answer the rest of your questions,' Shankar Singh told me, pointing at his third son, who introduced himself as Guddu Singh. When Guddu Singh clarified that the situation was not as grim and that things had been much better over the last few years, his father shot him down and asked me not to believe a word his son said. 'He belongs to the ruling party and will say only that,' the senior Singh quipped. When the son tried to counter him, the two broke into a heated argument in the local dialect, which I could barely follow. Looking agitated, the son rushed inside their two-storey home without even looking at me.

We both sat in silence for a while. The hut I sat in, Shankar's modest home, the mango orchids and wheat fields behind us, the constant chirping of birds from the bamboo groves, the gentle roar of water flowing through channels bordering the fields—everything was so soothing that I felt no urge to say or do anything. I gobbled up all six or seven pedas that were on the plate before resuming our conversation. I asked Shankar, 'What do you think about the farm laws and protests by the Chandrahiya farmers?'

'Oh, I did not participate in any protests. I'm too old and did not see the point either. But yes, the farm laws getting repealed is a good thing. We do need the government to fix an MSP and control it. Otherwise, how do we know what price to sell our produce for? Besides, the government should also stand guarantee for selling our crops. I hear that such a promise has been made in other states. It should come here too. But just repealing some laws will not improve the life of the Indian farmer. Most of our farmers are born poor, live a frugal life and die with nothing in their hands,' he reiterated.

As is the case with most farmers I have come across, a majority of Shankar Singh's problems were local and needed local solutions. 'Life was much better when the sugar mill in Motihari was working. When the mill was taking our sugar cane produce, for one crop season, I could make up to Rs 1 lakh easily. But the mill is closed now and we have to send our sugar cane to far-off locations. Diesel and labour costs make raising sugar cane less profitable now,' he said, after pondering for a while over my question on what he thought about the protests of Chandrahiya farmers against farm laws. 'When a group of farmers meet anywhere, you will only hear them complain. Growing up in such households, why would anyone want to be a farmer anymore? We need food grains, so we continue to do this, but I don't know about the future,' Shankar concluded.

When I asked him what could be done to improve the life of farmers, the octogenarian laughed. 'If I knew, wouldn't I have improved my life first? I have no idea. I'm a simple farmer. More intelligent people should do something about it, though,' he declared.

On my way back, I recalled a recent visit to Coimbatore to meet a techie friend, a software engineer who worked with a top global software giant remotely from his home in the suburbs of Coimbatore.

He had recently purchased a 4-acre farm on the outskirts of the city and took me out enthusiastically on a tour, explaining the various innovations and improvisations he was experimenting with for the various crops he had planted. For my friend, buying a farm and growing crops on it for his consumption was the realization of his lifelong dream, thanks to his high-paying IT job. He spent most of his free time on the farm to live a life that Shankar Singh had led for the past eight decades—drinking fresh cow's milk, cooking food using pure ghee and homegrown organic vegetables, and gorging on homemade pedas. To my techie friend, that was bliss.

I know several men of my age who dream of owning a farm like my friend does and quite a few who have managed to achieve that dream. Perhaps that's the future of the Indian farmer. A hybrid professional who does farming out of passion alongside another profession to take care of the household expenses. From what I could perceive, farming as the sole occupation has evolved to be no longer viable in this day and age, at least for the small- and medium-category farmers.

---

If the lives of Ram Babu Yadav and Santosh Singh were unenviable and deserving of our attention, the plight of Kala Chandra Das, a second-generation Hindu Bengali migrant farmer from Dhaka, Bangladesh (formerly East Pakistan), is simply deplorable. His father, Buven Chandra Das, was rehabilitated in Bharaulia village near Surajpur (around 15 kilometres from Motihari) during the country's partition back in 1948–49, with 4 acres of land and around Rs 1,200 in cash, along with thousands of other Hindu Bengali families.

I bumped into Kala Chandra by accident. I needed to return to Surajpur and my cab driver had refused to turn up. So I hired Kala Chandra's electric auto rickshaw to take me there. During a casual chat along the way, I noticed his accent was slightly different and probed a little further about his roots, when he revealed that he was a Bengali migrant farmer who had given up farming and leased out his land because he could not avoid poverty while pursuing his inherited profession. After hearing about his plight and that of his fellow Bengali migrants, I decided to visit his village instead.

Bharaulia is yet another picturesque village, about 15 kilometres from Motihari, accessible only through a narrow concrete road flanked by lush wheat fields, greenish-brown lily ponds and marshes all along the way. In proportion to the increasing distance from Motihari, the condition of the road as well as the homes steadily dipped, as both transformed from pucca to kuccha. Kala and his neighbours in Bharaulia are among the three-lakh-odd Bengali migrants who were rehabilitated with land and cash assistance in West and East Champaran districts of Bihar after Partition. His father, Buven, who had received the land allocated on the banks of the Dhanauti river, worked on it day and night. He made a modest living and raised his four sons on it. But the land allocated to him as well as the other migrants in this region was in a low-lying area and remained flooded for six months in a year when the river overflowed. 'We could never grow more than one crop during the entire year as the land remained flooded for at least six months. I don't remember all the details of my childhood well, but I remember that we had a shortage of everything in my home. There was never enough money, food or even clothes, and my father was always struggling,' Kala Chandra recalled. When Buven's sons grew up, he partitioned the 4 acres among his sons and each of them received an acre. 'Farming is simply not sustainable with just an acre of land,' pointed out Kala, who has two sons now and drives an electric auto rickshaw in Motihari to get by. 'We cannot employ farm labour to till the land, nor rent equipment, which are all expensive and need investment. You need money to even sow seeds, rent equipment and use fertilizers, etc., for which we have to borrow from moneylenders. If the crop fails for some reason, we are in debt and have to work twice as hard the next year to pay it off. By then, new debts accumulate and it becomes a never-ending loop. Bigger farmers with 10 acres or more and those who have their own equipment can work the land and make money, but not people like me. We have no choice but to lease our land out to other larger farmers and do other jobs to make a living,' he explained on our way.

When we reached the giant banyan tree outside Kala's home, a small crowd of young and old men and a handful of boys gathered around us. Most of the houses in the village resembled makeshift tents and were built out of mud bricks and bamboo sticks, usually used for housing livestock in other areas. Without exception, all the men and children were bare-bodied above the waist. To the left of the banyan tree was another hut built entirely of bamboo sticks, including the walls and entrance gate. The locals updated me that it was the government primary school building, where about fifty children studied. The school building was suited for regular classes only during good weather days. Too much rain or sun made it extremely uncomfortable for the children and teachers.

Until the Covid-19 pandemic struck, most able-bodied men in this village worked and lived in New Delhi, Mumbai and other cities, doing odd jobs and visiting their homes two or three times a year, mostly during Durga Puja. 'In Delhi, I earned between Rs 15,000 and Rs 20,000 a month if I worked all thirty days, a sum I can never imagine making as a full-time farmer here,' continued Kala. 'Due to the pandemic, I returned home and bought an auto rickshaw with my savings. We have completely given up farming now. The 1-acre land in my possession will have to be split between my two sons in a few years, which will be just enough for them to build a house and grow vegetables. What will they do for money?'

Of the 100-odd families residing in that remote village, which has no decent health facility or a high school, ninety families are in the same situation as Kala Chandra. While a few still hold on to their lands and try to cultivate whatever little they can, it is mainly the womenfolk who take care of farming, while the men head outside for casual labour, or drive auto rickshaws/taxis, or even do construction work in other states to make ends meet. For second-generation migrants, owning even an acre of land is a big deal as the 4 acres allotted have already been partitioned more than once in most cases.

Among the few residents here who have managed stay above poverty levels is Jeevan Kumar, son of another Bengali migrant. It was obvious that he was slightly better off from the moment he came, as he was the only one who wore a T-shirt and had a headscarf on. He was also the only one who spoke to me freely, besides Kala Chandra. Jeevan owns 10 acres of land, a tractor and other farm equipment—with all those, he is able to make some profit, but that's not his only source of income. 'The only reason I could continue farming is because I am also an artist and make sculptures that I sell in Motihari. Since I was doing well in that business, I could develop my farm and expand it,' he explained. Jeevan is also a small-time politician working for the BJP, which gives him considerable leverage among the local officials. 'You can see our plight; there is nothing more to explain. Look at our government primary school here,' he said, pointing at the flimsy structure. 'Approval of funds for a proper school building came three years ago but the local administration is still sleeping on it. If our children don't get quality education, how will we ever get out of this trap?' wondered Jeevan, whose home behind the school was the only one with a concrete roof and plastered walls.

Among the 100-odd families, only five to six youngsters have completed their graduation, and only two of them have secured government jobs. Without many employment opportunities, the promise of a decent life for these youngsters always lies elsewhere.

For those who depend on farming alone in Bharaulia, life continues to be a one-way trip down the path of poverty.

---

Having travelled on the Motihari–Muzaffarpur highway back and forth multiple times over the past few days, hopping in and out of one picturesque village after another, I had one item left on my Motihari itinerary: A visit to the George Orwell memorial.

Besides attaining fame for hosting the Mahatma, this rustic town in the foothills of the Himalayas is also the birthplace of one of the English language's most iconic writers, George Orwell.

On my last evening in Motihari, which was two days before Holi, I decided to soak in the variegated vibrance of the busy Gandhi Chowk bazar and walked towards the memorial, approximately 1.8 kilometres from my hotel according to Google Maps, along with hundreds, perhaps thousands, of people who brushed past on motorcycles, cars and even pushcarts, as they inched their way through the bazar area. Kurtas, pajamas and T-shirts were out on display at every second roadside vendor's shop, along with Holi pumps hanging from colourful nylon ropes right next to the clothes. Watching out for oncoming motorcycles, dodging past avid shoppers to my left and right, I reached Jaunlal Chowk, a four-way junction, from where the memorial was around 300 metres to the right. The road that turned right was much wider, with fewer shops, and walking became pleasant against the backdrop of the setting sun. After about five minutes of walking, Google Maps alerted me that I had reached my destination. But there was no such memorial in sight. Instead, I spotted a chain of shops, including a bangle outlet and a furniture mart. A little inquiry to both the shopkeepers yielded nothing—they had never heard of a George Orwell or any memorial on that road. For the next few minutes, I stood there and checked the Google reviews of the memorial for pictures, hoping to match the location. But that didn't work either!

After walking about 100 metres both ways and checking with more shopkeepers along the way, I decided to give up my search. After all, if the famed Gandhi Memorial in Chandrahiya had just one caretaker and was in a state of decay on the seventy-fifth anniversary of Independence, one couldn't possibly expect anything but a missing George Orwell monument. Or perhaps I was simply too overwhelmed and tired after interacting with dozens of farmers over the past few days and didn't feel like pushing myself any further to trace the George Orwell memorial. What more could it reveal anyway?

# THREE

# Bilga, Jalandhar District

BILGA, AN INNOCUOUS VILLAGE IN THE DOABA REGION of Punjab, is unlike any other patriotic landscape I have visited: Nothing of significance has happened here to propel the country's freedom movement—no major protests, violent uprisings or satyagraha have taken place here, nor has any great national leader triggered a mass movement from here. And yet, locals claim that Bilga is the Bardoli of Punjab, and to validate that belief, they supplement it with a count of freedom fighters from Bilga who committed their lives to their country's independence.[1] But that's not what's endearing about this enchanting region: Bilga, then and now, continues to be known for its non-resident patriots who fought for their country's freedom on foreign soil. The Doaba region, as the land between the Sutlej and Beas rivers is commonly known, is famous for the role of its resident as well as non-resident leftists in the national freedom movement, an episode that has by

---

1 Raakhi Jagga, 'The village of freedom fighters', *The Indian Express*, 21 October 2012, https://indianexpress.com/article/news-archive/print/the-village-of-freedom-fighters/

and large disappeared from the mainstream narrative of the Indian freedom struggle.

I reached Bilga, now a nagar panchayat, on a hot April afternoon when the sun was at its meanest and the roads largely desolate, with locals preferring to stay indoors to escape the heat. But for a few tractors driven by turbaned men and passing by in the opposite direction, I hardly came across any vehicle on our way. The ride was smooth, thanks to the freshly laid road. As in most parts of this bountiful land, the drive from Nakodar, where I was staying, to Bilga was a treat for sore eyes, with a seemingly endless stretch of wheat fields flanking the winding road. The crops, almost mature, had turned golden yellow, with their spikelets protruding well above the stem and tilting to the side, unable to bear the weight of the grains that were almost ready for harvest. When there was a good breeze, these crops danced in the air, forming gentle waves, just like they are captured in the countless romantic Bollywood songs shot in such wheat fields. Occasionally, sprawling mansions also sprouted up out of nowhere in the middle of these wheat fields, just as we have seen in Yash Chopra's romantic blockbusters. Later that evening, I found out that the iconic Hindi film director also hailed from the Doaba region and the sets he created or shot at for his films weren't purely conjured out of his imagination—the unbelievable mansions are real and are also quite common out here. Besides the wheat fields, I also noticed a few patches of sugar cane and some vegetable cultivation here and there.

The vast stretch of farmlands ended with a tea shop, an open-air taxi stand and a bus stand. The wall diagonally opposite the taxi stand was adorned with colourful posters of at least half a dozen private institutes coaching students for the International English Language Testing System (IELTS), arguably the world's most popular English-language test for higher education, besides one or two posters belonging to the Aam Aadmi Party, which had recently swept the Punjab state elections. From the taxi stand, a narrow road led to the town centre, where the Baba Bhagat Singh Bilga Memorial Library operated out of the ground floor of a modest two-storey home.

Baba Bhagat Singh Bilga, a prominent leader of the second phase of the Ghadar movement who passed away in 2009 at the age of 102, had wanted his home to be converted into a library dedicated to the people.

Inside the airy library room, I found a frail, elderly man seated on a sofa, wearing sunglasses and a denim cap, like some ageing Bollywood star. A little behind him, a group of women sat in a circle chatting with each other, rather loudly for a library setting, and filling out some kind of form. The library's walls were covered with photographs and portraits of bearded, fierce-looking freedom fighters from Bilga and other parts of Punjab. Apart from a handful of well-known freedom fighters' portraits, like that of Shaheed Bhagat Singh, Mahatma Gandhi, etc., I couldn't recognize most of the men in the images. The library was also stacked with racks and racks of books in Hindi and Punjabi. As a stranger from the south who had just walked into a village library, I was conscious of everyone watching me, probably whispering about me, and moved stealthily, gazing at the pictures and portraits mounted on the walls. After a while, when nobody bothered to find out who I was, I approached the elderly man with the cap and asked for the librarian.

'There is no such posting in this library. This is a public library where people come and go. If I'm here, I open and close it in the evening; if I'm not here, someone else opens every morning,' the elderly man said in English, with a heavy British accent. 'This is for the people and is maintained by them. Villagers come here to prepare for exams or even for meetings as it is nice and cool here. Sometimes they just come here to read the books, and that's what this is meant for! This used to be the home of Baba Bhagat Singh, and, as per his wish, it is now used to serve the local community and belongs to the people,' the man explained.

Intrigued, I told him I wanted to meet the family members of Bhagat Singh Bilga or other descendants of Ghadar Party members. The man requested me to sit down next to him and introduced himself as Prem Singh, the younger son of Baba Bhagat Singh Bilga. 'If you're looking for Baba Bhagat Singh's family, you should speak to me or my elder brother, Kulbir Singh, who lives a few blocks away,' he said.

Prem Singh, now eighty-two, and his elder brother, Kulbir Singh, eighty-four, live in Birmingham, UK, and visit their village every year for a few weeks. Sometimes the holiday extends for a few months, too. After the Covid-19 pandemic struck, since they couldn't visit India for two years, the siblings had come on an extended vacation this year. While Kulbir lives in a mansion just a few 100 metres away from their father's memorial, Prem Singh lives on the first floor of the Bhagat Singh Memorial whenever he is in Bilga. 'My wife recently passed away, and since I'm alone, I like to stay here, spend time at the library during the day and retire to my room upstairs,' he said, and offered to help in whichever way he could.

I spent the rest of that afternoon in the company of the two brothers, listening to stories of growing up with a father who had travelled the world as a youth and was largely underground until Independence, but later preferred to remain in his native village and continue working for the Ghadar Party, which he had joined as a young man. Despite living in the UK for around six decades, Kulbir and Prem, too, in a way, never left their native village, as Bilga, and only Bilga, had occupied their mind all these years.

Bhagat Singh Bilga was born in 1907, a few years before the Hindustan Ghadar Party was formed in distant Astoria in Oregon, US, in 1913. But the seeds for India's freedom struggle were sown from foreign lands a few years earlier—after the first batch of Indians, mostly Punjabis, landed on the West Coast of America, seeking a livelihood in the early 1900s. Back in Punjab, the condition of peasants had deteriorated drastically during the second half of the nineteenth century due to increased land revenue, heavy indirect taxes and debts, while the British government, interested primarily in generating revenue, exported only raw materials produced in Punjab to British companies at cheap rates and sent back finished products from England at prices fixed by them. Due to poverty caused by several flawed government policies, Indians became easy victims to diseases like plague, smallpox, cholera, etc., and people were dying of hunger like fleas, while the government was exporting food grains to England ceaselessly. The impoverished peasants, driven by hunger, had no other option but to leave their homeland and either become military recruits or knock on the doors of foreign countries.[2]

As a passport system had not been established during the early years of the twentieth century, peasants took credit or mortgaged land and went to Malaya, Singapore, Penang and China without any major hurdles. Some were also recruited into the British police and taken to work in these lands. In these non-White British colonies, Indians were accepted without resistance by locals as well as their colonists, as the economic and slave conditions were similar to that of India at the time. These men found work as chowkidars, guards, railroad workers, watchmen, etc., and earned a meagre sum. While working in these countries, Indians employed in the ports of Singapore, Penang and Shanghai interacted frequently with passengers from Canada and America, who boasted of the prosperity of those countries. Thus, Indians, mostly Punjabis, working in these

---

2 Sohan Singh Josh, *Hindustan Gadar Party: A Short History* (Jalandhar: Desh Bhagat Yadgar Committee, 2007), second ed., p. 52.

port cities began dreaming of going to places where they were told they could earn nine to ten times their present salaries.

Besides these workers, a large number of retired Indian soldiers of the British Army, who had travelled to various British colonies for the army, also intended to settle down in those colonies. These soldier emigrants, proud subjects of the British Empire who had fought shoulder to shoulder with the British Army in distant lands, had often heard from their officers that they held the same status as British subjects in any of the Empire's other colonies. With such dreams, several former soldiers migrated to White British colonies seeking a better life. While there are no exact records on when the first Indian emigrants reached Canada, a survey published in 1905 recorded their number as forty-five.[3] In 1906, that number went up to 387, and in 1907, it became 2124. However, upon landing in those countries, the early immigrants found out that they were looked down upon and not treated equally, even in colonies like Canada.

Meanwhile, immigrants from Japan and China had been entering Canada for many years and in much larger numbers; their figure stood at more than 50,000 around the same period.[4] Some of those migrants had acquired property and had even employed young White women to keep accounts and look after their businesses—a move resented by the local White population. The locals also resented losing manual labour jobs to these migrants, who agreed to work for cheaper rates and were hard-working.

While large-scale resistance against all non-White migration was generally the case both in the US and Canada, what had shocked the Indian migrants was that the Canadian government was far more stringent about accommodating Indians, while going easy with the Chinese and Japanese immigrants. The reason given for that was

---

3 *Hindustan Gadar Party*, p. 57.

4 Ibid.

that Indians were dirty and uncivilized, and would not blend into Western society as well as the Japanese and Chinese.

Both British India and Canada agreed that the migration of Indians to Canada should end, and thus introduced strict measures to curb their entry, which included the admission of immigrants who came only through continuous journey, as back then there were no ships that went all the way to Canada from Indian ports. Apart from these new restrictions, the Indian Emigration Act (13 of 1883), already in place, had restricted Indians to go only to Ceylon and Straits settlements. This law made migration to Canada illegal, and if any Indian still dared to go, they were not allowed to land unless they shared the sum of 25 dollars, which was later increased to 200 dollars. The situation was similar in the US, where Indians had begun to migrate around the same time.

More than the harsh rules laid down by Canada and the US against the immigration of Indians, what irked Indians the most was that the Chinese and Japanese were allowed to migrate more easily and even bring their wives and children with them. Despite Canada being a British colony and Indians being British subjects, this deliberate insult to Indian immigrants, most of whom had served in the British Army as loyal soldiers and had even travelled across the world to fight for the British, shocked them.

Among the various reasons attributed by both Indian and Western historians for such discrimination was that the top British officials in India and England felt that close familiarity of Indians with Whites, which would inevitably take place in North America, was not good for British control over India, and that it was by projecting an air of superiority over Indians alone that the country was held and not by force.[5] Since most Indian men went without their families, they were invariably bound to enter into relationships with White women, which could further deplete their awe for the

[5] *India's Struggle for Independence*, p. 147.

White race. Furthermore, they were worried that these immigrants would get contaminated by socialist ideas, and that the racial discrimination to which they were bound to be subjected would then become the source of a national agitation back in India.

Indian students who had by then begun to trickle into North America realized that while the British wanted Indians to go to Fiji and work as labourers, they did not want them to go to North America, where they might be infected by ideas of liberty. These immigrants also realized that the main reason why the Chinese and Japanese migrants were less discriminated against was because they belonged to free countries and their governments could take up the cause of their citizens if they were made to suffer. India, a British colony, had no government of its own. The early immigrants soon realized that the root cause of all discrimination was British rule in India and that unless their country was freed, they would not be respected anywhere in the world.

These thoughts spread among several immigrant Indians and set forth a flurry of political activity both in North America as well as back home. Several publications also came out during this period, such as *The Free Hindustan* newspaper published by Taraknath Das and *Swadesh Sevak* by G.D. Kumar, both published in Vancouver to spread the message of the need for a non-resident struggle for Indian independence. Later, these groups formed the United India House in Seattle, US, where they regularly lectured Indian labourers on their rights both at home and abroad every Saturday. Close links also developed between the United India House group and the Khalsa Diwan Society in Vancouver, who approached the top British and British India officials to put an end to discrimination against Indians. All those efforts led to a collective nationalist consciousness among immigrant Indians, which was about to flare up any time.

During that period, a few other incidents, including the visit of a radical Sikh priest, Bhagwan Singh, to Vancouver and the bomb attack on Lord Hardinge, Viceroy of India, in Delhi, eventually paved the way for meetings of immigrant Indian groups thirsting for freedom of the kind they witnessed in foreign lands. A decision was taken by top immigrant leaders on the West Coast of the US to not fight the Americans for the discrimination they suffered in their land and, instead, use the freedom available there to fight for their motherland. These groups, at a meeting held in Astoria, Oregon, in July 1913, vowed to overthrow the British in India through armed revolt and to start a weekly newspaper called *The Ghadar* from their headquarters, the Yugantar Ashram, in San Francisco to spread their message. Thus, the Ghadar movement had begun.[6] When the First World War began and the British were busy fighting the German Army, the first batch of Ghadarites returned to India to free their country through armed struggle.

---

I met Kulbir Singh, the elder son of Baba Bhagat Singh Bilga, later that afternoon in his expansive mansion just about 300 metres away from the memorial on the same road. Despite the short distance, I lost my way and stood outside at least two or three other bungalows, looking for an NRI senior citizen from England, which matched the profile of most homeowners there. While the main road was full of two-wheeler mechanic shops, insurance showrooms, pharmacies and other petty outlets, every street that turned inwards was filled with large mansions surrounded by 10- or 12-foot-high compound walls and giant wrought iron gates. Asking around, I found that all the owners are all living in London, Birmingham, etc., and come to these homes once a year, sometimes once every two years. After ringing the doorbells of a few empty bungalows, I called the eighty-four-year-old, who came to the main road and took me to his home.

6 *India's Struggle for Independence*, p. 149.

The large grey iron gates at the entrance to Kulbir Singh's property did no justice to the grandeur of the bungalow and gardens behind. As we walked in on a tiled pathway, I noticed two huge fountains surrounding a neatly maintained lawn, with tall palms and other ornamental trees and plants of different species forming a boundary to the garden area ahead of the entrance to the bungalow. Inside, the ground-floor living area was vast and empty but for a three-seater couch flanked by smaller couches occupying the right corner of the living room. A spiral staircase, just as the ones seen in big-budget Bollywood movies, led to the first floor, where multiple bedrooms were kept locked. The kitchen was on the other end of the living room, away from the sofas, where Mrs Singh was cooking. Kulbir and I settled down on the sofa; he adjusted his hearing aid while inquiring about the purpose of my visit and I turned on the voice recorder, bracing myself for an exciting brush with history. Mrs Singh, who looked frail, her back arched like a question mark, brought lemon soda and a plate of biscuits, and sat next to him.

Kulbir began with a little anecdote from his father's schooldays. 'My father studied at the Khalsa High School in Ludhiana, one of the very few good schools in the region. When he was in class nine, the Viceroy was expected to visit the school for an event, and the headmaster prepared the boys to welcome and cheer him when he arrived. Ludhiana, especially the village where the school was situated, was famous for Ghadar Party heroes, and the son of the Ghadar Party fighter who was imprisoned for life was my father's classmate. So he knew about the party and the fight for the country's freedom at the time. When the Viceroy came, my father and a few of his friends shouted, "Down, down with the Viceroy!" They were badly beaten up for that act. That was his first act of defiance, which continued to be a lifelong affliction,' he recalled, as the various episodes from his father's life unravelled.

Historians have split the Ghadar movement into two phases: The first phase ending with the defeat of the Ghadarites, following the First World War, when they returned to India and tried to overthrow the British; and the second phase beginning a few decades later, when the Kirti Kisan Party was formed. The first batch of Ghadarites, who, according to some estimates, numbered around 8,000, returned to India to free the country from the British. However, only 5,000 of them were allowed to proceed freely, while precautionary measures were taken against some and severe restrictions were enforced on the more active members' arrival in Punjab.[7] The returning Ghadarites were also surprised to find people in Punjab were in no mood for the revolution they had envisioned and got no cooperation from the locals. Disappointed, those Ghadarites approached the Indian soldiers to mutiny against their officers and trigger a revolution. While that idea met with some success in isolated pockets, the soldiers were also not as geared up for a mutiny as in 1857.

After that attempt also failed, the remaining Ghadarites, under the leadership of Bengali revolutionary Rash Behari Bose, planned to begin a full-fledged revolt on 19 February 1915. However, with several government spies joining the movement by then, the police came to know of the developments beforehand and arrested most of the leaders. At least forty-five revolutionaries were sentenced to death and over 200 condemned to life imprisonment. With that defeat, the first phase of the Ghadar movement ended. Bhagat Singh Bilga and his generation of youth who grew up in Punjab's villages listening to those tales were thus infused with revolutionary thoughts from a very young age.

When Bhagat Singh completed high school, his family couldn't afford higher studies and he had to begin working. Uninterested in government service due to his political stand, the youngster decided to follow in the footsteps of his fellow villagers and relatives, most of whom had travelled to different parts of the world to work and make

---

7 *India's Struggle for Independence*, p. 153.

a decent living. Since Bilga was already blacklisted by the British for the revolutionary activities of its citizens, Bhagat Singh went to Kolkata, got a passport ready and boarded a ship bound for Chile in South America along with two other men from his village because he could not get a visa to North America. 'During those days, wages in Argentina and Canada were almost similar, and several Punjabis were already living and working in Buenos Aires. So after getting down at Chile, my father and his associates went by road to Buenos Aires, where he lived and worked for some years. This was in the early 1930s,' Kulbir continued.

In Argentina, his father came in close contact with Ghadar Party leaders and played an active part in the movement. This was around the time when Ghadarites were becoming attracted to the communist ideology that had flourished in Russia, and two prominent party leaders, Ratan Singh and Santok Singh, even went to Russia to study the socialist form of governance.

After returning to Argentina, Ratan Singh and Santok Singh convinced the Ghadar Party leaders to select forty young men and send them to the Soviet Union, where they would also study Marxism and socialism. It was around that time that the Kirti Kisan Party was formed, marking the beginning of the second phase of the Ghadar movement. 'The two [leaders] were very impressed with what they had seen in Russia, and the Ghadar Party resolved that it would follow communism and work towards establishing a socialist government in India, as was the case in the Soviet Union then,' Kulbir recalled from his father's autobiography.

Bhagat Singh Bilga was among the forty men selected and was sent to Russia. He stayed there for two years, studying the new form of governance that appeared, at least to them, to have a solution for most of the problems in India. After the programme was completed, all the trainees were free to return to the countries they had travelled from or go back to India and lay the groundwork for a Marxist revolution. Bhagat and several of his associates chose the second option and took different routes to reach India, as they were already being tracked by the British Intelligence as revolutionaries who could trigger a leftist revolt in India. Arriving in Colombo, Ceylon, under a different passport, he spent the next several years in hiding under assumed names while organizing workers' unions in Kolkata, Kanpur and even Amritsar in Punjab, without even getting in touch with his family. As these gatherings were illegal, Bhagat Singh often organized the meetings in the Golden Temple premises to escape the police radar. However, sometime during 1935–36, the police arrested him outside the Golden Temple for anti-national activities and took him to Lahore, where he was detained for two months and interrogated.

Upon his release, Bhagat Singh Bilga returned home and continued party activities. 'I was born in 1938 and, as a child, I had seen my father go underground many times for various reasons. He edited a banned publication, as a result of which the police were always after him and forced him to remain elusive. Later, my father formally joined the Communist Party and was its provincial member. For a brief while, he also joined the Congress when it became inevitable for all forces to work together for Independence. He was constantly lecturing and spreading the communist ideology even during that period,' Kulbir reminisced. His wife observed him keenly, often correcting and double-checking the dates and years as he spoke.

After Independence, the Indian economy began creating new job opportunities and scope for establishing businesses. But the globe-trotting spirit of Bilgans did not wear out. In 1963, when Kulbir was around twenty-five and had just completed a course in electrical work, he came across a job posting for electricians in England. Growing up in a family where men had travelled the world since a time when there weren't even passports, he immediately applied for the job. 'In a few weeks, I got a visa and left for England to work as an electrician,' he stated.

In England, Kulbir had no trouble settling down, as there was ample support from his father's friends and relatives who had been living there for generations by then. Upon his father's advice, he joined the Indian Workers' Association (IWA), Great Britain, which worked for the welfare of Indian workers in the country and fought against racism and other forms of discrimination. 'I grew up in a home where fighting for workers' rights and revolting against unfair authority was the norm. So naturally, when I went to England, I wanted to join the IWA and work for the people. I also joined the Communist Party of Great Britain and kept in touch with the party leaders here,' he said.

Thus continued the saga of protests and demonstrations in Kulbir's adopted home, even as he held on to his day job as an electrician for a contractor who did electrical wiring for Rover cars. Soon, his younger brother, Prem Singh, also joined him, and the two settled down in Birmingham, where a branch office of the IWA was also opened later and continues to work for Indian workers' rights.

Life in Birmingham turned out to be good for the siblings. After working for several years with the contractor for Rover cars, Kulbir got an opportunity to take up electrical contracts independently and became a business owner. He proudly proclaimed that most of the Rover cars in the market today have electrical units built by his firm. Becoming a business owner has not stopped the octogenarian from working for the IWA or raising his voice for hapless workers. 'Like Bilga, it is in my blood. You cannot take it away from me,' he said with a chuckle.

Most young men from Bilga still leave their homes and travel to distant lands in search of a better livelihood. To the left of Kulbir's home were two huge bungalows whose owners lived in Lancaster, UK. Beyond these bungalows was a third, larger home, whose owner lived in London. Every street had locked homes maintained by locals for the homeowners, who were hardly there except for a few weeks every year. Today, Bilga remains a town of large homes that remain locked for most part of the year. 'It's the same case in any neighbourhood here,' clarified Kulbir. 'All the shops and businesses you see here are owned by NRIs like me, but they have been rented out. In almost every home, there is at least one family member who lives in a foreign country. In some homes, everyone has moved out.'

Does this mean the revolutionary spirit of their fathers and grandfathers has also left the country?

'No way,' he asserted. 'Bilga is no longer just a village for us, it's a state of mind. Wherever we go, we take Bilga with us. It's just the way things have been with us for generations now. Even now, when the Kisan Sabhas were fighting the farm laws introduced by the Modi government, it was our support that turned out to be a game changer. So many Bilgans participated directly and indirectly. A vast majority of the protestors were from villages in the Doaba region. The IWA protested for the Indian farmers back in England. Whenever there was a development, the IWA reacted. In fact, I have personally contributed Rs 2.5 lakh towards the Kisan Morcha. The IWA collected lakhs and lakhs of rupees and sent money to the farmers' homes. How else do you think the farmers survived one and a half years outside New Delhi? We, the overseas workers from Punjab, supported them and will extend our support whenever workers and farmers protest. It's who we are and what we do,' he said emphatically, no longer sounding like an octogenarian with health issues.

'In fact, during that period, when we heard that Prime Minister Modi was visiting Glasgow, I booked an entire coach in a train and some thirty-five to forty of us went to Glasgow and held a demonstration in support of the protesting farmers. It is our farmers' fierce resistance that made the government retreat. He [Modi] has never taken back anything in the past, but the farmers and their supporters have shown what resisting authority means. That's the reason the Ghadar Party was formed, and the Kisan Morcha is proof that the spirit of the party remains alive to this day,' he thundered. By then I had been treated to a tall glass of lemon juice and two cups of tea with biscuits by his wife.

Before parting, I asked him about the Bilga of today. 'It's still very much the same. The most popular exam in Bilga is the IELTS. Almost every youngster prepares for it and tries for a job abroad. They go abroad, settle down and earn money for their families. This is our life, and the story continues.'

Before seeing me off, Kulbir showed me photographs of his sons, Amanbir Singh and Jagbir Singh, daughters-in-law and grandchildren. While his elder son was now running the electricals business, his younger son was employed in a private firm, and almost all his grandchildren were in the medical profession.

'Do they participate in the IWA activities?'

'Of course, they are my children! They grew up hearing stories of protests, resistance and revolutionary movements. They do and so will their children at the right time. It is our way of life,' he asserted.

From Kulbir's home, I went to meet Santok Singh Bilga, district secretary of the farmers' association, Jamhoori Kisan Sabha, Punjab, and state committee member of the Revolutionary Marxist Party of India, at his residence about half a kilometre away and past several neatly paved and narrow lanes. Santok Singh was among the few from his generation who chose to stay back and make a life for himself. His family inheritance and active participation in local politics ensured that he did not have to go outside seeking a better life. Being a committed leftist and a champion of farmers' causes, Santok had participated in the 2020–21 farmers' protest against the new farm laws all through the fourteen-odd-month period. For the first few months, he had organized protests in Bilga and had later shifted to the NCR region, where he had stayed for eleven months and continued the stir until the Central government agreed to repeal the act. Not just Santok but thousands of farmers from Bilga had participated in the protest, which the leftist organizations had been instrumental in coordinating, ensuring that it did not fizzle out despite official pressure. Santok and the other residents of the Doaba region see the Kisan Morcha as an example of a long saga of struggle against the abuse of power.

Though not as grand and spacious as Kulbir's home, the farmers' association leader's home, located in the interior of the village, was still on a large campus, surrounded by a tall compound wall with a vast courtyard in the front, where his tractors, motorcycle and car were parked. His farmland was also on the same road, about 2 kilometres to the right, where he had built a small house of sorts to relax in and supervise the farm labourers from. Between his farmland and home was his provision store, which he had named 'Janta Stores'. The farmer-politician usually divides his time between those three properties, and I caught up with him at Janta Stores later that evening, while he was serving customers. They ranged from a twelve-year-old boy who came riding a Bullet to buy an energy drink named Hell to a septuagenarian looking for wheat flour and coconut powder. Now in late middle age, the tall, slim man with a flowing beard dyed black preferred a white kurta and matching turban on most days. Kulbir and Santok, in many ways, were two sides of the same coin.

According to Santok, the lives of those who stayed back in Bilga have only turned out to be worse. With hardly any employment opportunities available to the youth even seventy-five years after Independence, along with the drug menace, driven by unemployment and despondency, rising to alarming levels, Santok worries for his village and people. The mass exodus of youth for several decades now has, in a way, partly been responsible for the state of affairs back home. 'It is true that every family has someone abroad who keeps sending money back home. Seeing their success, all that our youth here want is to go to a foreign country and settle down. They either go abroad and do well in life or do drugs and destroy their lives. There is absolutely no future in this village, and the youth of not just Bilga but the entire Doaba region are in the grip of drugs,' he declared. 'From teenagers to thirty-year-olds—they all do drugs. Synthetic drugs are so common here that you will even find them in the hands of children. It's a scary situation!'

For a land so replete with tales of valour and resistance, I could not understand why the younger generation had turned to drugs in such a big way. 'Did they not participate in the morcha?' I asked.

'All children raised here grow up listening to tales of struggles of their family members against the British, against successive governments and against injustice and discrimination of various forms anywhere in the country or the world. It is just the way of life here. And yes, they did come for the morcha in large numbers in the beginning, but after a while they all backed out and went to what they were doing before—getting intoxicated,' he explained.

The Kisan Sabha secretary blamed the 'rise in' drug abuse on the abundance of overseas money in the hands of youth who have no jobs and nothing else to do but get high and party. 'Now there is a new government that has promised a lot. I don't know how they will deal with the problem of drugs and get the younger generation back on track,' he said.

But that's not the most worrisome part for Santok. People like Kulbir who come back regularly and want to contribute to their hometown are now very few, and their numbers are drastically dipping. 'Unlike during the Ghadar movement days, most locals who go abroad these days lose all connection with their homeland and get busy with their own problems in a new country. After a generation or so, the connection is totally cut, and the people who stay back are left to fend for themselves. If you've been around the village, you've seen the palatial homes that remain locked for most of the year. Nowadays, if a local NRI returns, it is mainly to dispose of their property and leave for good. That is the situation in Bilga right now,' he said.

Citing his family as an example, Santok said that although he owned a big house, farmland and other businesses, all of which were sufficient for the family to lead a comfortable life, neither of his two sons wanted to settle down in Punjab. 'My elder son went to England, got married to a girl there and has settled down in that country. My younger son married a local girl. But he, too, wants to settle abroad, and now he and his wife are in England on a tourist visa. If he finds a job, they will stay back in the UK. It's not that we need the money, but youngsters just don't want to stay back. For generations, we have seen that the ones who go out do well in life. It is a fact!' Santok's concern is shared by a majority of parents in the Doaba region, who have little choice in this matter.

On the way back to my hotel in Nakodar later that evening, once again I passed by so many large, palatial homes built right in the middle of farmlands, with lush wheat fields surrounding them in picture-perfect locations. The only difference, as dusk set in, was that unlike in Bollywood films, where these homes glowing with colourful lightbulbs could be seen from far, not even a 40-watt bulb illuminated most of the bungalows, which disappeared into the darkness at night. Big, fat Punjabi weddings in sprawling mansions do take place here, but only once every five years or so, when these mansions turn into homes bustling with adults and children of all ages.

Earlier that afternoon, Kulbir Singh, who loves gardening, had complained about how he struggled to maintain his large garden. 'It's just the two of us now, and when we are gone, the garden is hardly maintained. I come, make it alright and leave, only to see it completely destroyed when I return,' he had said. The last time his grandchildren visited Bilga was five years ago. 'Now, they have their own commitments and are busy with their professions or school, and hardly find time to return to their homeland,' he had confided. Kulbir hoped that he and Prem would continue to visit Bilga twice a year, as long as their health permitted.

'After that, who knows ...' he had said, looking up at the roof of his bungalow.

When I reached the hotel lobby around 8.30 p.m., loud music blasted from one of the guest rooms and a group of tattooed youngsters, both boys and girls, hopped from one room to another, chatting loudly among themselves. I had noticed them one or two nights earlier, too, but hadn't bothered to observe closely and had moved on. After my conversation with Santok Singh about his concern for the current youth, the presence of young boys and girls in the hotel corridor during late hours, the blaring music, the discomfort on the faces of the reception staff, and the rooms getting occupied on an hourly basis suggested a slightly different, not-so-palatable drift.

---

On the Jalandhar Cantonment–Jandiala Road, opposite the MBD Neopolis Mall, in Jalandhar city is the Ghadar Party Martyrs Memorial. An expansive library on the ground floor, a museum on the first floor, along with a modest office room complete the two-storey building, painted red and yellow, in a 3.5-acre green campus. While the government has its Jang-e-Azadi Memorial in another part of the district, the Ghadar Party Martyrs Memorial has been funded by the Desh Bhagat Yadgar Committee, comprising thirty-seven members from various leftist organizations in Punjab. The memorial, as claimed by its members, preserves the history of the people who fought for the freedom of this country from this region 'in their own words'. 'We have not accepted any funds from the government. It is fully funded by the committee, hence, there has been a delay in its completion. But we are proud of its independent nature,' said Gurmit Singh, general secretary of the Desh Bhagat Yadgar Committee, on a pleasant weekday evening when I visited the campus.

A few other committee members gathered at the memorial took me on a tour of the campus while explaining the various monuments and records on the struggle of the Ghadarites put out on display. At least 3,500 original documents pertaining to the Ghadar Party, as well as the Kirti Kisan Party, were gradually getting digitized with the intent of putting them up online for research, and the IT wing of the committee was busy with that task. In the library, at least a dozen-odd students from various universities across the country sat and pored over books and documents as part of their research. Surinder Kumari Kochhar, a dynamic, bubbly revolutionary in the sunset years of her life, dressed in a salwar kameez and wearing sneakers, enthusiastically explained the significance of the various phases of the Ghadar movement and the relevant monuments on display. 'While there are fewer people interested in the history of the Ghadar Party nowadays, we still get a lot of interested students from various universities who want to do research on the movement. They are given free access, and even accommodation in some cases, to help them spend their time in valuable research,' Surinder explained as we walked past the library containing wooden bookshelves stocked well with books in Punjabi and Hindi on the Ghadar movement. 'There is still a lot of curiosity among students regarding this movement!'

Surinder Kumari Kochhar is from Nurmahal, about 15 kilometres away from Bilga. Her father, Comrade Gandharv Singh Kochhar, was active in the Kirti Kisan Party activities and later became an important member of the Naxal movement in this part of the country. Raised with these philosophies since childhood,

Surinder, with a Boy Scout haircut and gleaming eyes, remains single and is glad to have followed in her father's footsteps in joining the movement and contributing to it in her own way. She even recalled fondly how her father spent most of his life underground and evading the police, while sticking his neck out for poor farmers who were being exploited. 'The party and the committee are just for that purpose: To empower the powerless, to fight for those who cannot fight for themselves. We did whatever we could do, now it's up to the next generation,' she summarized for me as we finished our walk through the museum.

At the end of the tour, we halted beneath a giant portrait of at least half a dozen men of different ages, handcuffed and chained. The caption mentioned that they were all hanged for their conspiracy against the British. The men, who were all hale and hearty, had probably come from different parts of the world, leaving cushy lives behind to fight for the freedom of their homeland. The woman who explained all this to me too could have easily chosen a simpler life. But she had not.

We stood under that image and chatted for a while. Upon finding out about my southern background, Surinder confided that she liked south Indians a lot. 'A lot of comrades from the south come here, especially from Kerala. Even now, a delegation has gone to Kerala to attend a few events. Earlier, we used to be proud of our diversity, but now I am worried,' she said. 'I have never seen this kind of distrust among Indians for one another. It's very scary. Even out here at this memorial, we are never sure of when we might come under attack or tight scrutiny. There are so many girls who come and do research here for several days. Their safety is important, and I'm here 24/7 to protect these young children. I spend my time making sure that they are not disturbed and are allowed to work freely,' Surinder said as we walked out, her feet wobbly and hands shaky.

# Don Parewa, Nainital District

'WE SHOULD LEAVE EARLY AND RETURN BY 5.30 P.M.,' my cab driver said. 'It's too risky to drive on that road after dark. Elephants, leopards and tigers frequent the road we'll be driving down. During the day, we can spot them easily and they can spot us just as easily.' He also boasted of how he had lost count of the number of times he had spotted a tiger or a leopard while passing through Jim Corbett National Park near Ramnagar, about 65 kilometres from Nainital.

The taxi, arranged to take me to the memorial of freedom fighter Shaheed Diwan Singh Bisht in Parewa village at 7 a.m. the next day, was booked by the OYO guest house in Ramnagar where I was staying. The guest house, originally a farmhouse belonging to a retired politician, was run by four men, all in their late twenties to early thirties, who took pride in calling themselves 'Pahari log' (mountain men) and agreed with the cab driver, also a Pahari.

The Kumaon region, as this part of Uttarakhand is called, is renowned for its salubrious climate, majestic sal trees and India's first national park, named after the famous hunter-turned-conservationist Jim Corbett. As tourism is the only source of employment for most residents of this resort town, named after the former British Commissioner Sir Henry Ramsay (and not Lord Ram, as most tourists believe), topless Maruti Gypsy cars, parked on almost every street corner during tourist season, begin rumbling on the roads even before the jungle rooster's morning call. When we set out for Don Parewa at half past seven, dozens of Gypsy cars packed with tourists, their binoculars and DSLR cameras hanging from their necks, ready to be put to use upon spotting that elusive tiger, leopard or even some deer out to graze, had already begun their morning sorties, puffing out white smoke into the crisp air. What was easier to spot, though, was the town's love for renowned hunter and naturalist Jim Corbett, as Ramnagar was full of business establishments named after the man: Corbett hotels, Corbett homestays, Jim Corbett breakfast centres, Corbett salons, Jim Corbett textile showrooms—the man's name had been printed all over town and with good reason, as he is still the Kumaon region's most popular mascot.

The ghat road to Don and Parewa villages began soon after we crossed a bridge over the Kosi river, which had been reduced to a slim stream trickling between layers of large, yellow-brown, egg-shaped boulders by mid-April. The road followed the course of the river for a while, cutting through Jim Corbett National Park and its surrounding reserve forests in many areas. On this bank of the river, tall, leafy sal trees filled most of the area, along with occasional patches of wild jackfruit, almond and other native trees. The other bank of the river bordering Ramnagar was home to all the multi-star resorts, boutique hotels and outdoor sports activity centres, with gleaming hoardings advertising river-rafting, paragliding and even bungee jumping for the more adventurous among the tourists.

We rode on a winding tar-topped road for several kilometres. Thanks to the dry weather, dry yellow, orange and brownish-grey leaves shed by those tall trees covered the soil completely, awaiting a random cigarette butt or a lit beedi to flare up into a forest fire.

At least 15 kilometres of the 31-odd-kilometre ride to Don Parewa passed through such forests, known to be frequented by tigers, elephants and other wild animals. Elephant herds blocking road traffic for several minutes and tigers crossing the road randomly to the other side are a common sight for villagers here, my Pahari cab driver apprised me along the way. Though we did hear some deer and peafowl calls, I couldn't spot a single animal or rare bird all the way to the hills that morning.

As the sedan started climbing uphill, manoeuvring steep slopes and curves, the vegetation gradually changed to tall grass and thorny bushes, but the heat remained. Unlike in the plains, water still trickled down the rocky slopes through the cracks during morning hours and cut across the road to flow down and join the river. In such spots, the condition of the road, which had gradually worsened as we went uphill, was in very bad shape, with hardly any tar topping, making the ride extremely bumpy. I also noticed that despite the steep uphill ride, there were hardly any road signs to watch out for hairpin bends or to alert drivers to accident-prone areas as on other ghat roads. Except for an earthmover, we did not encounter any heavy vehicle all the way up to Parewa village. I also noticed that despite the bad road and the remoteness of the location, dozens of mountain resorts and log cabins had come up over the past few years in many of the tiny hamlets all along the way, including a swank five-star resort recently built by a Goa-based chain of hotels.

After about an hour and a half of riding past rolling hills and cutting across mountain streams, we reached Parewa village, a tiny hamlet perched on terraced land overlooking a steep, green valley. At the entrance to the village was the Ronsla Devi Temple, an ancient shrine recently renovated and believed to be associated with the Ramayana period—a few broken pieces of antique idols recovered from the temple premises during the renovation had reiterated the locals' belief that their village has existed for thousands of years. Next to the shrine was a home-cum-general store with no customers. At the store, fresh vegetables were displayed on large wooden trays, behind which were glass jars containing grains, toffees and other essentials. When we stopped at the store, a slender boy, who had been sitting among the trays and reading a textbook, jumped and ran inside his home behind the store. A few seconds later, a middle-aged, lean and athletic man, whose hair had just about begun to grey, walked out and introduced himself as Rajinder Singh Bisht, the up-pradhan (deputy chief) of the village. When I told him that I had come to find out about the freedom movement in these mountains and about Shaheed Diwan Singh Bisht in particular, his face lit up.

'The memorial is in the inter college campus named after Shaheed Diwan Singh. He was also a Bisht like me,' Rajinder Singh said in a coarse voice, as if he were recovering from a sore throat.

When we asked for directions, he offered to take us there and immediately got into the car, leaving the shop unattended. We drove farther uphill for about 200–300 metres and arrived at the entrance to Shaheed Diwan Singh Bisht Adarsh Rajkiya Inter College. As the campus had been closed for several months due to the Covid-19 pandemic, the front gates were chained, and the college, also perched on the flattened slope of a steep hill, was empty. 'This institution was built several decades ago and used to be a primary school when I was a child. I studied here up to class five and then shifted to Ramnagar,' Rajinder, who was fifty-two then, pointed out. 'When it was upgraded to an intermediate college, we asked the government to rename the institution in memory of the young freedom fighter from our village who was martyred at the age of twenty-four, and they readily agreed,' he elaborated.

Bisht and my driver unchained and opened the rusty iron gates and we walked past several classrooms, climbed down a staircase and walked down another corridor, where the principal's room was located. Rajinder led us past more low-roofed, brick-walled classrooms to a pink, rectangular memorial structure with a bust of a young man wearing a white Nehru cap at its centre. Beneath the statue was a tablet with the names of the fourteen freedom fighters from Don and Parewa villages who had participated in the Quit India movement and had been imprisoned. 'Diwan Singh was just twenty-four when he died in Bareilly Central Jail, unable to bear the torture by the prison officials. He was arrested sometime in 1944 and died on 23 August 1945. Since then, 23rd August has been observed as "Shaheed Diwas" in this village, and all the residents come here to pay their respects to the village's freedom fighters, who sacrificed their lives for the country. It is also the only day when our politicians remember this village and make it a point to come here to honour the freedom fighters' families. Even former chief ministers N.D. Tiwari [when Uttarakhand was a part of UP] and Bhagat Singh Koshyari have come to our village and visited this memorial,' Rajinder highlighted as we sat on a flat piece of rock outside the memorial, an open, tent-shaped structure with just a parapet around it.

Just seven months old when his family moved to the village, Rajinder Singh Bisht had been a resident of Don Parewa gram panchayat since he was a toddler. His father worked in the Border Security Force, serving mostly in the Northeast, owing to their Pahari background. Growing up in a defence family, Rajinder's ambition as a child was also to become an officer in the Armed Forces. As the government school in Parewa went only up to class five, his father sent him to Ramnagar to complete high school, which was rare back in the early '80s, as most villagers couldn't afford the accommodation and education expenses. Until class ten, he stayed in a private dormitory and completed his schooling. Back then, there were no pucca roads between Ramnagar and the villages in the mountains, and one had to walk about 30 kilometres to get to Ramnagar. 'Every Monday I would leave home at 5 a.m. and walk all the way downhill, about 30 kilometres, to reach school. After staying in the dormitory for five days, I would walk all the way back on Saturday to spend Sundays with my family. Our lives, those days, were full of hardship,' he recalled.

After completing school, Rajinder applied for jobs in the Indian Army and even got called for interviews on quite a few occasions, but he couldn't get past that stage. When the army jobs didn't work out, he tried for other employment with the state government. 'This was during the '90s, and getting a government job was impossible without offering bribes. Even back then, I was asked to pay Rs 40,000 to get a job at a tehsildar's office, but I could afford just Rs 6,000. Hoping that I could do something about it, I went to Lucknow and spent several months trying to get a job in vain,' he said. When nothing else worked out, Rajinder returned to his village, got married and set up the kirana store outside his house, which he continues to run. With the income from the store and a little farming on the land his family owns, Rajinder has managed to raise four sons.

As the primary school in the village had been upgraded to a high school by then, he educated all four sons in the local government school, and then sent them to Ramnagar for their higher studies. 'My two elder sons, Ravishankar and Vivek, stayed in Ramnagar and studied. As an inter student, my eldest died in a road mishap in Ramnagar. My younger son, troubled by the incident, refused to study further and returned home. I tried to persuade him to return to studies, but he just refused and, instead, began to work in the hotel industry. Until the pandemic, he worked as a chef in Rohtak,' he said. Rajinder is now trying to convince his second son to take up a course in pharmacy or some other trade and get himself a job. He does not want his sons to lose hope looking at his plight.

'The biggest problem in this area is the lack of employment. We can deal with everything but not lack of jobs. Even seventy-five years after Independence, young and educated boys in the village cannot find decent employment. People here hardly have any money to go to bigger towns and study in colleges. Boys who finish school have only one choice: Go down to Ramnagar and work in the hotels that have mushroomed there. Despite all the attention Parewa has received, including visits by two state chief ministers on Shaheed Diwas, there are no jobs. Even tourism hasn't picked up here yet, mainly due to the lack of proper roads. For the past three days, none of the villagers have slept. There is a tiger on the loose, attacking our cattle at will. We have informed the district administration, but no action has been initiated yet. Until something is done, we have to be vigilant. Nobody has jobs or money, and if our crops get destroyed or livestock get killed, we will not even have food. Such is the plight here,' the middle-aged farmer rued. If this was the life of an up-pradhan with a slightly more affluent background, one can only imagine the plight of the less fortunate in Parewa.

My interest in Don Parewa gram panchayat had been triggered by a documentary on forgotten freedom fighters' villages, which highlighted the complete lack of development in these destinations. I had stumbled upon the documentary accidentally, while researching for this book. Available on YouTube, it was first released in 2016, highlighting the pathetic condition of the roads, lack of employment and scarcity of basic amenities for the locals. Six years later, I could see that nothing much had changed: The roads were still terrible, no health centres or doctors were available but for a government-run Ayurvedic clinic manned by a pharmacist, internet was still a mystery here and no form of employment was available to the youth besides a little terrace farming that the harsh climate and the wild animals permitted.

If this was the plight of Don and Parewa villages in 2022, more than eighty years ago, when there might have been nothing resembling civilization in these villages, how did a group of young men get together, sacrifice their lives and families, and fight the British? What could have driven them to such a calling?

For several centuries the people of Kumaon were cut off from the rest of the country, developing their own culture and tradition distinctly unique from that of the plains below. By the second half of the nineteenth century, thanks to the spread of education, development in transportation, etc., political awareness about British rule and the quest for freedom spread among the people in this region, largely due to the visits of eminent personalities like Rabindranath Tagore and others. By the early twentieth century, Kumaon no longer remained isolated, and unjust British policies, such as the Coolie–Begar system, where villagers were required to carry the luggage of touring British officials and their families for a pittance, or at times no pay at all, were resented bitterly by the people.[1] The villagers also had to supply good grains and other provisions to the visiting British free of cost, a practice called 'Bardaish', which was also widely despised.

Around that period, i.e., during the early 1900s, a few educated youth among the Kumaon residents joined the Indian National Congress, as a result of which the Home Rule League and leaders like Lokmanya Tilak became topics of discussion in several villages there. Thanks to the growing political awareness, a local body known as the Kumaon Parishad was also formed to address local issues, and Gandhi become a household name in the region. While the developments in the Kumaon region had been closely followed by Mahatma Gandhi since the early 1900s, he could stay in Kumaon only in 1929, between 13th June and 14th July.[2]

When Gandhi arrived in Nainital, he stayed at a house called Moti Bhavan on the outskirts of the town. The hill station, which had been inhabited mostly by educated upper-middle-class people and had been traditionally less reactive to developments across the

---

1 Anil K. Joshi and Prema Bisht, 'Footprints of Gandhi in Colonial Kumaon', *Proceedings of the Indian History Congress*, vol. 79 (2018–19), pp. 501.

2 Ibid., p. 502.

country against British rule and oppression, was awakened with the arrival of Gandhi, as was evident with the crowd that thronged to get a glimpse of the leader. During his stay in the region, Gandhi visited Ranikhet, Almora, Bageshwar, Kausani, etc., where he spread the message of Swaraj and the practice of using Swadeshi goods, and initiated social reforms to uplift the lives of local people. All these initiatives had a significant impact. Gandhi's stay in Kumaon charged the atmosphere and the Congress Party began to get more and more patrons. It was evident when he launched the civil disobedience movement, as the people of Kumaon responded overwhelmingly to his call.

After provincial autonomy was granted in 1935, the Congress swept to power in the provincial elections and Govind Ballabh Pant, a close associate of Jawaharlal Nehru, became the premier of the United Provinces (later known as Uttar Pradesh). A devoted Gandhian, Pant helped spread the movement further, and as a result, when the Quit India movement was launched in 1942, there was a groundswell of support from the region. As the movement spread to the hills, volunteers began to defy the British in both Gandhian and non-Gandhian ways, especially in Almora, Nainital and parts of Garhwal, which became hotbeds of protest.[3] The British Army unleashed a reign of terror in retaliation, and thousands were imprisoned, many fined and a few even killed. Several nondescript villages became famous for its residents who fought against the mighty British, and Shaheed Diwan Singh and his team of thirteen volunteers were among them. All of them had been instigated by a wave of nationalism that spread like wildfire in the hills of Kumaon.

---

3 Vineet Upadhyay, 'Kumaon gave its children to the 1942 Quit India Movement', *The Times of India*, 9 August 2015, https://timesofindia.indiatimes.com/city/dehradun/kumaon-gave-its-children-to-the-1942-quit-india-movement/articleshow/48415227.cms

Around that time, the British officers and bureaucrats had built quite a few bungalows in the Kumaon hills and had taken up residence there, mostly during the summer months. Stirred by the movement against the British occupation raging across the country, Diwan Singh, who was unmarried, got together with like-minded men in Don and Parewa villages and planned attacks on the bungalows occupied by British officers. The idea was to force the British out of the hills, as part of the raging Quit India movement or August Revolution. The group smuggled kerosene and petrol from the nearby markets, and after hoodwinking the guards, who were mostly local villagers, they set fire to several British-occupied buildings in the region at night.

Family members of the other freedom fighters claimed that soon after the arson attacks, all the men went into hiding in the surrounding forests, fearing arrest, and would visit their homes only at night and that too disguised as women. As most of the lower-level police personnel were also Paharis from the surrounding areas, and the fighters got their support clandestinely and managed to evade arrest for a while. Eventually, all fourteen of them were arrested and taken to various prisons. Diwan Singh, who was taken to Bareilly Jail, could not endure the torture and succumbed on 23 August 1945. The other men returned to their villages after serving their prison terms and continued with their lives.

---

While Shaheed Diwan Singh Bisht died a bachelor, his younger brother Maan Singh Bisht continued to live in the village post-Independence and had two sons, Jeevan Singh Bisht and Gopal Singh Bisht, who worked as helpers at the government Ayurvedic clinic in Parewa. Jeevan Singh had recently retired from service, but Gopal Singh still worked at the clinic, and I was told we could meet him there.

The government Ayurvedic clinic, built inside the inter college premises, and an Auxiliary Nurse Midwife (ANM) centre are the only healthcare options for the 150-odd families in the Don Parewa gram panchayat. The clinic is a large building with a consulting area, two other rooms for treating patients who need beds and a pharmacy room, where about half a dozen white cardboard boxes were stocked with Ayurvedic medication to treat patients for acidity, fever and other basic ailments. While the clinic has sufficient space for at least half a dozen beds for patients, there were hardly any staff or medicines available when we walked into the clinic that afternoon. A young pharmacist, Mukesh, who came from a nearby village, helped ailing villagers with the medication available when the doctor wasn't present, which was more often the case. On that morning, too, the government Ayurvedic doctor was absent but his office room was wide open, with his white coat draped over the back of a rotating chair behind a large table. As the doctor's room was cleaner and more spacious, I was offered a seat there and asked to wait for Gopal Singh, for whom word had been sent out.

About fifteen minutes later, two other villagers, Madhav Singh and Pratap Singh, came to the clinic to meet me after they got to know I was looking for freedom fighters' family members. Their grandfathers were among the fourteen 'Swatatra Sangram Senanis' whose names were printed at the memorial. While Madhav Singh's grandfather Hyat Singh Koshali died soon after he was released from jail, Pratap's grandfather Bache Singh Lohalla lived for a few years with the family. However, neither of the two remembered anything about their grandfathers or what they had done. 'Our fathers might have known something, but they are too old now to recall what happened. Besides, who has the time for all that,' wondered Madhav Singh, whose dry, pockmarked face and frail body suggested a lifetime of hard labour. Like most of the villagers, both the men were farmers, making best use of the little land they owned. As the income generated from the land was hardly sufficient, they took up casual labour in and around the village, besides signing up for MGNREGA work every year. 'When nothing works out, we go to other cities in search of work,' said a famished-looking Pratap Singh, wearing a faded, torn cotton shirt and dirty dhoti.

Within just a few minutes of talking to those men, I realized that the poverty and hard life that those villagers had been subjected to did not allow them a strong political stand or even to reminisce about the contributions of their grandfathers to the country's freedom. When I asked them how they felt about the country and whether their grandfathers' contributions to the freedom movement were justified seventy-five years later, both laughed. So did Rajinder Singh, who had been patiently listening to our conversation until then. 'We don't even have a proper road after seventy-five years of freedom. Until 2004, if someone fell sick, we had to carry them 31 kilometres downhill to Ramnagar for treatment. Our people do not have any jobs. If you need work, you must go to some other city. What kind of freedom are we talking about?' Rajinder pointed out. 'The saddest part is that this generation does not even have the luxury to think of indulging in politics or joining political movements. Getting on with life is a challenge by itself,' he said. All the other men, including pharmacist Mukesh, nodded in agreement.

From the Ayurvedic clinic, we drove a little farther uphill along the winding ghat road and past a few more narrow bends to reach Don village. As most of the affluent Senani families had already moved out of the hills and settled down in different parts of the country, and the few remaining ones did not have the means to seek a better life elsewhere nor any knowledge about the contribution of their ancestors, just a handful of Senani kin were left in the villages for me to interact with. Among them, the Binwal brothers, I was told, were the most prominent. The three Binwal siblings, who went to prison for their role in the attacks on British bungalows, were listed right below Shaheed Diwan Singh Bisht at the memorial.

Upon reaching Don, we parked the car next to a steep cliff, from where we had to walk uphill, along a narrow, rock-laden path and past several tiny huts, terrace gardens and tile-roofed homes to reach the residence of Ambadutt Binwal, also a former pradhan of the gram panchayat. When we reached the modest tile-roofed home of the Binwals, Ambadutt was sitting with his legs stretched out in the front portico, both knees bruised and bandaged following a recent fall from his bike while on the way back from Ramnagar. His son, who had been riding with him, had also fallen and broken his leg. Having seen the road just that morning, I was hardly surprised, as one could easily imagine how a two-wheeler rider would struggle to climb that mountain road, especially at night.

Ambadutt's father, Haridutt Binwal, and his elder brothers, Shobharam Binwal and Dighardev Binwal, had participated in the armed attack on the British officials who stayed in the bungalows in and around that region during the Quit India movement. 'Led by Diwan Singh, they set fire to British bungalows and offices to force the British to leave India. My father and his brothers, who were very young at the time, used to hide in the jungles during the day and attack those places at night. My father did not share a lot of details about that period, but he did tell us about them forming groups and setting homes on fire by filling glass bottles with oil, lighting them on fire and throwing them inside buildings through open windows. When the police would come after them, the men would escape into the forest, returning home at night, only to leave for the forest again in the morning. The locals provided these rebels with food and information on British troop movements, and some of the local policemen even tipped them off before raids in forests. It was the support of all the villagers that gave these people the courage to attack the British,' Ambadutt recalled as he tried to explain to me the role played by his remote village in the freedom struggle. 'In that sense, the entire village and its surrounding settlements participated in the movement indirectly. Despite being so far away from everything and going through so many hardships daily, our fathers and grandfathers decided to participate in the freedom movement and played their role. Somehow that spirit is lost among the youth today.'

Rajinder also agreed with Ambadutt's observation. 'They all aspire to leave this village and find a better life elsewhere. Nobody is interested in improving their village. It's probably all the hardship that we have seen growing up. If someone in the village falls ill and we call for an ambulance, it would not come until recently. Only now has the 108-ambulance service been offered to us,' Rajinder added, also clarifying that vans and other SUVs were only now operating regularly, allowing villagers and shopkeepers to reach Ramnagar and transport merchandise farther on.

Ambadutt is among the slightly well-off villagers, with his elder son working at a private firm in Gurugram and the younger one, who got injured along with him on the motorcycle, studying in a polytechnic college. He is among the few villagers who could even afford to educate his children beyond intermediate, a luxury for most young men around there. To send a child to college in Ramnagar, one had to spend at least Rs 3,000 for accommodation, a few thousand rupees as fees and some more money to commute to the village and back. Overall, at least Rs 10,000 a month would be needed to educate children beyond intermediate—most of the villagers could not afford that sum. Hence, children who pass out of school go out seeking work and land up in Gurugram, Rohtak or other towns and cities, mostly in the hospitality industry. Both Ambadutt and Rajinder believed that the difficult lives they led and the lack of access to quality education and employment probably drove youngsters away.

As we discussed the mindset of the youth in their villages, another youngster in his early twenties walked in and was introduced to me as Girish, grandson of another freedom fighter, Durga Ram. His family was also among the few that remained in the village despite all the odds. Girish immediately pointed out that the decision of other Senani families to move out was right and that one should leave when there is a chance to do so. Like most youngsters in his village, Girish had also studied only up to intermediate and then left for the plains in search of a job in the hospitality industry. He worked at a hotel in Rohtak until the Covid-19 pandemic forced all hotels to close. Since then, he hasn't looked for a job. 'Unlike the rest of the country, we have problems that are difficult for others to understand. For instance, there is no mobile tower anywhere in the vicinity. If I need to access the internet or just check my email, I will have to go 30 kilometres downhill. How is it possible to get a job in such a situation?' Girish fumed. 'Sometimes, when the wind is blowing in the right direction and other weather parameters cooperate, we get feeble access from the Almora region towers, but it is unpredictable. The biggest problem youngsters face here is connectivity. We are completely disconnected from the rest of the world and, thus, aren't able to update ourselves with anything. The government should do something about this,' he insisted. 'Otherwise, only old people will be found in the village and the rest would all have to move out for good.'

Another issue in the region had been the absence of a major political leader, since N.D. Tiwari, to take up their cause. With such a small vote bank (approximately 150 ration card holders), the residents of Don and Parewa are hardly a priority for the politicians in the state. The only option available for economic upliftment, according to the former pradhans, is tourism. They see tourism as their way out of misery, but none in the village have the money to build and operate hotels. 'We openly invite anyone who can to come and set up hotels and we will support them, as that is the only way to retain the youth here: By generating employment. All other problems can be solved then,' Rajinder said, while Girish nodded. Until then, the exodus of youngsters would have to continue.

By early evening, Rajinder Singh ran out of people he could take me to meet in Don Parewa. In just a few hours, we had covered almost everyone who could give me some insight into their Pahari lives, past and present. We drove back to his kirana store, dropped him there and began our return journey. My cab driver, glad that we would make it well before driving on the road became too risky, offered to take me to a few tourist destinations in Ramnagar before wrapping up for the day.

The return journey was also largely devoid of any action, as we could not spot a single animal or bird from the car windows. But for a few SUVs taking tourists to the resorts nestled in the ghat areas, we did not encounter any vehicles on our way down either. Back in Ramnagar, the evening safaris into Jim Corbett National Park had begun and open Gypsy cars overflowing with tourists appeared to be all over the park. I stopped at the national park too and took a tour of the visitors' centre along with a few Bengali families who had come on their annual holiday. After the national park visit, we stopped at the Garjiya Devi Temple perched on a single rock by the Kosi, upon the insistence of my driver, who found it weird that I wasn't interested in praying. Thousands of pilgrims walked up the rock in a long queue, worshipped the deity and then took a dip in the meandering river. After spending a reasonable amount of time people-watching by the river—to the satisfaction of my driver—I returned to the OYO homestay surrounded by wheatfields ready for harvest on the outskirts of Ramnagar.

Upon noticing that I was back earlier than usual, one of the men running the homestay, a thirty-one-year-old from a village near Almora, asked me if I had had a good time at the national park, assuming I had come to visit it like other tourists. When I expressed my disappointment at not spotting any animals throughout the day, he said jeep safaris were of no use. 'If you really want to see the jungle, you need to go with one of our men. If you're interested, I will show you the forest for free on my motorcycle,' he offered.

With nothing else to do, I immediately agreed, and within the next few minutes, I was off to the national park in a Honda Splendor, sandwiched between two slender men. Within minutes of leaving the homestay, we were cruising on a dirt path in the national park —no gates were present, no entrance tickets needed—by the bank of the depleted river. A little farther away, among isolated bushes, we spotted at least two sambar deer that crossed our path from a distance and continued deeper into the jungle. We went past dense shrubs and a tribal hamlet, all the way to a remote pond, that was well shrouded by a thick canopy of tall trees. After parking the two-wheeler near the pond, my homestay owner and his friend guided me to a rock by the pond, where we sat and smoked. Two spotted deer that were drinking from the pond dashed into the thicket upon noticing our presence. 'This is where I come and sit to clear my mind,' my homestay owner said, taking in a deep puff. 'I have seen tigers and leopards drink from this pond so many times. It is in this part of the jungle where you find the animals, not where the safari jeeps take you,' he said.

I asked him if we were violating the law and what would happen if the forest watchers spotted us.

'What forest watchers? They are all our people, Pahari log. This is our forest and we have all known each other since we were children. Who can stop us from roaming our land?'

Perhaps it was that spirit that drove Shaheed Diwan Singh and thirteen other men to set fire to the British bungalows more than eighty years ago.

## Tamluk, Purba Medinipur District

I REACHED TAMLUK RAILWAY STATION, WHICH WAS deserted, barring the station master and a couple of stray dogs, on a weekday evening around 7.30 p.m. The Howrah–Haldia local train had been packed with office-goers and vendors when it had left Howrah Station, but it had almost emptied even before rolling into Tamluk, when three other passengers and I deboarded. Outside the station, too, just two tuk-tuks (or totos, as e-auto rickshaws are called in this town) were parked to transport passengers to their destinations. The other passengers—an elderly woman, her son and her daughter—walked towards one of the tuk-tuks, had a little chat with the driver and climbed inside. The tuk-tuk driver, who also asked me for my destination, suggested that I get into the next vehicle when I told him the name of the guest house I was to stay at.

If one were to simply go by first impressions, Tamluk should be known as the medical hub of not just West Bengal but the entire nation, for all I could see during my fifteen-minute journey from the railway station to the guest house were hospitals, small and large clinics, medical shops, diagnostic centres and more hospitals. Even as the tuk-tuk turned left from the railway station, we were greeted by the three-storey Balaji Nursing Home, followed by a medical shop and the one-room clinic of a doctor with a neon billboard as large as that of the multi-storey hospital. The railway station road ended at the Tamluk–Haldia multi-lane highway, where I spotted more one-room general and dental clinics, two- and three-storey nursing homes, speciality care centres, biomedical testing laboratories and a few large healthcare facilities on both sides of the road. There was a one-room dental clinic even outside the guest house where I was staying. With so many healthcare facilities, I was hardly surprised when the front office manager of the guest house asked me if I was a medical representative on tour. 'The only guests we get are medical representatives or patients. We hardly get any tourists, as there is not much to see here,' the middle-aged manager told me before checking me in. A little online probe later revealed that Tamluk is indeed a major medical hub, offering healthcare services to patients from Howrah, Purba Medinipur, Paschim Medinipur and even Odisha. Doctors and specialists from Kolkata and other cities often drive down daily to treat patients here.

Tamluk is also a city of statues: Life-size images and busts of Mahatma Gandhi, Subhas Chandra Bose and other national leaders competed for space with those of local heroes such as Khudiram Bose, Satish Chandra Samanta, Ajoy Ghosh, Sushil Kumar Dhara and Matangini Hazra at pretty much every major road intersection and street corner. Besides healthcare centres and statues, I also noticed plenty of ponds, both large and small. The ponds were as common as the banana plants that formed the boundaries of the numerous canals that fed those waterbodies from the grand Rupnarayan river, which separated Purba Medinipur district from Hooghly district.

But Tamluk is not just popular for its medical facilities, statues and ponds. This ancient town and its surrounding areas are best known for its people, who have played a key role in shaping

Bengal's destiny, from prehistoric times to the nation's struggle for Independence, and right up to the most recent assembly polls in 2021.

---

Credited with almost continuous human habitation since the Neolithic period (7000 to 1000 BCE) by the Kolkata Circle of the Archaeological Survey of India, Tamluk has been known by different names over the centuries, such as Tamralipta, Damalipta, Tamralipi and Velakula—an important port town, from where seafaring vessels established trade with distant kingdoms. The region was visited by Chinese travellers Fa Hein, Hiuen Tsang and I-Tsing, who have recorded vivid accounts of their travels to this ancient land. This city has also been mentioned in the works of Pliny the Elder (first century CE) and the geographer Ptolemy (second century CE) as Taluctae and Tamalites respectively. In Hindu religious texts, this city has been referred to as Bhivas or Madhya Desh.

Having come to a region so soaked in antiquity, I decided to begin my sojourn into Tamluk's tryst with history at the Government Archaeological Museum, managed by the Archaeological Survey of India, Kolkata Circle. Ironically, when I reached the spot that Google Maps led me to, there was no museum but a vacant ground on which buses and other large vehicles were parked. The sweetmeat shop owners and other small-time vendors nearby had no clue of a museum in their neighbourhood either. Just as I was about to give up, a youngster who had come to drink tea at a soft drinks parlour told me that he knew the location and led me to the first floor of an old, worn-out building, where a faded, dust-smeared name board announced the presence of the museum housing antiques from the region dating back to 100,000 BCE.

While the ASI mentions the excavation of antiques from the Neolithic period, the Government Museum had stone scrappers, stone cleavers and axes carved out of stone dating to the Paleolithic period (100,000 BCE to 20,000 BCE), excavated from this region and carefully preserved. On display at the barely locatable museum were: blades from the Mesolithic period (10,000 BCE to 5000 BCE); stone celts and bone tools, harpoons and fish hooks from the Neolithic period (5000 BCE to 2000 BCE); pottery from the Chalcolithic period; terracotta plaques and figures from the Sunga dynasty (second to first century BCE); amphoras from the first century CE, establishing possible trade contacts with the Roman Empire; and scroll paintings from the late twentieth century.

After taking in as much detail as possible about the antiques on display, I approached the museum staff for more insight into the region's past and found, to my surprise, there was neither an archaeologist nor an assistant archaeologist present, unlike what their website had mentioned. The scant staff present at the museum on that weekday afternoon had no clue about the region or its past. 'You can get all the details from Dr Kamal Kundu,' suggested a young helper present at the museum. He also gave me an address. 'You can also try at our head office in Kolkata, but it is unlikely that anyone there will be able to help you either,' he said.

---

It all began in a room in a rented house. A group of history buffs scavenged the Rupnarayan riverbed every morning looking for antiques before heading to work and deposited them in the room, recalled Dr Kamal Kumar Kundu, a retired bank official and history buff who lives in a modest, unpainted two-storey house right next to the Tamluk Rajbari, a centuries-old palace in ruins, presently under the Archaeological Survey of India.

Born and raised in Paschim Medinipur, Dr Kundu came to Tamluk in 1966 to study at the government college. After completing his graduation in history there, he proceeded to Kolkata to pursue higher studies. Six years later, he returned to Tamluk after getting a job at a State Bank of India branch there. It was then that his passion for the ancient history of Tamralipta drove him to collect antiques from the region as a hobby. Soon, he brought together fellow history buffs from the region—some of his professors from Tamluk College and colleagues at SBI who shared similar interests—and raided the Rupnarayan riverbed and the various ponds in the neighbourhood, looking for antiques.

Dr Kundu and his team carefully collected the antiques—mostly terracotta figurines—and preserved them in the room he had rented at his relative's home. 'In many ways, it was the beginning of the Tamluk Museum that you visited,' he told me, sitting behind a large table cluttered with books and files of various sizes on the ground floor of his home. Of late, Dr Kundu spends a lot of his time researching the ancient history of the Medinipur region.

When the collections grew and he ran out of space, Dr Kundu and his associates approached the Tamluk municipality to allocate adequate space for them to store and showcase the antiques to the public. Since professors at Tamluk College were also part of the group, the municipality staff offered them a two-room facility for the collections, which was later turned into a museum gallery. It was much later that the ASI took interest in the artefacts collected by these amateur excavators and took over the museum, adding more material from the ASI excavations of the region from 1940 onwards and opening it to public viewing in its present location.

However, as is the case with everything else out here, the museum and its origins have also become a political subject, and successive governments and parties have tried to take credit for it. 'The situation now is such that my associates and I, who originally came up with the idea of a museum, are no longer involved with it and are not even consulted on anything,' he rued. To illustrate his point on how the history of the region was being coloured by the politicians of the day, Dr Kundu cited the Rajbari next door as a classic example. 'The ruined palace is well known to everyone here. As a youngster, I used to walk in and out of every corridor on its ground and first floors and even studied it with my professors. It was constructed by a tax collector appointed by the Mysore Empire and is just about 300–400 years old. But now people are associating it with a period much earlier than that and are giving different versions of its past to suit their interests. It's the way things are these days,' he said, and then clarified that while the ASI has taken over the building from the original owners and is renovating the premises, the family have moved the court already and a suit is still in progress. Before we parted, Dr Kundu also handed over a couple of books on the history of Medinipur region for my reference.

When I went to the Tamluk Rajbari after my interaction with Dr Kundu, ASI-appointed workers were painting the compound wall with red oxide and inspecting the other sections of the dilapidated structure. The palace, in a state of shambles, was behind a large courtyard covered with tall grass bushes and other weeds. A notice board put out at the entrance by the Government of India proclaimed that the monument has been declared to be 'of national importance under the Ancient Monuments and Archaeological Sites and Remains Act, 1958 as amended by the same Act in 2010' and that 'whoever destroys, removes, injures, alters, defeces, imperils, or misuses the monument shall be punishable with imprisonment up to 2 years or fine up to Rs. 1 lakh or both'. A little away from that notice board, another board displayed by the ASI, Kolkata Circle, claimed the ruined structure exhibited the architectural brilliance of the late medieval period, specifically the Indo-Islamic style.

The main entrance to the palace had a wide courtyard that had almost crumbled, creating giant craters in the wall. The left and right wings of the structure were double-storey barrack-like formations, of which the left barrack was demolished. Built mostly using bricks, with occasional red sandstone for the pillars, the palace also had a large basement with rooms, entry and exit routes and possibly tunnels, as in most buildings constructed in that period. In one corner of the main hall were the crushed, stained remains of the national flag stuck to a thorny bush. Behind the flag lay a dog that began barking as soon as she saw me trying to enter the interiors of the complex, as if she were guarding the Rajbari and its secrets. I peeped inside and found three puppies: One brown, another black and a third also brown but with patches of white. The dog was so aggressive that I gave up the idea of exploring the palace and retraced my steps until I was outside. Behind the palace was a giant banyan tree whose trunk was surrounded by a raised platform. A plaque erected on the platform mentioned a date that had been almost erased and some information related to the freedom struggle. Beyond the tree were the busts of two freedom fighters, but details of their names or their deeds on the tablet beneath were also so worn out that I couldn't read anything at all. I recalled Dr Kundu telling me earlier that it was from this monument that Tamluk's satyagrahis began their march during the Salt March. Before we had parted, he had also mentioned that like everything else, 'Even the role of the people of the Medinipur region in India's freedom struggle has been twisted and tweaked to suit political interests.'

---

This nondescript healthcare town's role in India's long and complex freedom struggle is usually associated only with the formation of an independent national government known as the Tamralipta Jatiya Sarkar (which lasted almost two years, from 1942 to 1944), heeding Mahatma Gandhi's call for the Quit India movement. But the struggle for independence had begun to intensify in the Medinipur region way back in the early twentieth century, when Lord Curzon sought the first partition of Bengal. That proposed 1905 Partition proved to be a turning point in the history of India's national awakening, with the appalled nationalists in Bengal organizing protests and stirs that found instant resonance in Tamluk, barely 100 kilometres away from Calcutta.[1] It was around the same time that Khudiram Bose, a young revolutionary from Medinipur (then undivided) district, inspired by the speeches of senior revolutionary leaders of the region, volunteered for the freedom movement at the age of fifteen and made a plot to assassinate a British judge, Magistrate Kingsford, with the help of an associate. However, the two ended up throwing bombs at a similar carriage outside the magistrate's home in a case of mistaken identity and killed two British women instead.[2] The arrest and execution of Khudiram Bose further stoked the movement in and around Medinipur—making him a local hero. He was just eighteen at the time of his execution.

Around that period, the Tamluk subdivision of Medinipur district covered an area of 687.25 square miles (1,779.97 square kilometres) and had a population of just a few lakhs. Six police stations were under its jurisdiction: Panskura, Mayna, Tamluk, Mahisadal, Sutahata and Nandigram. The economy of the subdivision was primarily dependent on agriculture (rice and betel leaves were the chief agricultural produce) and the standard of literacy was poor, only 29 per cent in the pre-Independence days. However, with respect to political activities, Tamluk subdivision always occupied the forefront in all the movements for independence. That was reflected yet again during the 1920 non-cooperation movement, when Tamluk and its surrounding areas once again were hotbeds of protests and agitations along with other parts of the country. Voluntary memberships in the Indian National Congress witnessed a steady growth as a result.

---

1 *Sarbadhinayak: Freedom Struggle in Tamluk* (Tamluk: Tamralipta Swadhinata Sangram Itihas Committee, 1982), p. 3.

2 Calcutta High Court, Khudiram Bose vs Emperor on 13 July, 1908, Indian Kanoon, https://indiankanoon.org/doc/1765978/

After the non-cooperation movement was called off, many of those volunteers moved on to doing constructive work in the rural parts of the district—trying to impart education, improving the living conditions of villagers and laying the groundwork for a larger political movement among the masses.

When Mahatma Gandhi began his famous Dandi March to break the salt law on 6 April 1930, the movement found instant resonance in the eastern part of the country. A camp for volunteers was opened at the Tamluk Rajbari (memorial stone and tablet inscriptions that I had noticed behind the palace referred to that) and hundreds of young men joined the camp to participate in the movement.[3] As there was no sea coast near the subdivision, the Tamluk satyagrahis marched from the Rajbari to the banks of the Haldi river near Narghat village and broke the salt law. All the top Congress leaders from the region, including Ajoy Kumar Mukherjee and Satish Chandra Samanta, were arrested and imprisoned for two years. During the following years of relative inactivity, the voluntary public welfare work resumed once again.

In October 1940, when Gandhi started the individual satyagraha movement to protest against the British government dragging Indians into the Second World War unwillingly, a large number of Congress workers volunteered from Medinipur, including fifteen from Tamluk subdivision alone. The British attempts to supress the satyagraha movement only caused more widespread criticism of the government across the country, and discontent was so high that the region became a fertile ground for a much larger movement.

Unrelated events from across the globe also paved the way for the movement. It was a time when the Allies were on the backfoot in the Second World War, with Britain and France struggling to contain Hitler's German forces. On the Eastern Front, the

---

3 *Sarbadhinayak: Freedom Struggle in Tamluk*, p. 22.

Japanese were advancing towards India and the Britishers were preparing for a successful retreat, as they had done in Myanmar and other colonies. The British had anticipated that if the Japanese were to attack India, the district of Medinipur, skirting the Bay of Bengal in the south, would be the ideal destination to attack from the sea because they would find favourable landing ground there due to the widespread angst against the British government. Thus, the southern and eastern parts of Tamluk subdivision were declared emergency zones and all forms of transportation were banned and vehicles seized. Moreover, all food grains, including rice and paddy, were procured on an extensive scale and exported out of the country by the British without any regard to local requirement.

It was in that milieu that the Congress announced the Quit India movement on 8 August 1942 in Bombay, with Mahatma Gandhi as its leader. Even as political leaders across the country were getting arrested for their participation in the movement, called the August Revolution, Midnapore Congress workers did not jump in right away. On 8 September 1942, a month after the movement was launched, the owner of a rice mill in Danipur village faced protests from villagers for allegedly exporting rice to Britain without any concern for fulfilling local needs. As thousands of villagers protested, the police, in an attempt to silence the protestors, ended up killing three locals. The shocking incident aggravated the public even more against the rulers and led to a lot of debate on the course of action to be taken forward. It was then that the local Congress leaders resolved to block all government machinery in Tamluk subdivision.

On 28 September 1942, all major roads in the subdivision —Panskura–Tamluk Road, Tamluk–Narghat Road, Tamluk–Mahishadal Road and Kukrahati–Balughata Road— were dug up at several places, big trees were felled and dumped on the roads, at least thirty culverts were blown up, and telegraph and telephone lines were cut off over a length of 43 kilometres to prevent any exchange of information. All ferry boats on the Kosi and Haldi rivers were sunk or removed. All this action took place over the course of a night, with the sole intention that no military or police personnel should reach Tamluk subdivision from outside.

Local officials who came to know of these developments the following morning tried to repair the roads and managed to clear only the Panskura–Tamluk Road for military trucks to arrive in Tamluk. However, by 2 p.m. on 29th September, large processions of disgruntled people guided by Congress leaders approached Tamluk town from five different directions, and the military forces, who had arrived by then, clashed with the public. At least ten civilians were shot dead in the melee, including Matangini Hazra, who died holding the national flag in her hand. Meanwhile, public processions and clashes with military and police officers broke out in other parts of the town as well. Of the six police stations in the subdivision, the protestors could capture only one without any bloodshed. At all the other police stations, lives were lost as thousands of protestors took over the stations. At the Nandigram police station, at least four people were shot dead, as masses seized the station premises.

The next phase of the blockade consisted of taking possession of various seats of government authority at the local level, such as the Union Board, Debt Settlement Board, Rent Collection Centres, etc., to wipe out all traces of foreign rule from the countryside. As these activities proceeded in a relatively smooth manner, a devastating cyclone ravaged the region, causing unprecedented damage.

On 16 October 1942, heavy rains accompanied by a strong wind thrashed the region—uprooting trees, felling houses, overturning rooftops and bringing widespread destruction. An official report by the subdivisional officer of Tamluk clarified that a total of 3,873 persons died, 1,972 persons sustained injuries and 1,10,346 houses collapsed in the cyclone.[4] Due to the Second World War and the political situation in Tamluk subdivision, the British government tried to ignore the destruction caused by the cyclone and carried out no relief measures, despite several appeals from local officials for help. While the government indulged in criminal neglect and reluctance, widespread looting, raids and torture of the revolutionaries continued. According to reports, on the night of 24 October 1942, just seven days after the cyclone, a police party swam through the flood waters and raided Putputia, a village in Tamluk, searching a number of houses, arresting a few, looting several thousand rupees in cash from local businessmen and triggering complete outrage among the public.

Against that backdrop, the Congress workers under the leadership of Satish Chandra Samanta took the momentous decision of establishing the Tamralipta Jatiya Sarkar (Tamluk National Government) in order to establish law and order in the countryside, end the widespread anarchy and make proper arrangements for the relief and rehabilitation of the flood-stricken people. The Jatiya Sarkar was formally established on 17 December 1942, with Satish Chandra Samanta as its sarbadhinayak (commander-in-chief). It was also announced that volunteer corps, 'Vidyut Bahini', would be proclaimed as the national militia of the Jatiya Sarkar—in charge of law and order, besides defence of their territory. This national government was to eventually become a part of the federal state of India during Independence.

After the formation of the Jatiya Sarkar, the sarbadhinayak formed his cabinet of ministers and ran the administration. In a similar fashion, smaller Thana Jatiya Sarkars were formed at the Nandigram, Mahisadal, Sutahata and Tamluk thanas, and an adhinayak was appointed with the authority to run the administration in the respective areas with the help of ministers

---

4 *Sarbadhinayak: Freedom Struggle in Tamluk*, p. 33.

appointed by them. Under the national government, cyclone relief was initiated to help victims get back on their feet, courts operated freely to provide justice to the public and food grains were rationed during a famine that broke out during that period.

Even as the independent government was functioning successfully, the British Army and police were constantly trying to disrupt it and reclaim territory, leading to several skirmishes. In May 1943, Satish Chandra went to Calcutta to establish the Jatiya Sarkar's contacts with the outside world. However, he was arrested there and imprisoned. In his absence, Ajoy Mukherjee was made the second sarbadhinayak and the Jatiya Sarkar continued. He remained in power till 19 September 1943, when he was also arrested. Following him, two others became sarbadhinayaks and continued with the government.

On 6 May 1944, Mahatma Gandhi was released from his detention. A few days later, he called off the Quit India movement nationally. Heeding his call, the sarbadhinayak at the time, Barada Babu, ordered the suspension of all activities of the Jatiya Sarkar on 8 August 1944 and was arrested on the following day while participating in a peaceful protest in Tamluk town. From 1 September 1944 on, the Tamralipta Jatiya Sarkar ceased to exist and all activities of the national government were brought to a close.

The Jatiya Sarkar in Tamluk is among the very few independent governments that were successful for almost two years, besides the Prati Sarkar in Satara, Maharashtra (that went on till 1945),[5] in British India and remains a remarkable achievement in the history of India's freedom struggle.

---

5 *India's Struggle for Independence*, p. 466.

Exactly sixty-five years after Jatiya Sarkar was formed, as the nation geared up to celebrate the sixtieth year of independence from British rule, a similar situation played out less than 50 kilometres away from Tamluk in Nandigram and its surrounding villages in January 2007. The Left Front government, which had been in power in West Bengal for thirty years, was to embark on an industrialization spree by bringing Tata Motors to Singur for their Nano car project and the Indonesia-based Salim Group to Nandigram, a CPM stronghold then, to set up a Special Economic Zone for chemical industries.[6] The All India Trinamool Congress (TMC), in Opposition, led by Mamata Banerjee, had been successful in forcing the state government to scrap the Nano car project, but Nandigram was considered a safe zone for large-scale industrialization, considering the clout the Left Front enjoyed in the region.

Local villagers who were set to lose their land were aggrieved and planned to resist the government's move to set up an SEZ. They formed a committee known as the Bhumi Uchhed Protirodh Committee (BUPC) and decided to resist the government's move tooth and nail. The TMC, fresh from their success in Singur, supported the farmers and joined hands with the BUPC in spreading awareness and organizing protests.

On 2 January 2007, the farmers, with the help of TMC activists, clashed with around 250 CPI(M) cadres after getting a letter on land acquisition from a CPI(M) MP. Six people died in the clash and the farmers blocked the entire region earmarked for the SEZ. Protestors dug up roads, destroyed bridges and cut off all communication

6 Swagata Sen, '2007-Nandigram violence: A state of failure', *India Today*, 25 December 2009, https://www.indiatoday.in/magazine/cover-story/story/20091228-2007-nandigram-violence-a-state-of-failure-741632-2009-12-23

with the rest of the state, just as was done in September 1942.[7] Nandigram and its surrounding villages became isolated, with no police or any state government machinery being able to reach the villages or pacify the protestors. For almost two months Nandigram remained cut off from the rest of West Bengal.

On 14 March 2007, West Bengal Chief Minister Buddhadeb Bhattacharjee allegedly sent 2500 policemen to 'recapture' Nandigram.[8] However, according to various sources, they were accompanied by hundreds of suspected CPI(M) cadres. As per official records, the violent clashes that took place between the villagers, who were supported by TMC activists, and the police and CPI(M) activists resulted in the death of fourteen farmers. But over a hundred persons were declared missing after the violence; homes were looted and set on fire; and women were allegedly raped and held hostage, as the violence escalated to unprecedented levels. According to media reports at the time, bodies were found strewn around in villages, and several of them were even allegedly dumped in the Haldia river. The state police claimed that they were attacked from several quarters and had no choice but to retaliate. The casualty, worst in the thirty years of the Left Front's rule in West Bengal, left the nation stunned. For the next several months, violence continued to break out in the region between villagers and CPI(M) activists.

Eventually, the SEZ project was shelved and the March 2007 violence turned out to be the beginning of the end for CPI(M) rule in West Bengal. The TMC largely swept the local body elections in Nandigram that were held after the violence. In the 2011 assembly elections, Buddhadeb Bhattacharjee lost his seat

---

7 'Nandigram turns blood red', *The Economic Times*, 15 March 2007, https://economictimes.indiatimes.com/news/politics-and-nation/nandigram-turns-blood-red/articleshow/1764786.cms

8 Swagata Sen, '2007-Nandigram violence: A state of failure'.

and the Left Front was defeated by the TMC, after ruling the state for a record thirty-four years.

---

Debu's paranoia was evident soon after he picked me up from the guest house on the Tamluk–Haldia Road. 'It's a nasty place. *Bahut maar-peet hota hai.* I won't accompany you outside the car and will remain inside. You will call me only if you're in trouble,' he instructed, even before we left for Nandigram.

Barely a few minutes into the drive, he began giving me advice on how to behave when we reached there. 'Don't ever talk politics. Don't ask anyone which party they belong to. Don't ask any questions that make people uncomfortable ...' Then he asked me what I wanted from there in the first place. 'Do you really want to go to Nandigram? There are many people who have moved to Tamluk from Nandigram after the 2007 violence. You could interview them here.'

Debu's concern was justified as just the day before, two factions of the TMC had clashed in Nandigram and the violence had ensured that a curfew was still on. My local contacts claimed that with the 2021 West Bengal assembly elections witnessing a pitched battle between Mamata Banerjee and her second-in-command, Suvendu Adhikari, who had shifted camp to the BJP ahead of the elections and defeated her, Nandigram had been on the boil. The constituency and the Purba Medinipur region as a whole had witnessed clashes almost on a daily basis since then, and it was the cause of my newly married driver's worry too.

After about an hour and a half of driving along mostly empty roads and highways on account of the Poila Baisakh festival, we reached the bustling Nandigram market next to the bus terminus when the clock struck twelve and the muezzin's call alerted all Muslims—who were in significant number in the market—that it was time for prayer. The political tension in the market was evident from the number of ropes strung with colourful party flags that criss-crossed over the main bazar junction. Since both the TMC and the BJP flags had significant portions of saffron and green in them, differentiating the flags was difficult unless one took a closer look. Much more easily identifiable and sparsely available were the red flags of the Marxist Party that were found fluttering on isolated street corners, outside locked roadside shops a little away from the auto rickshaw and toto stands in the market, which were predominantly occupied by the saffron-green shades of the TMC and the BJP flags.

The mid-April heat was relentless; everyone in the market was sweating it out, whether they laboured hard or not. I got out of the car and Debu, who had changed his mind about staying inside the car after reaching Nandigram, tagged along as we went to a sweet shop, bought two tetrapaks of mango-flavoured soft drink and tried to have a conversation with the store's owner, a middle-aged, fit man with strong vocal cords, like most opinionated people.

I told him about the purpose of my visit and asked him to suggest whom to talk to. After staring at me for a while and making it clear that he would not answer any personal questions, such as revealing his name or other details, the man said, 'In Nandigram, there is no one you can talk to. If you ask a TMC person, you will get one type of response, and if you ask a BJP person, you will get exactly the opposite. No one speaks the truth here! And there is no one who can claim to be apolitical. If you don't belong to a party and are under the protection of their goons, you just can't live here in Nandigram. This is the situation of our town.'

When I asked him about the 2007 violence and whether his town and the surrounding villages had got over the massacre, the man claimed that things out there had gone from bad to worse over the past fifteen years. 'Now the situation here is like what it used to be in Bihar some twenty or thirty years ago. Every other day, there is a violent clash. Either TMC and BJP cadres clash, or different factions of the TMC clash with one another, or BJP cadres fight among themselves. The CPI(M) here is too weak to fight anymore but they are still around in small numbers,' he lamented.

According to the sweetmeat vendor, the political situation had dwindled to an all-time low during the 2021 assembly elections in the battle between Mamata Banerjee and Suvendu Adhikari. 'Cadres from both parties used to come every day before the polls and ask each of us about whom we would vote for and who was likely to win. The political goons kept such a close watch on every voter that the sheer attention left many disturbed mentally. Eventually, with the BJP clinching the constituency despite losing the overall polls, the TMC leaders' distrust of the voters of Nandigram worsened further and has remained so since then,' he explained. 'They now look at everyone with suspicion.'

When I began probing a little further on the local politics, I noticed that both Debu and the shop owner were getting uncomfortable as a couple of auto rickshaw drivers from the stand adjacent to the sweet shop came and stood behind me, listening to our conversation. Not wanting any further trouble, I thanked the vendor and left for Sonachura village, where a large number of people had gone missing or were killed in the 2007 violence.

---

Sonachura is about 10 kilometres away from the Nandigram bazar. A winding road flanked by one- or two-room homes with unplastered walls, lush vegetable fields, small ponds and occasional eucalyptus and banana plantations cut across several identical and sparsely populated hamlets and led us to the Sonachura bazar, where most shops were closed due to Poila Baisakh. We halted at the bazar area and asked for the house of the village pradhan. The pradhan for the reserved ward, Gita Rani, belonged to the TMC and lived in one of the very few two-storey homes in the village, past a 6-foot-wide concrete road behind the bazar. On the way to her home, we passed at least a dozen mud homes that were similar to the ones I had seen in the remote villages in Unnao district.

As I had anticipated, upon asking for Gita Rani, a shirtless sixty-year-old man with a huge pot belly, which he proudly kept massaging, came out and said he was Raj Krishna Mondal, Gita Rani's husband, and that we could talk to him. However, unlike in UP and Bihar, the councillor Gita Rani did join her husband in a few minutes and was equally vocal once she came and sat in our midst. Raj Krishna and Gita Rani live with their three sons, daughters-in-law and several grandchildren, two of whom were in the room with us. Raj's elder brother, Nishikant Mondal, was among those killed during the police firing in 2007. He was one of the village leaders and had headed the protests in Sonachura.

When I asked them about life in their village after the 2007 violence, both Raj and Gita Rani claimed that the past few years had been peaceful. 'We have no complaints and have got good roads, food. Our Didi takes good care of us,' Gita Rani asserted. She went on to extol how several schemes that had been introduced by the TMC government, like the Kanyashree, Rupashree and Lakshmir Bhandar schemes, had benefited families in their village. She added that they even get a few essential items like rice, etc., free of cost in rations.

Two of Raj and Gita's sons are educated up to high school, while the third son even went to college and earned a degree. The two elder daughters-in-law are graduates too. Yet, none in the family have a steady job. Raj's political influence has ensured that he got all contracts from the local body and the family did not have to live a hand-to-mouth existence, unlike most other families in Sonachura. While their eldest son was into farming, the middle son was engaged in pisciculture. The youngest had tried to find a job but had eventually resorted to farming due to lack of job opportunities. Unlike their parents' generation, hundreds of youngsters in this village of 8,000-odd residents had completed their graduation but had no jobs. 'It's the only problem here. There are no jobs for youngsters anywhere in this region. Didi has given us everything but jobs,' Gita Rani concluded.

Raj's martyred brother, Nishikant Mondal, had four children —two sons and two daughters—of whom two had managed to get teaching jobs in government schools. 'The other two are unemployed and take up odd jobs,' Raj said, and went on to clarify that his brother's family members had shifted their allegiance to the BJP and that they no longer kept in touch with them.

---

From Sonachura we proceeded towards Gopalnagar, where we were to meet the pradhan of that village, also belonging to the TMC. We passed through more impoverished villages and desolate roads, and reached a sharp bend just ahead of Gopalnagar with a couple of cigarette and tea shops still open for business. Debu and I stepped out of the car and asked an elderly woman at a cigarette shop for the Gopalnagar pradhan's address. She came out and led us to a shack, which was the office of the INTTUC Toto Autorickshaw Union. At least half a dozen rods with TMC flags were stuck to the roof of the shack.

A tall, lean man with dark, oily skin, dressed in a long-sleeved cotton shirt fully buttoned up to the collar and black jeans, wearing shiny brown leather shoes, came out of the shack and walked towards us. He was clean-shaven and his shiny black hair had been combed back. A younger woman draped in a saree also stepped out with him. The man shook hands with me and introduced himself as Konkon Adhikari, a former associate of Suvendu Adhikari.

After requesting, his female companion to bring out three chairs, he began to speak about the political situation in Nandigram, especially after the 2007 violence. When the chairs came, the three of us—Debu, Konkon and I—sat, the chairs placed on a corner of the road, and Debu tried to translate his statements into Hindi as fast as he could. As the man continued to speak, his voice grew louder and the rhetoric gathered pace. Debu, who tried to keep pace as well as he could, often kept silent as he couldn't match the man's discourse or vigour. After a while, I noticed that Debu had become extremely uncomfortable. A few other locals who were passing by stopped their vehicles, gathered around us and began listening to the man's oration, which had by then become even louder, as if he were addressing a public meeting. When Debu could no longer stand it, he excused himself and walked towards the car. Even with no translator and knowing well that I couldn't understand Bengali, the man continued to talk—it was clear that his oration was not meant just for me.

A few minutes later, I interrupted him, excused myself from the situation and walked away. Thankfully, he stopped after I got up, and joined me at the cigarette shop, where he ordered the elderly woman to give him a pack of Gold Flake cigarettes and some bananas. After lighting up a cigarette, he offered me a banana, which I refused. I walked towards our car.

After getting in, I asked Debu what the man had been harping on about. 'He is also a TMC guy, sir, and was praising Didi while abusing Suvendu Adhikari. He claims Adhikari switched parties at the last minute and that's why they left him. He also claimed that he has killed many people, thrown bombs, etc., and that the police are all in his pocket. He wanted you to go to the police station and verify all that about him.'

'What did he say about Didi?'

'He was bragging that he will be loyal to Didi till his death. I couldn't tolerate it after a while; that's why I walked to the car,' Debu said, starting the engine.

As we returned to Tamluk, I asked Debu if he belonged to any political party. 'Of course, sir, the BJP. Even my boss, the owner of this car, belongs to the BJP,' Debu replied. For the rest of the journey, he kept hurling abuses at Didi and her governance.

---

Later that evening, we drove to the Tamluk Smriti Soudha, a memorial building constructed along NH 41, near Nimtouri, to honour the heroes of the freedom movement in the region. At the entrance to the memorial building, bright bold letters engraved on the front wall screamed: 'Dedicated to the Freedom Fighters of Tamluk'. Since we had arrived on a public holiday, the memorial office on the ground floor of the four-storey building was locked. In the parking lot, a few young men were taking turns and diving into a pond right next to the Smriti Soudha building. I asked them if they knew the office-bearers of the memorial but did not get any favourable response.

On the first floor of the building was a large hall with tables and chairs strewn around in a haphazard manner. The walls of the hall were covered with paintings depicting incidents from the freedom movement, coated in a thick layer of brown dust. At the far end of the hall, a loud meeting was underway—about a dozen men and women sat in a circle and chatted about some civic issues in the locality. Upon noticing me, one of the men came up and asked what I wanted. I told him I was looking for the office-bearers of the Smriti Soudha. The man was clueless and suggested I go and try upstairs.

On the second floor of the building was a public library, which was again locked. A notice board was stuck outside, informing visitors about the change of some committee members, and a phone number was listed under the Smriti Soudha address. I took down the phone number and climbed to the fourth floor, which appeared to be a dormitory, where clothes were hung on ropes in long lines on one side and bedding was strewn around clumsily on the other. Unable to find anyone to speak to, I walked back to the car and called the phone number I had noted down. There was no response.

As we drove back to the guest house, I got a call from the Smriti Soudha contact number and a woman spoke in Bengali. Since I couldn't understand what she was saying, I passed the phone to Debu and asked him to talk. After a brief chat with her, Debu told me the man to whom the phone number belonged was dead. 'His daughter is using the phone now. She said that she has nothing to do with the Smriti Soudha and that it is under new management now.'

# Tentuligumma, Koraput District

IN HINDSIGHT, THE RIDE FROM JEYPORE TO BOIPARIGUDA, along a scenic countryside and past quaint villages with single-storey homes, rustic kirana shops and modest eateries with open kitchens, was comparatively smooth. From Boipariguda, we needed to make a right turn for Govindpalli and then proceed to Tentuligumma, my destination, in Koraput district of Odisha. But we were forced to stop the car after crossing Boipariguda because a large group of women, draped in colourful sarees and with their noses pierced with large rings, blocked the road with a thick bamboo pole. Their children swarmed around our car as soon as we halted and crowded behind both the front windows, tapping the glass panes. Munna lowered the window and handed a ten-rupee note to one of the women who stood behind the children. 'Today is their festival. It is customary for the villagers in this area to collect a little money from all vehicles that pass through their villages,' he explained apologetically, and proceeded to drive. He could sense my discomfort at what had just happened—people with no political affiliation or the backing of any recognized outfit blocking roads and collecting money from strangers without giving a receipt for the sum is generally known as extortion. I had witnessed this once earlier while travelling from Tezpur in Assam to Tawang in Arunachal Pradesh: Women and children blocking the road and demanding money.

The ride up to Govindpalli was mostly along a deserted two-lane road that had been recently re-laid. A little before we reached, Munna was forced to stop the car again: Between fifty and sixty khakhi-clad men of all ages blocked the road and stopped all four-wheelers. When Munna lowered the window, a mob gathered around the car and started talking to him rather rudely. When he tried to respond, they seemed to get more agitated and wanted him to get out of the vehicle. Just before getting out, Munna warned me to remain seated in the car irrespective of what happened outside and assured me that we would proceed in a bit. The khakhi-clad men dragged Munna to the rear of the vehicle and had an intense argument with him, with the decibel levels increasing alarmingly. From what little I understood, Munna was trying to convince them that he was the owner of the car and not a driver. He made his way back to the car, but the men were not convinced and rounded him up once again. I got a little restless and tried to open the door on my side, when a middle-aged man peeped in through the driver-side window, saluted and said 'Jai Hind'. He gestured at me to remain seated and blinked his eyes a couple of times as if to tell me everything was okay.

The argument between Munna and the crowd continued until he was forced to record a video on the mobile phone of one of the group members saying that he was from Jeypore and that he was the owner of the car he was driving, not a driver. The mob let him go after his video statement, with a warning that they would soon verify if he was indeed the owner of the car and then deal with him later if needed.

'There is a drivers' strike today and they are not allowing any commercial vehicles to operate. I had to tell them that it was my own car [he was driving a white-board Maruti Swift Dzire] and that I was not a driver but taking a friend to Tentuligumma. After I allowed them to record me on camera saying that this car belonged to me, they let me go,' Munna, my driver, said. We continued.

By then I had begun to feel very uncomfortable with the way the day was proceeding. About ten minutes later, the ghat section of the road began and a forest department notice board warned us to look out for animals, especially at night. The winding road criss-crossed the course of the almost dry Sabari river on the one side and dense foliage on the other. After the incident with the mob, Munna had stopped his small talk and drove quietly, focusing on the road. To change his mood, I asked him if there was any genuine threat of wild animals in the ghat section as I had been warned in Uttarakhand's Don and Parewa villages. 'There is no threat of animals in this area. But sometimes armed bandits or dacoits attack vehicles and loot whatever they can get,' he said. 'Not always, but armed bandits are known to operate in this area,' he casually stated and continued to drive.

I had been quite concerned about visiting this region, a known Maoist hub with several attacks reported even in the recent past. Usually before visiting such destinations, I try to reach out to local leaders and alert them of my travel as a precautionary measure, just in case of any trouble during my stay. With Tentuligumma, due to my hectic schedule, I hadn't made any such preparation. My hope had been that leftist friends in Kolkata would have some insight on the region. When I told my journalist friend in Kolkata, a CPI(M) card holder known to have connections with extremist groups, he dismissed my concern. 'You won't get into any trouble there. You're a Mallu and a journalist. They'll consider you one of their own. Don't worry about going there,' he assured me. He hadn't told me, though, about armed bandits roaming these jungles and the surrounding villages.

I had been charmed by Tentuligumma since reading about this quiet tribal hamlet and its heroes of the freedom movement. The unusual name—Ten-tuli-gumma—also added to my intrigue. Comprising just about 150 houses, the village was home to a tribal hero of the freedom movement, Saheed Laxman Naik, who had spearheaded the Quit India movement following Gandhi's call in this tribal belt. He was sent to the gallows at Berhampur Jail in 1943 following a hasty trial, as had been the case with most freedom fighters at the time, and has been celebrated posthumously for stirring up the tribal population in this belt to join the country's freedom struggle in the footsteps of Mahatma Gandhi.

But Tentuligumma and its surrounding hamlets have transformed drastically over the past seventy-five years. Today, the region is better known as a major hub of banned Maoist outfits. While Koraput, Malkangiri and a few other districts have been well-known Maoist bastions, Laxman Naik's village surrounded by rocky hills grabbed headlines in March 2016, when Gobardhan Bhumia, former sarpanch of Tentuligumma, was hacked to death by suspected Maoists at Sarangajodi ghat road under Boipariguda police limits. The local police had claimed that the murder of the former sarpanch was the result of rivalry among Maoist groups. In January 2016, Bapi Samanta, a suspected police informer, was murdered by the extremist group. The banned outfit had left a poster at the murder spot in which they had named ten people from the village who were warned to refrain from anti-Maoist activities. Two of those in the list, who were also Maoist supporters, had then approached Bhumia for a mediation with the rival group but allegedly did not receive much help. Suspecting the former sarpanch of misguiding the rebels, the two arranged for the murder of Bhumia, a known sympathizer. Dozens more have lost their lives by being caught in such violence in the region over the past few decades.

Extreme left organizations penetrated the tribal belt of Odisha several decades ago and deaths due to clashes with law enforcement peaked during the early 2000s. A report tabled in the Parliament of India in 2016 revealed that Maoist killings had peaked in Odisha in the year 2008, when 109 persons were killed. The killings had shot up from twenty-four in the previous year, a fourfold increase. The following years also witnessed a significant number of deaths, with eighty-two persons killed in 2009 and eighty-nine the following year. But since then, it has been largely following a downward trend.

The extent to which Maoists controlled the region was revealed in an attack on police stations in 2009, when several teams of the banned organization attacked the Boipariguda and Machkund police stations—blowing up the two stations simultaneously and setting fire to several vehicles.[1] A police outpost was also attacked at the same time. In April 2009, hundreds of Maoists raided the fire station and magazine room of NALCO, a Central public sector enterprise in the Damanjodi mines area. Ten CISF jawans and four Maoists were killed in the gun battle. These attacks forced law enforcement to step up surveillance in the jungles, and since then the numbers have been steadily dipping, with sixty-four persons losing their lives in 2016.

However, the threat remains and local support for extremist organizations continues unabated in the region, which was evident as recently as November 2022—five months after my visit there. A team of officials from the Special Operations Group conducted an anti-Maoist operation in the forests of Atalguda, Malipadar and Badli Pahad villages under Boipariguda police station limits

---

1 Satyanarayan Pattnaik and Sandeep Mishra, 'Second major attack in 2 months shocks Koraput', *The Times of India*, 8 June 2009, https://timesofindia.indiatimes.com/city/bhubaneswar/second-major-attack-in-2-months-shocks-koraput/articleshow/4633048.cms

and came across ten to fifteen Maoists camping in the vicinity of Malipadar village. Both sides exchanged fire, following which police recovered three country-made guns, tiffin bombs, detonators, Maoist uniforms and ten packets of cannabis. Two of the suspected Maoists died in the operation.[2]

---

Munna continued to drive in silence. On that sunny afternoon, thanks to the drivers' strike, there wasn't another soul or vehicle on the ghat, road except for some malnourished cows and their bouncy calves that had come out to enjoy their day on the empty highway. After about fifteen minutes on the road, I noticed a sign that said: 'Ghat Road Ends, Drive Pleasantly'. By then, both sides of the road were filled with the bright green mahol (mahua or butter) trees that abound in this region. Of every ten trees I noticed along the way, at least seven were mahol trees. There were also significant numbers of palm, wild teak and other trees. As we passed more tiny villages on the way to Tentuligumma, I noticed BSF checkposts all along the way. For more than a decade now, the BSF had deployed at least four battalions each in Koraput and Malkangiri districts to take on the left extremists in the region.

About 3 kilometres from Govindpalli, we were again stopped by a different group of drivers, who were a lot more passive and tried to convince Munna to join the drivers' union, explaining to him the benefits one could get by becoming a unionist. One of the men even told him that though he was driving his own car, he could still be a part of the union. However, Munna managed to convince them yet

---

2 Debabrata Mohanty, '2 Maoists killed in gunfight after SOG team comes under fire in Koraput: Police', *Hindustan Times*, 11 November 2022, https://www.hindustantimes.com/india-news/2-maoists-killed-in-gunfight-after-sog-team-comes-under-fire-in-koraput-police-101668183568666.html

again, and we continued. 'But they've asked us not to return before evening as they have not allowed any other vehicle. If others see, they will fault the striking unions,' he explained as we proceeded.

Just before entering Tentuligumma, we saw a pickup truck with 'Jai Shri Ram' painted on it parked right across the road, blocking us. After we didn't get a response to shouting for someone to come and move the truck, Munna and I got out and walked to a nearby shop to inquire. It was the drivers' strike again. 'For two days, no vehicle can pass this way,' said the shopkeeper. 'See if you can squeeze your way through the side; two-wheelers and auto rickshaws can manage,' he said. Thankfully, the Swift Dzire, too, could just about wriggle through the gap, and I was finally in Saheed Laxman Naik's village.

A concrete road led to the interior lanes of the remote village, lined with modest homes, cowsheds and mounds of dung. Loud Odiya music blared out of large, antiquated party speakers placed under a giant mahua tree outside the village community hall. But we couldn't spot a soul anywhere around us. 'It's probably due to the local festival. Everyone will be drinking and dancing through tonight. The music is to prepare the villagers for the evening festivities,' Munna explained as we rolled past tiny shacks with unplastered walls and tiled roofs. A little ahead, we noticed a skinny, bare-bodied man in his late fifties or early sixties and asked him for directions to Saheed Laxman Naik's home. The man immediately offered to take us there and joined us in the car. We continued along the narrow concrete road for another 100 metres or so, turned right and halted by a cluster of little huts on a dry piece of land. The man, Sukuru, got out of the car and limped towards a locked one-room hut surrounded by at least six other larger, better furnished huts and claimed it was the house of Saheed Laxman Naik.

Munna and I exchanged glances because we didn't believe what Sukuru was saying—the hut looked so tiny and was in shambles.

Looking around, we spotted a young girl operating a sewing machine in the house opposite the tiny hut. She confirmed it was indeed the deceased freedom fighter's house and that Laxman Naik's grandson, who still lived there, had gone to the forest to gather mahua flowers and would return only at night for the festival.

After Laxman Naik died in 1943, his son, Raghunath Naik, had lived there, but he had also passed away long ago, and his adopted son, Madhu Naik, was occupying the house now. The surrounding huts on that piece of land were occupied by close relatives of the Naiks, and the young girl's mother, who was Raghunath's niece, opened the door of the tiny hut and asked me to wait inside.

I walked in and sat on a shaky, dust-coated stool made of solid country wood. Considering Laxman Naik had lost his life at a young age for the freedom of this country, his progeny were surviving under shockingly abysmal conditions. The hut's flooring was made of cow dung paste, the walls were built of bricks gelled with limestone paste and the roof was tiled. A couple of deer horns protruded from the walls at the far end of the house, near which was a dirty bulb holder with a 40-watt bulb clinging to it. The hut had very minimal electrical wiring and one or two incandescent bulbs. The only indicator of Laxman Naik's connection with the house was a framed photograph of the Odisha government's note on his contribution, which hung on the front wall.

Soon, about a dozen relatives of Laxman's gathered outside his hut and looked at me curiously. I asked them to tell me whatever they knew about his contribution to the freedom struggle, and, unsurprisingly, none had a clue. They all knew that he had done something for the country's freedom and that the district collector, local MLAs and MPs came there to garland the freedom fighter's statue at the public park and pay respects at the memorial, but none had bothered to find out what he had done to deserve this recognition. They were more up to date on current affairs concerning their own lives and soon began the tirade of complaints against the local administration.

As we chatted, the village sarpanch, Buddra Naik, who was also a relative of the freedom fighter, arrived. He was dressed in a checked shirt and trousers and was younger than most of the others around me, probably in his early thirties. Buddra Naik lived in a separate hut with his wife, Manmati, and son, Raj Kumar. An active politician, he was the most articulate among them and the only one in touch with the block-level and district officials. After complimenting Buddra Naik on his choice of clothes, I asked him why none of the other men even had shirts on and still lived in structures that looked more like cattle sheds. Buddra said that the situation was much worse until a few years ago and that things were slowly getting better. 'Now there is some progress. The road from Jeypore to the village was laid only about a year and a half ago. There is a government school up to class seven, a health centre with an auxiliary nurse midwife clinic now. What we still don't have are mobile connectivity and a bus service, and villagers have to travel 35 kilometres to Mathili to reach the closest bank,' he elaborated.

Even after seventy-five years of Independence, the residents of Tentuligumma can only boast of those few amenities. Barely one or two homes in the village had concrete structures and those, too, were built using funds from the PM's Housing for All scheme. The homes had electricity but no televisions or other gadgets. After class seven, children still travelled 5–6 kilometres to nearby villages for high school and to Mathili for higher studies. The roads were laid but had no streetlights. 'We have called for the 108-ambulance service thrice from the village so far and they have come once. On [the other] two occasions, they refused to come, citing a lack of vehicles,' Buddra Naik said. Quality education even now remained a far cry, as the village still had just one or two graduates. Girls who wished to pursue higher education had to stay in hostels in larger towns, which most villagers were uncomfortable with. But neither Buddra nor the other villagers saw these issues as the government's shortcomings, for they are so used to a life devoid of any development. Even more tragic was that none of these people had a clue of their past or any hope for a better future.

Though the freedom movement started gathering pace across the country in the early 1900s, people in Koraput and its surrounding tribal hamlets got involved in the Indian National Congress initiatives only by the mid-1920s, after government employees and other prominent locals in touch with the outside world plunged into the movement and brought the campaign back home. Laxman Naik, born in November 1899 in Tentuligumma village, was exposed to tribal issues and their welfare even as a child because his father, Padlam Naik, was the mustadar (tax collector or government representative) of four villages, including Tentuligumma.[3] During his growing years, he also learned tribal witchcraft and about herbal medicine, and worked as a dishari (tribal priest). He also acquainted himself with using guns and other weapons during that period and got in touch with the local Congress leaders, which eventually led to his admiration for Mahatma Gandhi.[4]

After his father's death in 1930, Laxman was appointed as the mustadar and became more popular among the villagers due to his influential position and healing powers. Around this time,

---

3 S.C. Padhy, A.K. Padhy and S.C. Pathy, 'Lakshman Naik Tribal Freedom Fighter and Martyr', *Proceedings of the Indian History Congress*, vol. 59 (1998), pp. 587–94.

4 'The Life and Martyrdom of "Gandhi of Malkangiri" Laxman Nayak', Newsroom Odisha, 13 August 2022, https://newsroomodisha.com/the-life-and-martyrdom-of-gandhi-of-malkangiri-laxman-nayak/

the Congress movement was also gradually gaining popularity in the Koraput region. Several meetings and public gatherings took place in Koraput, Malkangiri and other smaller towns and villages to spread the message of the Congress Party. As a prominent local leader, Laxman Naik was also invited to such meetings, where he was further exposed to Gandhian ideals. In 1936, during a Congress drive to enrol primary members in the Malkangiri area, Laxman Naik came in contact with Radhakrishna Biswaroy, who was a prominent leader in the district and had been working for the party since 1929, after quitting government service. Under Biswaroy's guidance, Laxman enrolled himself as a 'four-anna' member of the Congress Party (party membership fees had been reduced to four annas to help poorer people enrol in the party) and inspired many others from the surrounding tribal villages to join the party too. Under his guidance, hundreds from Malkangiri joined the Congress and devoted themselves to the movement. These workers would go to the villages to promote khadi fabric and made people aware of the Congress Party initiatives towards achieving freedom. Such initiatives helped in setting up a base of support for the party among the tribals, who were now infused with a new energy, especially after the Congress formed a ministry in 1937. Consequently, minor scuffles with the police and those in power began frequently breaking out as the public were emboldened by then.

The Quit India movement of 1942 came at a time when people in several parts of Odisha were already yearning for a revolution. In Koraput, the movement created an unprecedented public awakening and the message of the nationwide revolt spread in tribal villages like wildfire. Spontaneous hartals and incidents of arson broke out in and around the district, even as all the major leaders, except Laxman Naik, were imprisoned for their role in the movement.

Mathili, on the Jeypore–Malkangiri Road, became a prominent centre of the national movement, thanks to the relatively more developed status of the town. Thus, with other leaders in prison,

Laxman, who had a good rapport with the Bonda tribes inhabiting the remote hills under Mathili police station limits, took up the initiative of marching to the Mathili police station and peacefully hoisting the Congress flag atop the station building on 21 August 1942.[5]

On the planned day, thanks to Laxman's influence among the tribals, people from several villages in the region joined the procession and marched towards Mathili waving Congress flags and chanting the Ramdhun. At least a thousand volunteers were reported to have attended the event and walked to the police station to hoist the flag. Police reports claimed that some of the marchers carried wooden logs and were engaged in a minor scuffle with the police when they were denied entry into the Mathili police station premises. The police ordered a lathi-charge and the demonstrators were beaten up by them. Laxman was also among the severely injured in the melee. Following the police attack, the demonstrators, most of whom belonged to the Bonda tribe, retaliated strongly and broke the bamboo fence of the police station—resulting in indiscriminate firing by the police.[6] Five persons, including the man who tried to hoist the Congress flag atop the station, died, while seventeen others were recorded as injured. Laxman Naik was thrown into a ditch near the police station in a severely injured condition. Among the government officials, a forest guard was also killed.

After the incident, hundreds of tribals who had taken part in the march escaped into the hills to evade police arrest. Laxman Naik was taken to back to Tentuligumma and treated. However, the police reached there looking for him on 2 September 1942 and arrested Laxman along with his son and other Congress workers. After initial interrogations, all of them were imprisoned in Koraput Jail on 18 September 1942. After the hastened trial that ensued,

---

5 *Proceedings of the Indian History Congress*, 'Lakshman Naik Tribal Freedom Fighter and Martyr', vol. 59 (1998), pp. 587–94.

6 Ibid.

Laxman Naik was sentenced to be hanged for the murder of the forest guard, while forty-nine others were given a life sentence. Once his appeal to the Patna High Court was turned down, Laxman Naik was hanged for the murder of a forest guard on 29 March 1943.

---

After meeting Laxman's extended family and the village pradhan, Munna and I wandered farther inside the village looking for anyone we could talk to, but found none. The men we came across were too old and spoke in a dialect that even Munna couldn't make proper sense of, and the women simply refused to engage with us. Unlike the homes, the roads in Tentuligumma were tar-topped and wide. At the village centre, a memorial structure for Saheed Laxman Naik had been built with a bust of the freedom fighter as part of it. The building of the primary school as well as that of the community centre were modest and recently painted. But they were all deserted. After hanging around with us quietly for a while, Sukuru came up with a possible explanation: 'It's the drivers' strike; all the men have gone for the strike. The women are getting ready for the festival.' Both his sons were also drivers and had left for Bhubaneswar to meet the chief minister and press for their demands. Apparently, driving was the most sought-after occupation among the youth in the village and, thus, young men rarely stayed home and mostly travelled across Odisha or its neighbouring states for work.

Having exhausted ourselves walking around in the sun all afternoon, Munna and I were running out of choices on how to spend the rest of the day in Tentuligumma, when Sukuru suggested that we visit the public park named after Saheed Laxman Naik. We followed him on foot yet again to the public park, which, for an impoverished village, was a revelation. The Saheed Laxman Naik Park was a well-maintained, large campus with varieties of trees and shrubs, surrounded by a tall compound wall. The hoarding mentioned that the park was sponsored by the energy firm Meenakshi Power Private Limited, which had also built a small 25MW hydroelectric power project over the Kolab river. The park was a community service initiative.

The lavish green haven had a large play area to the right of the entrance, with seesaws, climbers, sliding boards and other play equipment necessary for children, neatly painted in red, yellow and blue. Varieties of trees, including mahua, which was abundant, ashoka, a couple of large banyan trees, tall elephant palms and smaller guava trees, besides several flowering plants and shrubs of various sizes, provided sufficient shade and respite from the heat even during summer afternoons. At the far end was a tall statue of Laxman Naik with a plaque displaying his birth and death dates. The facility for a flagpole was also available ahead of the statue. To its right were the samadhis, tombstones, of Laxman Naik, his son, Raghunath Naik, and two other family members, built on a neat amphitheatre-like memorial painted blue. The floor of the memorial resembled a brown-and-yellow chessboard. Near the centre of the park was a large, raised circular platform built around two large trees, perhaps for the villagers to sit and enjoy their evenings. An elderly man wearing just a langot lay supine on the platform, half asleep. Sukuru walked up to the man and woke him up. He was Soniya Naik, watchman of the park.

Soniya Naik was eighty and lived in the park, although he had family back in the village. He was a schoolmate of Laxman Naik's son, Raghunath Naik, and had heard about the freedom fighter and his activities from his friend. 'He is not what you think; he is a very rich man. He earns Rs 10,000 every month just to sleep here,' Sukuru told us. 'He has money, sometimes more than men half his age.' Soniya Naik laughed at the description and nodded in agreement. Then the two began speaking in a local dialect that Munna couldn't catch.

Next to the Laxman Naik Park was the Tentuligumma BSF camp, with large wrought iron gates guarded by two gun-wielding personnel atop a watchtower near the entrance. When I expressed my wish to visit the BSF camp to Munna, he was initially reluctant to accompany me but agreed when Sukuru and Soniya Naik also joined us. However, as we walked closer to the BSF camp, all three got equally concerned about getting too close to the gate. Clearly, the paramilitary personnel were not welcome in the village, and the locals were just as suspicious of the BSF folk as they were of the villagers. 'Aren't they for your safety? Why are you afraid?' I asked Sukuru and Soniya. The two men looked at each other and laughed. They told me they would wait about 50 feet away from the camp, under a tree, and asked me to go alone.

The BSF guards in the watchtower, too, looked relaxed after I started walking alone towards the camp. When I told the guards that I was a journalist from Chennai, they immediately welcomed me inside and gave me filtered water and biscuits. Two senior officers came out of one of the tents and bragged about the developments in the village since they had arrived and how peaceful the village had been since. One of the officers even pointed out that a direct road to Koraput was also in the works and would be completed soon. When I asked them about the Maoist threat and the popularity of the extremists among locals in these parts, both officers refused to comment, as they were supposedly engaged in some 'secret operation'.

After the officers were done bragging about everything they could stake a claim for, I sat in silence for a few uncomfortable seconds before walking out. By then, young women draped in colourful sarees were on their way to a local temple, holding bowls made out of thatched green leaves containing rice and other eatables. The number of loudspeakers blaring filmi music had increased, and their beats echoed in the rocky hills that surrounded the village. 'Soon everyone here will be drunk. Let's get out of here before that,' Munna suggested.

On our way back, Munna was a little concerned about the striking drivers in Govindpalli who had advised him not to return early, because we were, in fact, returning quite early. However, nobody was present on the road all the way back to Jeypore. The ride was smooth and swift.

# FOUR

# Panchalankurichi, Thoothukudi District

THE TWO-TIER AC COACH OF THE PEARL CITY EXPRESS to Thoothukudi, formerly Tuticorin, was largely empty, with just one or two passengers in most of the cabins even as the train rolled out of Chennai Egmore Railway Station. While sparsely populated coaches are usually a boon on long-distance trains, they can be a dampener if you're someone who loves to eavesdrop on your co-passengers' conversations to kill the boredom of travelling alone. Fortunately, there was company around, and they happened to be two elderly women returning home after a family event. They occupied the two lower berths of the cabin to the right of my lower-side berth. A young north Indian man occupied the upper-right berth, while the one on the other end was still empty.

Draped in bright silk sarees, the women gobbled up their dinner—idlis and onion-tomato chutney neatly packed in steel tiffin boxes—by 8 p.m. while discussing which chutney was best for train journeys and which to avoid. After the meal, one of them pulled out a Bourbon biscuit packet from her leather handbag, and the two leisurely munched on the chocolate biscuits one after another.

Once the biscuits were dispensed with, the women prepared their beds. One of them, slimmer and more active than her companion, got up and said to the north Indian man in a stiff, loud voice: 'You can keep the lights on. No problem!'

The man, who was fiddling with his phone while lying on his side and facing the cabin wall, immediately turned around and replied, 'Thanks, but *neenga lights off pannikonga* (you can turn off the lights), no problem!'

'Oh, so you know Tamil?' Both women seemed amused.

'*Aama*, madam. *Koncham koncham kathikitu iriken* (yes, madam. I'm learning little by little). Living in Chennai for some years now!'

'Very good, *aana naanga Hindi kathika maatom* (but we won't learn Hindi)!' Pat came the reply. Then she turned to her friend and they both laughed. The young man, too, laughed at the spontaneous, almost impulsive response and turned off the cabin lights. 'This MP ... goes around saying Hindi *theriyathu poda* (don't know Hindi, get lost) and all that. Without knowing Hindi what has she been doing in Delhi for so long? I'm sure even her son knows Hindi,' the slightly overweight woman informed her friend. She was referring to then Thoothukudi MP Kanimozhi's Hindi Theriyathu Poda campaign after the DMK leader was allegedly harassed by CISF guards at the Chennai airport for not knowing Hindi.

'But we will never learn Hindi anyway,' her companion reiterated, and drew the curtains together, shutting me out of the scene.

---

You could blame it all on the excessive salt buried under the soil if you chose to. In Tamil, there is a popular question often directed at shameless, unreactive people: '*Sothula uppu potu than sapudriya?*' Do you add salt to your rice and eat? Medical science also has ample proof to establish a correlation between excessive salt consumption and increased blood pressure. Thus, in a region known for its high-quality salt production, it is only natural that people's blood pressure shoots up and forces them to react whenever anyone tries to impose authority or attempts to subdue them. From the days of Veerapandiya Kattabomman, an eighteenth-century Polygar, or Palayakarar, who refused to pay taxes to the British government and was eventually hanged by them, to Snowlin, an innocent teenager who was shot dead by the police in 2018 while participating in a peaceful protest against Sterlite Copper—Thoothukudi and its surrounding areas are best known for its citizens' indefatigable urge to resist, deny and defy.

Several native rulers and chieftains from this region have challenged the British since the early days of their occupation. But the most potent symbol of that resistance to this day remains the Panchalankurichi chieftain Veerapandiya Kattabomman. If you need to understand the story of the deep south and its defiant leaders, Kattabomman's Panchalankurichi is a good starting point.

But that's not the most compelling story that I want to draw your attention to in this ancient land that has almost disappeared from the map in May 2022. Ironically, it is the pathetic living condition of Kattabomman's fifth-generation descendant Beema Raja, who, just a few years ago, publicly pleaded to the Tamil Nadu government to increase his freedom fighters' pension by at least a few thousand rupees so that he could feed his family three meals. How could a country forget the descendants of such a decorated hero? What could have forced Beema Raja and his family into such penury?

Two major highways cut across Thoothukudi town, and both pass through identical rectangular plots of land, laced with little mounds of milky-white crystals of sodium chloride between the months of March and October. The initial stretch of the Thoothukudi–Madurai highway, one that takes you to Panchalankurichi, is also dotted with acres and acres of salt marshes as far as the eye can see. If you're unaware of the climatology of the region and happen to travel in an air-conditioned vehicle at night, you might even mistakenly believe you're driving through snow-clad plains somewhere in the cold northern hemisphere.

From early dawn to a little after sunset, thousands of women, shielding their sarees and skin with thick, oversized, long-sleeved cotton shirts and long boots, wade through ankle-deep brine, sifting the salt from the water all day and collecting them along the bund of the plots. After all the brine has crystallized, the salt is then accumulated into little mounds—yet another sight to behold in the sweltering heat of summer months—before they are taken for distribution. With such large-scale production of the white crystal, the region is unsurprisingly known as the salt pan of Tamil Nadu, known to be the largest producer of salt in the state, which accounts for roughly 11 per cent of the total salt production in India. While the present salt manufacturing industry could be attributed to the modernization that arrived during the post-Independence period, salt production in and around Thoothukudi is just about as old as the town itself and finds mention in some of the earliest literature available about the region.

As you drive out of town, the salt pans get gradually replaced by shipping containers of different sizes and colours, dumped on dry, barren land along both sides of the highway—another symbol of Thoothukudi's rapid development, thanks to the V.O. Chidambaranar Port Trust. Thousands of containers painted blue, green, different shades of brown and maroon, in various stages of decay—some with their tops blown off, some with one side crushed in accidents and others just too worn out due to wear and tear—line the perimeter of the barren landscape as you drive along the smooth highway for the next several kilometres. Just ahead of a road over bridge, about forty-five minutes after leaving town, a narrow road turns to the left, where a huge tourism department notice board welcomes you to 'Panchalankurichi Fort, home of Veerapandiya Kattabomman'. Parked trucks with just the container-carriers line both sides of the highway as you approach the junction, from where you take a left towards the historic town.

Once off the highway, the containers and the trucks are replaced by gigantic windmills and a complex network of electricity transmission towers. The majestic windmills gently roll in the mild breeze of mid-May all the way up to Panchalankurichi Fort. The fort, built by Kattabomman and later rebuilt by his brother Oomaithurai, was completely razed by the British during various battles, and a diminutive replica of the same now stands in the same location and serves as a memorial for the martyred Polygar.

When I reached the fort's entrance at around 11 a.m., I was surrounded by an unusual hysteria: Busy people moving around everywhere with a definite purpose, like ants crawling over spilled sugar. The boy at the ticket counter provided an explanation: Every year, in the fourth week of the Tamil month of Chithirai (mid-May), members of the Thokalavar community, to which Kattabomman belonged, gather at the Sree Veera Sagadevi Temple located inside the fort grounds for the annual festival. The two-day celebration in May every year was just a couple of days away when I got there. Outside the fort, balloon vendors, pani puri sellers and even nomads selling all kinds of wares had already set up their stalls, luring children and youngsters to throw away some of their money. Loud devotional music blared out of the central music system through speakers erected at all corners of the fort premises.

The fort, a two-storey structure with dome-shaped gateways and windows that had been freshly painted in off-white distemper, was hardly imposing to the eye, unlike some of the others I had been to during the past few months. Hundreds of workers, mostly belonging to the community, were busy cleaning the fort walls, sweeping the floor, inspecting cooking arrangements and setting up the various tents erected outside the fort, where I was hoping to meet the fifth-generation heir of Polygar Kattabomman.

As I walked into the main hall, I noticed there were hardly any tourists present besides me. Members of the Thokalavar community, who had come from different parts of the state and country, were present in large numbers, explaining intricate details of the slain Polygar's life, which were depicted as paintings in the main hall of the fort, to the younger generation. The interiors of the main hall were full of such paintings depicting the life and times of Kattabomman and his younger siblings.

After taking a few photographs of the fort and jotting down some of the details described in the painting captions, I asked around for Beema Raja, the great-great-grandson of Kattabomman and the alleged direct heir to the throne if it was still, hypothetically, available. An elderly woman sweeping the floor of the main hall of the fort drew me away from the crowd, as if to share a royal secret, and gave me directions to a residential colony, the Kattabomman Santhathiyar Kudiyiripu (Kattabomman's descendants' quarters), situated just about 75 metres outside the fort, where Beema Raja and his wife, Pethiammal, lived in their one-storey home allotted by the government.

The quarters, constructed for members of the Thokalavar community, were immediately outside the fort entrance, to the right. Gifted by the state government as a tribute to one of the country's oldest freedom fighters and his kin, the entire colony now comprises over 200 homes, originally built for the Thokalavar community, who have now either improvised or rebuilt these structures to suit their economic backgrounds or familial needs. Several of them have even sold their homes to other members of the community and moved out.

Beema Raja's house was at the far end of the quarters, and remained an impoverished, asbestos-roofed, one-storey structure that resembled a shed rather than a home. On the wall facing the road, a shabby portrait of a solider with a curling moustache and a sword in his hand had been painted, along with some other caricatures. A few plastic drums partially filled with water and dirty laundry lay at the entrance, which was wide open.

I walked towards the open door and peeped inside, but there was nobody home. To anyone who is familiar with the legacy of Kattabomman and has admired the actor Sivaji Ganesan's majestic performance as the Panchalankurichi Polygar in the 1959 biopic of the same name, the sight of the home of his fifth-generation heir would indeed be a rude shock. Clothes were strewn all over the floor and a few mats were rolled up in a corner. But for a cot made of coir rope, there was hardly any furniture in the living area. Just as I wondered what could have gone so wrong for them, while trying to click some pictures of the home, an elderly, broad-shouldered woman wearing a red saree and matching blouse limped towards me and asked me to follow her to a one-room temple for Melmaruvathur Adhiparasakthi, diagonally opposite the house. Her forehead was smeared with kumkum and holy ash and she wore gigantic nose studs embedded with colourful gemstones.

'It's not safe to talk outside as I don't trust anyone here. My husband is Kattabomman's heir, Beema Raja, but all these people in the colony, my relatives, are torturing us to give up his claim as heir to the throne,' said Beema Raja's wife, Pethiammal, who was just sixty-four years old but looked much older. 'He has gone to Coimbatore for some work and will come only tomorrow. He will tell you all about it if you can come back tomorrow,' she whispered.

'Why are your relatives torturing you?' I asked her.

'The present leaders of our community now claim that Kattabomman has no direct descendants and that the entire community should share his descendancy. How can we allow that when my husband is still alive? He has lived for the past eighty-two years upholding Kattabomman's legacy. It is our misfortune that he still has to fight to hold on to his claim to royal lineage,' Pethiammal said with a deep sigh.

Soon, I found out from her that the genesis of the rivalry to claim Kattabomman's descendancy dated back to several decades. Back in the 1970s, when Beema Raja was a young man, he took up the task of popularizing the freedom fighter for his role in the freedom struggle, highlighting the Thokalavar community's participation in the movement. When the late M. Karunanidhi was a PWD minister under the first DMK government of Tamil Nadu, Beema Raja managed to meet and convince him of his claim to being Kattabomman's heir and also highlighted the plight of his community members, who were so harshly punished by the British that they were yet to fully recover from the suffering. When Karunanidhi became the chief minister of Tamil Nadu a few years later, he immediately sanctioned the quarters for Kattabomman's kin and also allocated homes, along with 3 acres of land, to anyone who could prove he or she belonged to the Thokalavar community. 'You tell me, was Karunanidhi a fool to allocate quarters and land just upon my husband's words? If he hadn't been convinced that Beema Raja was a direct descendant, would he have done that? Does the government not ask for proof? But our relatives now want to disown us because we are poor and they have all become very rich and influential,' Pethiammal said to me. 'They are now waiting for our death so that they can erase our claim completely.'

Beema Raja and Pethiammal have a son and a daughter, both of whom work at the fort as maintenance staff and make just a little more than MGNREGA workers. 'Members of the royal family are not allowed to work but we have no choice now. We are grateful that the state government has given both my children jobs at the fort,' Pethiammal said, in tears as she narrated her family's plight. Even as she sobbed, an elderly man peeped inside through the grill gate of the temple, took a good look at me and walked away.

Pethiammal became a little paranoid upon seeing the man and asked me to come back later, once her husband returned. Assuring her that I'd be back to meet her husband, I followed the man who had peeped inside. He was headed towards a giant tamarind tree by the shrine, where he went and sat on a raised parapet. The man gestured for me to sit next to him, as if he had something important to tell me. His name was Muthaiasamy, and he was also a member of the Thokalavar community and a neighbour of Beema Raja and Pethiammal.

Muthaiasamy lived in a larger, better-maintained home on the other side of the road, which he had bought from one of the original allottees in 1985 and later rebuilt to suit his needs. His son and two daughters were all married and settled in different parts of the district, and visited him once in a while. 'Did she claim her husband was a direct descendant of Kattabomman?' he asked me.

I nodded in agreement.

'It can't be true as there are no records to prove it. How can there be a direct descendant of someone who died over 200 years ago? We are all his descendants, and that family [Beema Raja and Pethiammal] cannot accept it. That's the main issue here. Some years ago, our community members [Thokalavars] appointed more capable people and better representatives as the president and the secretary of the Sree Veera Sagadevi Temple Committee, who are formal representatives of the community, but Beema Raja wants to keep it confined to his family. Now, that was a decision taken by all of us, but this family doesn't want to let go of their claim as the sole representatives of Thokalavars. That's the main issue here. It's not just their legacy, is it? Kattabomman could not have fought the British alone, could he?' Muthaiasamy asked.

He did makes sense, but the old woman's plight still deserved an explanation. So, to probe a little more into the matter, I headed back to the fort premises, where the frenzy and noise had only increased as the day had progressed. Tracking down the president of the temple committee, Murugaboopathy, didn't turn out to be a difficult task—he was the one in command and giving directions to everyone on what should be done and how. Dressed in a long-sleeved cotton shirt and trousers, Murugaboopathy was constantly smoking Gold Flake Lights as he oversaw the pandal construction and other preparations. However, he was only happy to engage with me. 'I'll be glad to clear any of your doubts regarding our community,' he assured me, and ordered for two chairs to be brought for us to sit and talk under one of the tents.

Just a few minutes into the conversation with Murugaboopathy, I understood why the Thokalavar community wanted him to represent them and not Beema Raja. He was a highly successful electrical contractor, whose three children were all doctors and well-settled in life. In contrast, Pethiammal and Beema Raja were living in abject poverty, piggybacking on a 200-plus-year-old legacy.[1,2] 'There is no true heir to our community's pride and saviour, Kattabomman,' Murugaboopathy asserted. 'If there was clear proof that he [Beema Raja] is the direct descendant, I would have fallen at the feet of that man for his ancestors have made our community proud. Unfortunately, there is no proof to this claim. There are no records of Kattabomman and his wife having any issues [children]. The only proof we have is that of Oomaithurai's [Kattabomman's younger brother, also a freedom fighter] wife and her family, who were taken to Poonamallee Jail, near Chennai, where they spent several years. There is a tale

---

1 S. Thirunavukarasu, 'Kattabomman kin upset for being ignored', *Deccan Chronicle*, 15 August 2014, https://www.deccanchronicle.com/140815/nation-current-affairs/article/kattabomman-kin-upset-being-ignored

2 J. Praveen Paul Joseph, 'Kattabomman descendant under shadow of poverty', *The Hindu*, 10 July 2014, https://www.thehindu.com/news/national/tamil-nadu/kattabomman-descendant-under-shadow-of-poverty/article6194849.ece

that she was pregnant when she was taken as prisoner and had a son, who is the direct heir, but there is no concrete proof of that either. In the absence of any direct proof, it is only fair that all Thokalavars, who are blood relatives in some way or another, share the legacy. Isn't it?'

Murugaboopathy also pointed out that while Kattabomman's role in standing up to the British can never be undermined, the incidents that took place after his death—the rescue of Oomaithurai from the Palayamkottai prison by the Thokalavar soldiers, the rebuilding of Panchalankurichi Fort in record time and putting up a fight against the British yet again—cannot be ignored either. 'How can one family hijack the entire legacy? Did all Thokalavars not fight against the British as Kattabomman's soldiers?' he asked me, before half a dozen men and one or two women surrounded him to receive further instructions.

Before parting, Murugaboopathy clarified that he planned to move the court soon and settle the dispute for good. 'I'm just waiting to free myself a bit,' he said, and pulled out another cigarette. 'You have to come to the temple tomorrow and watch the festivities. It will be a spectacle you won't regret!' he said.

What is this legacy that the Thokalavars are still fighting for 200 years later? As with most historical events of the time, I was faced with multiple versions of Kattabomman's encounters with the British and just a handful of established facts to go by. To clearly understand Kattabomman and his famed stand against the British East India Company towards the end of the eighteenth century, a backgrounder on the prevailing political and economic climate in southern Tamil Nadu is essential.

Back then, the southern part of the country was known as the Carnatic, a territorial nomenclature that went into disuse in the nineteenth century.[3] Geographically, the Carnatic comprised several districts and principalities along the Coromandel Coast—from Nellore in the north through Chittoor, Arcot principality, Fort St. George (Chennai or Madras), Fort St. David (present-day Puducherry), Tanjore (Thanjavur) principality and the smaller principalities of Ramnad (Ramanathapuram), Tinnevelly (Tirunelveli) and Madura (Madurai) in the south. Most of the southern districts were under the control of tribute-paying chiefs, known variously as Polygars or Palayakarars, Nayakars, Setupati, etc.

During the seventeenth century, the Carnatic fell under the Mughal ruler of Hyderabad, which, in turn, fell under the jurisdiction of the subedar of the Deccan. Following the fragmentation of the Mughal Empire after the death of Aurangzeb in 1707, there were two claimants, Saadat Ali Khan (1651–1732) and Anwaruddin Khan (1674–1749), to this rich and well-resourced region. Their claim over the region, and of their successors too, was directly tied to the interests of the French and the English, who were in conflict over trade and territorial acquisitions in the region. In 1763, the Treaty of Paris established the claims of the British and recognized Muhammad Ali of the Wallajah dynasty, a descendant of Anwaruddin Khan, as thc Nawab of thc Carnatic.[4]

Soon after taking control of the region, the East India Company began issuing lavish personal loans to the Nawab at extortionate rates of interest, for which they took large and fertile tracts of his domains as collateral. Among the earliest territorial acquisitions of the East India Company was the territory around Chennai (then Madras), known as the 'jaghire'. This was originally granted by the

---

3 Parvathi Menon, 'The Carnatic Debts and the Agrarian Crisis of the Eighteenth Century', Review of Agrarian Studies, 9(1) January–June 2019, http://ras.org.in/the_carnatic_debts_and_the_agrarian_crisis_of_the_eighteenth_century

4 Ibid.

Nawab of the Carnatic as a revenue assignment to the Company in 1765. The revenue assigned from the jaghire was intended to be a contribution towards war expenses undertaken by the Company in 'aid' of the Nawab. In the beginning, the direct administration of the jaghire was not in the hands of the Company and revenue was collected only by the Nawab. However, in 1780, the Company took over direct administration of the jaghire and let it out as fourteen large farms on nine-year leases at increasing rents. The Company kept pressing the lessees for advances that they were unable to muster. When the lessees repeatedly failed to pay their rent, their lands were appropriated.

This strategy was eventually extended to all other territories under the control of the Nawab of Arcot. In due course, the management and control of revenue collection from Tirunelveli district also got transferred from the Nawab to the Company, on the condition that he be allowed one-sixth of the revenues for his personal use. The Company's efforts to collect revenue from the local chieftains in the south did not yield results and it was forced to return the assignment back to the Nawab in 1785. But the revenue administration was once again taken over by the Company in 1790, after it established a Board of Assigned Revenue for the purpose. The board's initiatives were often so oppressive that it brought the Polygars or Palayakarars (or the local hereditary military chieftains) into open confrontation with the Company. During that turbulent period, when the political tension between the Polygars of the south and the Company was simmering, a young and ambitious Veerapandiya Kattabomman became the ruler of Panchalankurichi after his father, Jagaveerapandiyan, passed away in 1790.[5]

With the Board of Assigned Revenue completely taking over revenue collection from the Nawab, fresh surveys were conducted

---

[5] M. Gopi Saraboji, *Veerapandiya Kattabomman* (Chennai: Kizhakku Pathippagan Publications, 2022), p. 21.

on lands belonging to small rulers to increase taxes. This activity created a division among the Polygars—with some resisting the new survey and others succumbing to British pressure. A few Polygars, including Kattabomman, decided instead to appeal to higher authorities of the Company with the claim that the survey was erroneous and ill-conceived and stopped paying their dues to the Company. It was his first act of resistance against the British.

Kattabomman's growing contempt for the Company peaked soon after 1797, when Collector Jackson assumed charge and further intensified efforts to collect taxes and tributes from Polygars in his territory. Kattabomman consistently refused to pay his dues to the Company. Protesting against their intensified tax collection initiative, mostly to aid the British Army in its war in Mysore, several Polygars from the south stirred the public by holding gatherings, protests, etc. As a prominent ruler from the region, Kattabomman was among those who were instrumental in stirring the agitation.

Collector Jackson, who came to know of Kattabomman's role in the stir, wrote a letter to the Panchalankurichi chieftain on 26 October 1797, urging him to settle the pending 'chisti' dues to the Company.[6] But Kattabomman chose not to respond to the letter and ignored the collector's request. Jackson, however, continued to send letters urging him to settle the dues, which the latter also consistently ignored. When the demand for settling dues went unheard, Jackson urged Kattabomman to meet him in person to discuss all pending issues. Even this suggestion failed to yield a response. Eventually, when Collector Jackson threatened military action against Panchalankurichi for failing to pay tributes and disobeying his orders, Kattabomman agreed to visit him in person.

With a small band of about 4,000 soldiers and close associates, Kattabomman left for Ramanathapuram to meet the collector, who had by then purposely left town for a tour of various regions in his

---

6 *Veerapandiya Kattabomman*, p. 32.

control. Getting to know of the collector's field trip, Kattabomman decided to meet him enroute, but Jackson denied him an audience. Aware that Kattabomman was following him, he continued his tours to Thirukutrallam, Sekkampatti, Sivagiri, etc., for over 640 kilometres, without giving the Panchalankurichi chieftain an audience.

Upon returning to Ramanathapuram, Jackson agreed to meet Kattabomman at his headquarters. A fatigued and humiliated Kattabomman reportedly had a heated exchange with Jackson and categorically refused to settle his dues. Annoyed by Kattabomman's stubborn resistance to pay his dues, Collector Jackson sought further instructions from his superiors in Chennai and Trichy on what to do about the Panchalankurichi ruler's non-payment of dues. While he waited for a response, he asked Kattabomman and his loyal soldiers to stay put in Ramanathapuram. Suspecting Jackson's motive, Kattabooman and his soldiers launched an attack on the Company soldiers and stormed their way out of the Company headquarters. In the melee, a senior British official, Lieutenant Clarke and a few sepoys were murdered. While Kattabomman and his brother Oomaithurai managed to reach Panchalankurichi, they found that their minister Sivasubramania Pillai had been imprisoned by the Company soldiers.

Following the attack, Jackson sought his superiors' permission to take sufficient action against Kattabomman for the murder of Clarke as well as for the non-payment of tributes. Top East India Company officials in Fort St. George, Chennai, summoned Kattabomman to Trichy on 3 October 1798 for a detailed inquiry. After the inquiry, convinced with the response, they cleared all charges against him and even felicitated Kattabomman for being a loyal ally of the British. As a token of friendship, they also released his minister, Sivasubramania Pillai. In return, Kattabomman pledged to be a loyal subordinate of the Company. Jackson was replaced and another official, Lushington, took charge as collector.

Meanwhile, the Fourth Anglo–Mysore War began and the British forces were fully engaged in it. With mounting war expenses, the need for collection of tributes/taxes also soared, and Collector Lushington's full attention turned towards increasing revenue from the kingdoms they controlled. As a consequence, several Polygars in the region once again got together and plotted to overthrow the British, who were by then struggling to defeat Tipu Sultan's army in Mysore and were considered weak. When Kattabomman was approached by the other smaller rulers, he immediately volunteered for the cause. When the news of his activities reached the Company, Lushington summoned Kattabomman for a detailed inquiry. But as had been the case in the past, the Panchalankurichi chieftain kept ignoring the summons. The increasing demand for more and more taxes also prompted Kattabomman to meddle in the affairs of neighbouring kingdoms to increase his revenue. Due to that, a few neighbouring Polygars, who were loyal to the British, also complained about him to the Company and wanted them to rein in Kattabomman.

Even as top Company officials were mulling over strong punitive action against Panchalankurichi, a looting incident at a rice godown owned by the Company in Srivaikundam, allegedly by Sivasubramania Pillai to procure rice for a family wedding, ended up in a clash with the Company's security guards and resulted in the death of one of the guards. The British officials, when they came to know of that, immediately summoned Kattabomman to hand over Sivasubramania Pillai for the loot and murder. But Kattabomman refused to do so, claiming the Company had no jurisdiction over his subjects and that he had already conducted an inquiry.

With complaints continuing to pour in from all directions, the Company eventually decided to take military action against him and sent Major Bannerman with a large force, including soldiers from Madras, Travancore and surrounding kingdoms to

Panchalankurichi. Kattabomman was forced to make a choice of either handing over his minister or facing the British Army. On 4 September 1799, Bannerman's army attacked Panchalankurichi Fort and were faced with stiff resistance from the much smaller army of Kattabomman. In the early days of war, Bannerman's large army faced several setbacks and failed to breach Kattabomman's fort. However, with reinforcements flowing in from various quarters and additional ammunition brought from far-away destinations, Bannerman's soldiers began to taste success. When Kattabomman realized that his small army might not be able to hold on to the fort for long, he decided to escape to Trichy with a small group of soldiers to meet senior British officials and press for a truce with them. Under the cover of darkness, with a small team of guards, he fled the fort and managed to reach all the way up to Pudukottai, where he was nabbed along with his associates and brought back to Ramanathapuram. While historians have offered different interpretations of Kattabomman's arrest, most claim that he was betrayed by some hostile Polygars with whom he had an ongoing rivalry and who tipped off the British and even assisted in cornering him.

Kattabomman was brought to Kayathar, where a speedy trial was conducted, at the end of which he was sentenced to be hanged in public. Major Bannerman, who wanted to make a public spectacle out of his execution to serve as a warning to other Polygars and rulers who dared to defy the British, made elaborate arrangements at the execution spot for local chieftains and the public to witness the event.

Though the British intended the execution of Kattabomman to serve as a deterrent, the defiant manner in which he approached his end made Kattabomman a legend and inspired the people of Panchalankurichi and other local kingdoms to brace for more pitched battles against the British. In a report sent to his superiors on the execution a day later, Major Bannerman described the behaviour of Kattabomman during the trial as 'undaunted and supercilious'.[7] While walking up to the tree where he was to be hanged, Kattabomman 'walked with a firm and daring air, and cast looks of sullen contempt on the Polygars to the right and left as he passed,' the major had recorded. Kattabomman's only regret at the time of his hanging was that he had chosen to flee from his fort, instead of dying there fighting for it.

---

If one is asked to name an institution that has single-handedly propelled the growth of Thoothukudi and its surrounding districts over the past five decades, the answer would have to be the V.O. Chidambaranar Port Trust, one of thirteen major ports in India. At least that's what Google and the latest artificial intelligence sensation, ChatGPT, would say. Named after V.O. Chidambaram Pillai, another famous freedom fighter from the region, the port is considered to be a boon as well as the town's bane by the old-timers there. When I asked the critics of the port for a reason, they asked me to go on a ride to the port with my eye on the sky.

And I did exactly that. I rolled down the windows of my cab, looked up at the sky and asked my driver to go slowly on the drive from my hotel in Muthiahpuram to the VOC Port. The first few kilometres of the ride revealed nothing: Clean blue skies with occasional patches of grey clouds wandering aimlessly, as if they had lost their way, as we drove past the employees' quarters of various large firms, including Southern Petrochemical Industries Corporation (SPIC) employees' quarters. Just beyond those SPIC

---

[7] T. Ramakrishnan, 'Kattabomman's execution record to be digitised', *The Hindu*, 7 January 2021, https://www.thehindu.com/news/national/tamil-nadu/kattabommans-execution-record-to-be-digitised/article33515337.ece

staff quarters was the huge Southern Petrochemical Industries Corporation (SPIC) plant, from which giant chimneys protruded towards the sky and puffed out white smoke that dissolved into the crisp morning air without even leaving a clear trail. That white gaseous discharge, within a few metres from the mouths of the chimneys, becomes part of what people here inhale and exhale every minute to keep themselves alive.

Beyond the SPIC plant were the Tuticorin Alkali Plant units, with similar chimneys puffing out a slightly greyish smoke into the air. The number of chimneys protruding into the sky increases as one drives past the Thoothukudi Thermal Power Plant, a unit of the Neyveli Lignite Corporation, and a few other chemical plants—all puffing out gaseous discharge of different colours into the atmosphere at different times of the day. By the time I reached the port's entrance, I had a vague sense of what some people were worried about.

From the port, I headed towards Ottapidaram, a small town situated a little more than 3 kilometres away from Panchalankurichi, where V.O. Chidambaram Pillai was born in September 1872, exactly 112 years after Kattabomman was born. The road towards Ottapidaram from the Thoothukudi—Madurai bypass was also flanked by giant windmills, power transmission towers and occasional tall palms, swaying in the gentle late-morning breeze. But, unlike the road to Panchalankurichi, I also spotted a substantial number of chimneys of varying sizes and colours. At least a dozen chemical plants, each having one or two chimneys, dotted both sides of the road as we proceeded. 'We are now in the SIPCOT area,' my driver pointed out just as I wondered why so many factories had come up there.

A little farther along the way, I saw a much larger plant with at least seven chimneys that were taller, wider and appeared to have been out of use lately. All the outer walls of the plant were covered in brown dust, while the metal roofing had rusted almost completely.

A police vehicle was guarding the entrance to the plant, which had been locked.

'That's the Sterlite factory,' my driver informed me. I asked him to slow down the car so that I could click a few pictures on my mobile—after all, the Sterlite Copper plant was one of the reasons for Thoothukudi finding a place in my itinerary. I asked the driver to remember to halt by that factory on our way back.

Just a few minutes later, I had arrived in Ottapidaram, the shanty town where V.O. Chidambaram Pillai, popularly known as VOC, was born on 5 September 1872 into a family of lawyers. The modest two-storey home on a dingy corner street, where the veteran freedom fighter was born, had been converted into a memorial-cum-library. Barring a statue and a few photographs of the man who formed the first professional Indian navigation company by operating a fleet of ships, the memorial barely does justice to the contribution made by the eminent nationalist. None of the staff present at the memorial had any details of the family members of VOC, nor about his life, besides what was there in the public domain. I walked around the street, which still had 100-plus-year-old homes, and inquired about VOC—only to find that several locals didn't even have a clue about his contribution to the freedom movement, nor any memory of his family. The only person who apparently interacted with him during his last years was Sankaran, an office assistant at the VOC memorial, until his retirement in 1995. 'Now he lives with his sons and comes here once in a while. But we can't say when,' said the present librarian at the memorial, and handed me a mobile number, calls to which remained unanswered.

One can't blame the people of Ottapidaram for not having any connect with Chidambaram Pillai, because by the age of twenty-eight, he had moved to Thoothukudi, in 1900, to set up a legal practice after honing his skills at the Ottapidaram Sub Magistrate's Court for a few years. Pillai had cleared the Pleadership

Examination of the High Court of Judicature, Madras, held in Tirunelveli in February 1894 with a second grade.[8] Thoothukudi was quite an affluent town even back then due to the busy port, which had been in existence for several centuries, thanks to the natural harbour that opened into the Gulf of Mannar and remained calm throughout the year, even during the monsoon. For lawyers, that meant good business, and Chidambaram Pillai, well known for his sharp cross-examination skills, soon established a successful practice and garnered a name for himself in the legal profession in Thoothukudi.

Around that time, the partition of Bengal in 1905 by Lord Curzon had stirred the national consciousness of people across the country. This anti-British fervour paved the way for the Swadeshi movement, which began to echo even in the southernmost part of the country. VOC got in touch with Swami Ramakrishnananda of the Sri Ramakrishna Math and Mission, a strong advocate of Swadeshi work, during one of his visits to Chennai, and was soon convinced to take up the cause in Thoothukudi. After returning home, VOC started the Tuticorin Industrial Welfare Association, a Dharma Sangam for fostering Swadeshi industry, a National Emporium that sold Swadeshi goods, along with a Spinning and Weaving Centre. The success of those institutions prompted a few well-off merchants in the region to suggest that VOC start a Swadeshi shipping company of his own to break the monopoly of the British in the field.

During that period, the Thoothukudi port handled all India–Sri Lanka traffic, including cargo. Annually, a large number of cattle were exported to Sri Lanka, in addition to the usual movement of rice, cotton and salt. Besides Sri Lanka, the port also handled passenger traffic to distant places like Fiji, Mauritius, South

---

[8] R.A. Padmanabhan, *VO Chidambaram Pillai* (New Delhi: National Book Trust, 1977), p. 22.

America, etc., where indentured labourers were being shipped off in large numbers. Other exports and imports were also handled by the port in a big way, and the British India Steam Navigation Company controlled all operations.

When the influential merchants of Thoothukudi pressed Chidambaram Pillai to start a shipping service, all they had in mind was chartering a ship to transport people to Sri Lanka, but Pillai suggested the idea of floating a public-owned steamship company that would operate its own fleet. In October 1906, the Swadeshi Steam Navigation Company came into existence. With shares open to the public, the company raised a capital of Rs 10,00,000, divided into 40,000 shares of Rs 25 each, which could be held only by Indians, Sri Lankans and citizens of other nations of the East.[9]

After scouting around the world to purchase ships for the Swadeshi Steam Navigation Company, VOC managed to procure two ships from France along with two steam launches. The ships were then re-conditioned and fitted to suit their playing as passenger-cum-cargo vessels on the Thoothukudi–Colombo run. The ships had accommodation in saloons for forty-four passengers in first class, twenty-four in second class and another 1,000 third-class passengers, besides 2,500 tonnes of cargo. The arrival of two Swadeshi ships alarmed officials of the British India Steam Navigation Company and its patrons, the White merchants of Thoothukudi. When the Swadeshi Company was formed, the British rival ridiculed it as a nine-day wonder. But not only did the shipping firm survive the competition, it also began to thrive, as almost all Indian merchants and passengers only turned to the Swadeshi steam service between Thoothukudi and Colombo because these ships were not only more modern but also less expensive than the British vessels. This remarkable success of VOC in running the Swadeshi Steam Navigation Company and breaking

---

9 *VO Chidambaram Pillai*, p. 30.

into an industry that was the monopoly of the British earned him the title of 'Kapalotiya Thamizhan', the Tamilian who piloted a ship.

With the Swadeshi Steam Navigation Company up and running, Pillai's focus gradually returned to the Congress Party and its activities across the country. Along with the well-known poet Subramania Bharati from Ettayapuram, in the same region, he went to Surat and participated in the 1907 Surat Session of the Indian National Congress as a supporter of Bal Gangadhar Tilak, his political guru at the time. Returning from Surat, Pillai immersed himself in political work along with the affairs of the steam company. Another nationalist and mendicant, Subramania Siva, joined VOC during that period, and the two soon became the flag bearers of the Swadeshi movement in the Thoothukudi area. Between February and March 1908, Chidambaram Pillai and Siva addressed meetings at Thoothukudi Beach almost on a daily basis.[10] These meetings were attended by thousands of people, who were stirred by the revolutionary ideas of the two leaders. During one such meeting, Pillai and Siva urged the workers of Coral Mills (now Madura Coats) to go on a strike demanding better wages—an established trade union practice in Western countries but considered taboo in India at the time.

Stirred by their call, over 1,500 workers of Coral Mills participated in a labour strike that began on 27 February 1908. Chidambaram and Siva organized relief camps for the striking workers and conducted negotiations with the mill's owners on their behalf. With striking workers not wilting under pressure, they soon received the support of the ordinary people of Thoothukudi, who tried to help the workers in every possible way. In many ways, the Coral Mills protest could be called the first major workers' strike in that region. During that period, the people of Thoothukudi, including barbers, dhobis and other essential workers, refused to serve the officers of Coral Mills, to express their solidarity with the

10 *VO Chidambaram Pillai*, p. 56.

striking workers. All of that brought the owners to the negotiating table sooner. Historians allege that as a negotiator, Pillai took a reasonable stand, and the negotiations ended amicably and the strike was withdrawn—yet another feather in Pillai's Swadeshi cap. The Coral Mills strike paved the way for similar such strikes across the country in European-owned firms, demanding workers' rights, better wages, etc.

However, VOC's success in stirring up the working class did not go down well with the British officials, who slammed sedition charges against Chidambaram Pillai and Subramania Siva for their public meetings at Thoothukudi Beach, and summoned them to the district magistrate's office on 9 March 1908 to defend their case. Pillai, Siva and an acquaintance of theirs, Padmanabha Iyengar, presented themselves at the office of the collector of Tirunelveli, where they were treated with scant respect. However, what ensued in the meeting was an argument between imperialism and nationalism, details of which infused fresh Swadeshi fervour in the region, and Subramania Bharati, who wrote two poems based on the meeting, helped disseminate the details of the case to the masses.

The collector's inquiry went on for three days, at the end of which all three men were ordered to be remanded to judicial custody. As news spread of the arrest, Tirunelveli erupted in resentment. Shops were closed, businesses came to a halt, students marched out of colleges and huge crowds gathered in main areas and marched towards the municipal office, condemning the action. The mobs burnt buildings, police stations and even the Additional District Munsiff's Court.[11] Soon, the riots spread to neighbouring Thoothukudi and Tachanallur. Tensions were so high that many Europeans in the city spent nights in a ship anchored off the coast. The situation was brought under control only after three days, and by then, several lives had been lost.

---

11 *VO Chidambaram Pillai*, p. 64.

Chidambaram and the two others accused of sedition appealed to the High Court against the detention order and secured their release. But the district magistrate refused to oblige the court's order and instead chose to prosecute them for sedition. Pillai was then sentenced to two terms of transportation for life, each for twenty years, for the speeches he had made on 23 and 25 February 1908, while Subramania Siva was sentenced to ten years' transportation. Although the sentence was later reduced to six years of hard labour for Pillai, following an appeal, the ordeal he went through in prison, serving the full term, virtually ended the most luminous phase of his life as a Swadeshi campaigner.

Upon his return from prison, Pillai refrained from taking an active role in politics and focused his energy on literary and other pursuits. Meanwhile, the Swadeshi Steam Navigation Company was also forced to wind up after several unsuccessful attempts to keep it going, thus ending one of the most enterprising Swadeshi challenges to the British monopoly of the high seas. Nevertheless, several years after his death, historians continue to elucidate the important role played by V.O. Chidambaram Pillai in the Swadeshi movement, and the Thoothukudi port has also been named after him. That period is also known for the first successful public movement in the region.

---

On our return drive from Ottapidaram, my cab driver alerted me to the approaching Sterlite factory premises. 'If you want, we can halt for a little while and make some inquiries. The factory has been shut down for four years now and it is unlikely that you will find anything useful. But we could go to the closest village instead, where the locals began their protest,' he suggested. He immediately clarified that his knowledge of the villagers and their protest was limited to YouTube videos and other forwarded messages. 'Most of the people of Thoothukudi are well aware of the anti-Sterlite protests and the fallout, thanks to social media. But everyone pretends not to have any knowledge,' he said. I directed him to drive to Kumarettiyapuram in Therkku Veerapandiapuram panchayat, one of the villages closest to the Sterlite Copper smelting unit, a unit of Vedanta Limited.

Just as my driver had mentioned, Kumarettiyapuram turned out to be a tiny hamlet less than a kilometre away from the sprawling Sterlite campus. On that late weekday afternoon, not a soul was to be found as we drove along the dingy streets looking for someone to talk to. The modest homes, mostly single-storey structures, were all locked from inside. We finally stumbled upon four middle-aged men huddled together a little away from the tar-topped road, just behind the municipality park. Two of the men were lean, bare-bodied and squatting, facing each other, and smoking beedis, while the third man, whose disproportionately large belly indicated that he was suffering from some kind of disease, was sitting on the ground with his legs half stretched out. He was wearing a white vest that was full of holes and had turned brown due to the layers of dirt coated on the fabric. The man facing him was also seated, on his slippers, and was wearing a torn checked shirt and a lungi tied all the way above his thighs. Upon noticing the car halt, all four stopped talking and stared at the car suspiciously. A tall and lean Chippiparai hound, a breed found commonly here, lying next to the men stood up lethargically, let out two feeble barks at me and then moved away, disinterested.

I walked up to the men, introduced myself and asked them what they knew about the Sterlite factory.

The men did not respond and stared back at me.

I asked them again if they knew about the factory polluting their village and if they were participants in the protest. Again, no response from them. Just as I was about to walk away, the pot-bellied man asked me to stop. 'You want to know how Sterlite polluted our village? You should have come here four years ago, when the factory was functioning. You wouldn't be breathing fresh air like you are now.[12,13] The factory came here twenty-two years ago and we suffered for the past eighteen years. When the factory was open, you could not stand and talk like this. Your nose would always burn as if you had inhaled tobacco powder. We, too, felt the burning sensation in our noses soon after the factory opened, but our nostrils got so used to the polluted air that we no longer felt it. Some days, when excess smoke was let out, we used to feel heavy in the chest.' The pot-bellied man also appeared to be suffering from some kind of skin discoloration.

The slightly older man resting on his slippers intervened. 'We cannot tell you everything that is going on as there are too many spies in the village. After you leave, policemen will come and inquire who you were and what we told you. That's why nobody in the village will speak,' he said.

One of the squatters claimed that even the water in the ponds used to be oily some years ago. 'Now it's clean and fresh,' he said, and asked me to visit the Therkku Veerapandiapuram panchayat president. 'He will be able to tell you the correct situation. None of the villagers can be trusted anymore.'

I thanked the men, got directions to the panchayat president's house and asked the driver to get the car out of the village before the men grew even more uncomfortable. As we proceeded to Therkku Veerapandiapuram village, I looked around to take in the sights more carefully after my conversation with the villagers. The

---

12 M. Kalyanaraman, 'Has the Thoothukudi Sterlite plant been able to generate the medical oxygen supply it promised?', Scroll.in, 18 July 2021, https://scroll.in/article/1000181/has-the-thoothukudi-sterlite-plant-been-able-to-generate-the-medical-oxygen-supply-it-promised

13 Nityanand Jayaraman, 'Tuticorin Air Quality Improves Noticeably After Sterlite Closure: TNPCB Data', The Wire, 11 December 2019, https://thewire.in/environment/tuticorin-air-quality-aqi-sterlite-copper-smelting-pollution-sipcot-tnpcb

village ponds were brimming with water, the vacant lands were grass-topped and lush, even in the month of May, thanks to the frequent summer rain, healthy cattle fed on the grass, and the air felt light and easy. Tall and lean hounds with shiny yellow-brown coats roamed everywhere—I was unable to find any other type of dog, at least in those villages—and looked healthy. If the villagers were indeed speaking the truth, four years must have brought about a lot of relief.

When I reached the Therkku Veerapandiapuram panchayat president's home-office in the back alley of a tar-topped road after asking around, the president's husband, Subbiah, was waiting for me. After exchanging pleasantries, I shared the conversation I had had with the villagers and asked him if it was true that people had really suffered from health issues when the Sterlite plant was operational.

Subbiah had participated in the anti-Sterlite protest when it first broke out in Kumarettiyapuram and had even gone to jail for protesting. 'It's been a very complex issue. I don't even know what is true and what isn't anymore. Yes, there were some health problems and pollution issues, but did the effluents let out by Sterlite spread disease among people? I don't know,' he clarified. 'Honestly, as a politician and people's representative, I am with the people. If people want the factory closed, I will protest for them. If a majority of the people in my panchayat want it open, I will fight for that,' added Subbiah, cautious not to let a loose word out. 'To be really honest, I want to share this: Many of the villagers who protested earlier now want the factory to reopen. Those who wanted it to stay open then, now want it closed. The truth is nobody really knows why people change their minds. So now I maintain a neutral stand. I just go by what the majority of the people want me to do,' he reiterated, and also insisted that he had nothing more to add.

When I asked him if people had been threatened or bought into silence, he refused to comment again. Before parting, he told me that while all factories do pollute the environment to some extent, they are also a necessity. 'After all, we need employment too. The land here is not suitable for cultivation, as sea water has intruded into most areas. With no cultivation and no other source of livelihood, how can people live?'

---

With nobody in Kumarettiyapuram or any of the surrounding villages willing to speak about Sterlite's impact on their lives, I was left with no choice but to return to Thoothukudi. Once back there, I went to the tiny one-room office of Krishnamurthy, a.k.a. Kittu, on the first floor of a commercial complex on Levingipuram to understand the genesis of the protest, which ended up as one of the bloodiest in the state, consuming civilian lives.

Seated in a room that was almost empty, barring a wooden table and two chairs, Krishnamurthy introduced himself first as a trade unionist and then as a member of the Anti-Sterlite Thoothukudi District People's Federation. He was also among the few who had been active in the anti-Sterlite movement since its very beginning. 'It actually began way back in 1995, when we first heard that the Sterlite Copper smelting unit was getting shifted to Thoothukudi from Ratnagiri in Maharashtra, after locals over there protested and drove the factory out of their hometown. We were very young and in college at the time, but were made aware of the dangers of the plant that was coming to our hometown even back then,' Kittu recalled vividly. Led by a few senior environmental activists and academicians, students of V.O. Chidambaram College, where Kittu was studying, blocked the road from the airport to the venue on the day the foundation stone for the plant was laid by then chief minister Jayalalithaa. 'We even courted arrest. It was symbolic in a way that students of VOC College were at the forefront of that protest. In a way, it was a tribute to VOC, who organized and successfully conducted the first strike in south India against Coral Mills, now known as Madura Coats. I'll come to that later,' Kittu clarified before continuing. 'But the protest in 1995 was the first major resistance against Sterlite, and it was done by the common people of Thoothukudi alone.'

Nothing much happened after that protest, but as news gradually spread about the ill effects of the various pollutants that could be released into the air and water in their locality, members of the fishing community soon joined the agitation, which had begun to shape up quite well. They took the agitation to the sea by blocking large vessels that brought raw materials and other machinery to the port for the smelter unit by using their tiny fishing vessels to form an impenetrable ring surrounding the harbour. The ships had to eventually reroute to other ports to transport raw material for the factory, and business went on as usual once again. Soon, the construction of the plant was completed and the first unit was inaugurated in 1996 by DMK founder and then chief minister, M. Karunanidhi, amid rampant protests by environmentalists, academicians and even students.

While the protestors continued to canvass the ill effects of having a copper smelter in their backyard, most people in the surrounding villages still supported the factory as they were hopeful of large factories bringing overall development to the region, besides guaranteed employment. 'About a year after the plant became operational, a gas leak from the Sterlite plant caused widespread suffocation in and around Thoothukudi.[14,15] Around the same time, in August 1997, a blast killed two workers at

---

[14] 'The Great Smelting Pot: Coming A Copper', *Outlook*, 5 February 2022, https://www.outlookindia.com/magazine/story/the-great-smelting-pot-coming-a-copper/211512

[15] '84 gas leaks at Sterlite in 2013 alone, Tamil Nadu tells Madras HC', *The Times of India*, 21 June 2019, https://timesofindia.indiatimes.com/city/chennai/84-gas-leaks-at-sterlite-in-2013-alone-tn-tells-madras-hc/articleshow/69881981.cms

the plant. The fears of a repeat of the Bhopal gas tragedy struck Thoothukudi town and protests gathered momentum once again,' Kittu told me. However, that incident was forgotten soon, since in this coastal town strong winds from the sea blow away everything in their path, including people's memories.

Even as sporadic protests and concerns of increased respiratory ailments among the people living close to the plant emerged time and again, no major shift in the momentum of protests occurred and was largely confined to a small group of activists. A public interest litigation filed in the Madras High Court had made the court order the shutting down of the plant in 2010. When the case went to the Supreme Court, Sterlite was slammed with a heavy penalty of Rs 100 crore for polluting the environment, but there was no instruction to shut down the plant. The factory became operational yet again. A second gas leak that took place in March 2013, however, revived fears of an impending catastrophe. On that occasion, the Tamil Nadu Pollution Control Board (TNPCB) stepped in and ordered the closure of the plant, bringing relief to the locals.

'By now, rumours of polluted water in ponds and wells in villages in and around Kumarettiyapuram began making the rounds, and untimely livestock deaths were also associated with the contamination of groundwater. This began sometime around 2010, about thirteen years after the plant had become operational, and then the rural folk also joined the protests and strengthened the movement,' Kittu said, and added that in Kumarettiyapuram, the village closest to the plant, many people also developed skin diseases and other ailments in that period. 'Since then, whenever someone died of cancer in any of the villages, videos went viral on how it could be due to the pollutants in the air and water.[16] But there

---

16 'Protesters blame Sterlite for five cancer deaths in one week, demand its closure', *DT Next*, 1 May 2018, https://www.dtnext.in/

had been no conclusive study yet and we could not prove anything. Life went on, as the protestors continued to do their job.'

Sometime in March 2017, news came out that Sterlite was planning to double its production from 4 lakh tonnes to 8 lakh tonnes. That information shocked the activists and villagers alike. Upon verifying the authenticity of it, the villagers of Kumarettiyapuram decided to take concrete action and submitted a petition to the district collector, urging the state government to immediately stop Vedanta Limited from expanding its plant to double the capacity. The villagers marched to the collectorate, resulting in a minor scuffle with the police, and a few even courted arrested.

By then, people all over Tamil Nadu were just getting familiarized with the power of mass protests as it was the season of major agitations. The fisherfolk's protest against the Kudankulam Nuclear Power Plant right next door, in Tirunelveli district, was an inspiration. The more recent Jallikattu protests at Marina Beach in Chennai, when lakhs and lakhs of people converged and made it into a success, inspired the people of Thoothukudi, as well as those in other parts of the state, to take up causes of their own and stage peaceful protests to put forth their dissent. Thanks to social media, those messages spread like wildfire. It was against this backdrop that a small group of villagers from Kumarettiyapuram decided to sit on a chain protest at a public park in their village and resolved to continue their agitation until the Sterlite plant was forced to close down. Those few people were responsible for starting that 100-day relay protest in February 2018, which forced the government to eventually shut down the plant.

'In the beginning, the protest did not garner any widespread attention, except among the locals. No media, no officials bothered

---

tamilnadu/2018/04/30/protesters-blame-sterlite-for-five-cancer-deaths-in-one-week-demand-its-closure?infinitescroll=1 to check out these villagers and, except for a few police personnel posted at the venue for security reasons, none bothered to take the stir seriously. But, as I mentioned before, the people of Thoothukudi have been resisting Sterlite since 1995, and some of us had been a part of this movement since our student days. So, as news spread, more and more activists and concerned citizens joined the protests, and, in time, the media also turned their attention towards the chain protest that was growing in strength every day in Kumarettiyapuram. On the fifteenth day of the protest, several associations and unions from Thoothukudi joined the protestors and pledged their support to the cause,' Kittu said.

He continued, 'But the movement still hadn't grown into a big one. On 24 March 2018, the protestors got permission to hold a public meeting, in which over 150 organizations from across Thoothukudi district participated. During that meeting, women from Kumarettiyapuram took centre stage, while all the other leaders sat behind them and followed their lead. Several thousands gathered for the cause, yet the protest was completely peaceful, with no untoward incident reported. As the days went by, the protest grew in strength and the movement gained momentum. Naturally, the numbers began to grow. On 23rd April, we even picketed the local TNPCB office to force a closure of the plant. While protests were continuing on one side, any death of a local due to cancer or other ailments was used as an opportunity to campaign against Sterlite. Funeral processions turned into propaganda vehicles to campaign against Sterlite, and social media helped spread the message of any death or deformity among the volunteers.

'As the protest approached its 100th day, we decided to organize a mass rally to the collectorate. The plan was to march to the collectorate, hand over a petition to the collector and stage an indefinite fast at the venue. The people were ready now to go to any extent to force the closure of the plant. They were just waiting for the right time for a final face-off with Sterlite, when a thirteen-year-old boy from around here died of cancer. Just two days before he died, an audio clip of a conversation between the boy and his friend, in which he wondered why he had got the dreaded disease and talked about his suffering, got leaked online and went viral. The audio clip shook the conscience of the public. That clip really stirred the protestors, especially women, in a big way.' He added that the plan even then was just to hold a peaceful march.

On 22 May 2018, thousands of people, including activists, businessmen, trade unionists, fisherfolk, students and just common folk, gathered at predetermined venues and marched towards the collectorate. A skirmish between the police and protestors led to an altercation, which led to a lathi-charge and later escalated into a full-blown clash between the two groups—resulting in the indiscriminate firing by the police that took thirteen lives. Thoothukudi remained on edge for the next several days, until the Tamil Nadu government ordered the shutting down of the Sterlite Copper smelting unit on 29 May 2018 and the premises were sealed for good.

---

While Kittu had given me a ringside view of the 100-day protest, several questions remained. The most important among them had to be the following: How did all leaders of the dozens of organizations that participated in the anti-Sterlite protests manage to escape police bullets and not even suffer an injury? How was it that only anonymous, ordinary people were killed during the police firing in May 2018?

Seeking answers to those and several other questions, I rushed from Levingipuram to a private office in a posh and ancient part of the city besides Thoothukudi Beach, where the streets and buildings reminded me of Puducherry and other former White towns that have managed to retain their old-world charm. On a collision course with that charm was the construction work taking place in Thoothukudi town as part of the Central government's Smart Cities Mission, which had left most of the roads in that part of the town dug up and unmotorable. After getting out of the car by the beach due to the ongoing construction work, I walked towards the office of a private firm situated in another vintage building. Wooden stairs led to the first floor, where Prof. Fatima Babu was waiting for me in a room that was under CCTV surveillance. I figured the activist wanted to ensure that her words weren't misinterpreted, considering the various unpalatable events that had unfolded in the past.

As with most sustained movements and stirs throughout history, the anti-Sterlite protests also needed a face: a leader people could look up to, seek advice from and blindly follow during confusing times. And that face happened to belong to Prof. Fatima Babu, a retired English professor of St. Mary's College in Thoothukudi, who loves metaphysical poetry for its intensity and admits to quoting Nigerian author Chimamanda Ngozi Adichie whenever she gets a chance. Like Kittu, Prof. Fatima has also been an active member of the anti-Sterlite movement since the mid-'90s, when the factory first began in Thoothukudi, and identifies herself as a 'lifelong porali', warrior.

'We came to know about Sterlite and the dangers that the factory could bring to our community through veteran environmentalist Anton Gomez in 1995. Since then, I have been active in the resistance movement,' she told me. As an educated local woman, Prof. Babu was accepted by both the local fisherfolk and the Nadar communities, the two dominant groups in this region, who rushed to her whenever they heard of an accidental death or injury at Sterlite, confident of her ability to fight for the victims' families and prevent the multinational giant from burying the incident from the general public. 'The fishermen were always opposed to the factory as they were concerned that the effluents let into the sea would spoil their catch and affect their livelihood, but other communities here were generally supportive as they believed that a big firm setting up shop in their town meant employment and development. They remained unaware of the dangers of the copper smelter until 23 March 2013,' she said.

Prof. Fatima vividly recounted the events of the day even after so many years. She woke up to a strange irritant in the air that had penetrated her bedroom without her knowledge sometime during the night. In her garden outside, she found that the leaves of some of the plants had completely dried up overnight, as if someone had sucked the life out of them. Later, she found out that thousands in her hometown had experienced skin irritation, nausea and other symptoms of a gas leak.[17] By then, her mobile phone had begun ringing non-stop as panicked friends and neighbours called her one after another to find out what had happened the previous night. While most knew it had something to do with Sterlite, they wanted confirmation from Prof. Babu. She immediately rushed to the government hospital, where she witnessed scenes that she did not want to recount to me. 'However, the Sterlite officials denied any such sulfur dioxide leak from the factory. But higher than normal levels of the gas were observed across the city, and that was even confirmed by district officials.[18,19] The incident helped sway public opinion against Sterlite in a big way,' Prof. Fatima said.

---

17 Yazhiniyan Thoothukudi, 'Noxiouss gas triggers scare in Thoothukudi', *The New Indian Express*, 24 March 2013, https://www.newindianexpress.com/states/tamil-nadu/2013/mar/24/noxious-gas-triggers-scare-in-thoothukudi-461419.html

18 Nityanand Jayaraman, '10 years since Sterlite gas leak: Another reason why smelter was shut down', The News Minute, 23 March 2023, https://www.thenewsminute.com/tamil-nadu/10-years-sterlite-gas-leak-another-reason-why-smelter-was-shut-down-174940

19 'Sterlite copper plant in TN shut down after gas leak', *The Hindu Business Line*, 12 March 2018, https://www.thehindubusinessline.com/companies/

'On that occasion, the danger of a gas leak became real, and people could relate to what we had been warning them about for years. Around the same time, residents of villages in and around the Sterlite Copper smelting unit, especially Kumarettiyapuram, had also begun to experience increased prevalence of diseases and erratic behaviour among their livestock. Since there had been a resistance movement active for the past twenty years, it was easier to bring all the groups together in 2017, when we came to know that Sterlite was planning to double its capacity. With the villagers on our side, there was no looking back,' Prof. Babu recalled.

Like Kittu, Prof. Babu also credited the villagers of Kumarettiyapuram for triggering that phase of the protest on their own. 'After presenting their concerns to the district officials, the residents began their relay protest in early 2018. The agitation grew stronger by the day as several organizations lent their support for the cause. On 24 March 2018, we were able to bring at least two lakh people together. It was a milestone in the movement. By then, almost all the major unions and associations in Thoothukudi town had joined hands with the core team of the anti-Sterlite committee, and we were almost certain that we would force Sterlite to shut down for good this time. The 100th day of the protest was supposed to be another milestone for the resistance movement to graduate to the next level, and everyone was pepped up. All the activists, community leaders and unionists involved in the protest, and even the general public, were giving speeches and communicating the message of staying together to kick Sterlite out of Thoothukudi. The citizens were informed of the plans for the march to the collectorate on 22nd May well ahead of time. We wanted it to be a big show of strength, a kind of culmination of all these years of our agitation,' Prof. Babu said.

---

sterlite-copper-plant-in-tn-shut-down-after-gas-leak/article64115761.ece

By then, the stir had received wide coverage from almost every major media outlet in the state and the rest of the country, with Prof. Fatima Babu and other prominent leaders featuring on national as well as international media outlets. The developments in Thoothukudi were being watched with keen interest. As the movement became bigger and bigger, fissures began to erupt among the leadership of the committee, and many began to question the credentials of Prof. Babu and other leaders whom they felt were garnering all the publicity and staying in the limelight. Soon, the slandering followed. 'I was well aware even back then that there was a move to discredit me, and there were even attempts at publicly shaming me by putting out video footage, etc., on social media. I'm not sure who or which organizations were behind it, but I knew that we, the committee members, had lost trust in one another,' Prof. Babu revealed. 'But the cause was more important and we had to stick together.'

Two days before the planned march, on the ninety-eighth day of the protest, district officials summoned the leaders of all the major groups participating in the protest and suggested that they give up their march to the collectorate, citing-law-and order issues. They were asked to organize a sit-in protest at the S.A.V. School grounds in the city instead. 'When the police suggested this, most of the leaders agreed to the demand, claiming that since the police were formally allowing them a venue, it was better to stick to that place. I was quite surprised and even resisted in the beginning, as we had already mobilized the public for a massive show of strength in the heart of Thoothukudi. But all the other groups agreed one after another to the district officials' suggestion, while a few of us were singled out for sticking to the old plan of a march. With so many fissures already present in the anti-Sterlite committee, we all eventually agreed to a sit-in protest at the S.A.V. School grounds,' Prof. Fatima said.

But the general public that thronged every protest venue against Sterlite in large numbers had already geared up for a grand march to the collectorate and were not willing to believe any announcement regarding a last-minute change of plans. The groups that had agreed to a sit-in protest also failed to communicate effectively because every organization and its leader feared that he or she might be branded a traitor for backing out at the last minute. 'By then, so many groups and sub-groups had formed both for and against Sterlite, and so much misinformation had spread across social media and other platforms, that no one knew what to believe. We tried to send the message about the change in plans and that we were no longer going to march towards the collectorate as a procession, but people refused to believe us. They gathered at various points that morning as planned earlier and, when all the leaders and key activists of the anti-Sterlite movement were at the S.A.V. School grounds for the sit-in protest, a leaderless sea of people began marching towards the collectorate,' Prof. Babu explained. 'By noon, it was all over and hundreds were shot at by the police. I was at the S.A.V. grounds with the other leaders, among a small group of 1,000 protestors. I don't know where the others were but there were none among the marchers on 22 May 2018. I still wonder how that was even possible! People have now branded me a traitor, but what about the others? Where did everyone vanish that morning, leaving the people who trusted them to fend for themselves?' Prof. Babu pondered, as she often does on sleepless nights, which were quite frequent, she revealed.

---

The mood outside my hotel in Muthiahpuram, opposite Spic Nagar, was already charged by 9 a.m. on the fourth Friday of the month of Chithirai. Mahindra Boleros, Tata Sumos and Toyota Innova MUVs criss-crossed the highway outside my hotel. Yellow flags bearing the emblem of the Sree Veera Saghadevi Temple and Kattobomman's face fluttered above the cars' hoods. Excited young men craned their necks through the open windows of those speeding vehicles, screaming and shouting at one another; the usually dull and quiet restaurants and eateries overflowed with extended families that had come from distant places to attend the festivities in Panchalankurichi. The district police had already invoked Section 144 of the IPC in and around Panchalankurichi, restricting public movement as they anticipated trouble during the festivities. Yet, against my driver's advice, I asked him to take me back to Panchalankurichi that morning. 'I have to witness the festival today,' I told him as he drove out of the hotel parking lot reluctantly. 'If there is any damage to the car, I will take care of it,' I assured him.

The frenzy picked up pace the moment we turned off the Madurai highway, as dozens of police personnel of various grades guarded the road leading to Panchalankurichi. Members of the Thokalavar community, pouring in from across the state, were heading towards the fort's temple on foot or in cars, vans and buses. Most of the roads had been restricted to one-way traffic to avoid chaos by then, as almost every year clashes break out between groups of people during the festival. After getting diverted by the police in at least half a dozen spots due to those restrictions, we eventually reached Panchalankurichi Fort just a little before noon. After parking the car half a kilometre away, again due to police restrictions, I walked towards the fort's entrance, which had turned into a carnival site. At least three or four pani puri vendors were doing brisk business. A few nomadic families had also set up their stalls beyond the pani puri sellers, displaying bright, colourful beads, necklaces and even stuffed toys for children. A grand stage had been erected right outside the fort for the cultural events later in the evening, while loud devotional songs, frequently interrupted by announcements, blared out of loudspeakers planted on both sides of the scaffolding.

I walked past it all and into the fort to find that, in comparison with the numbers outside, only a modest crowd of people, mostly women and children, were present in the Veera Saghadevi Temple premises, where rituals and prayer chants were proceeding at a brisk pace. Adjacent to the temple, huge tents had been erected, where food was served to all the guests that had come to the shrine. Panagam (a jaggery-based drink popular in these parts) was being served out of large drums that were being constantly replenished. Volunteers poured panagam into colourful plastic mugs and handed them over to anyone who wanted to quench their thirst that sultry summer afternoon. At least two dozen women practising traditional palmistry had spread out their mats under the shade of the tall neem trees that abound in the fort's premises, waiting for customers keen on knowing their future—the Thokalavars are known to have the talent for foretelling future through palmistry.

As I wandered in and out of the fort's premises to soak in the festive atmosphere, Murugaboopathy, who was even busier than when I had last seen him, spotted me. Thanking me for making it to the festival, he immediately summoned an associate to get me a mugful of panagam. 'You have to stay till evening and enjoy the festival. It gets much better after sundown,' he assured me before he was summoned to take care of other arrangements. 'I'm a little busy, as you can see. We'll catch up at leisure later,' he said, and vanished into the crowd.

The purpose of my trip to Panchalankurichi that afternoon was neither to meet Murugaboopathy, nor to observe the festivities. I had risked Section 144 and come to Panchalankurichi to meet Beema Raja, the official heir to Kattabomman, and listen to his side of the story on his claim to the slain freedom fighter's legacy. So I looked around for Pethiammal in the temple premises, where she had asked me to come during my last visit two days ago. Since I couldn't find her, I called her mobile number. Pethiammal picked up but refused to speak after realizing it was me on the line, and cut the call abruptly.

About fifteen minutes later, Pethiammal called back and asked me to come to the Om Shakti shrine outside her home in the

Kattabomman Santhathiyar Kudiyiripu colony. 'My husband has returned from Coimbatore and is waiting inside the temple to talk to you,' she whispered before hanging up again.

I rushed to the Om Shakti temple at the far end of the colony and found a frail old man seated on a coir mat inside the shrine. In comparison to the chaos outside, the colony was an ocean of silence, with not a soul around in any of the 200-plus homes. At the age of eighty-two, Beema Raja still looked regal, with his majestic moustache that extended all the way to his sideburns after curling at the cheeks. It remained thick and black—an obvious outcome of years of careful grooming. He was dressed in a sandal-coloured cotton kurta and white cotton dhoti, with a white turban wrapped around his head. Pethiammal stood next to the cot and explained the purpose of my visit into his right ear—the left ear was not as effective—as he nodded enthusiastically.

After patiently listening to his wife recount my last visit to their home, Beema Raja signalled me to check if my voice recorder was functioning. 'This kind of tragedy always happens to people of royal lineage,' he said. 'We've always had to fight for the throne; traitors are all around us, trying to take it away,' he told me when I informed him about members of the temple committee planning to go to court over his legal heirship of Kattabomman. 'But I have all the proof that is necessary to convince the court. It would be good if they went to court—then I could get this resolved once and for all,' he said.

According to Beema Raja, he was the fifth direct descendant of Veerapandiya Kattabomman and heir to the Panchalankurichi throne, and, thus, head of the Thokalavar clan. 'Veerapandiya Kattabomman's wife was taken to the Tiruchy prison after his death, where she gave birth to a son, Jagaveera Rama Kattabommu, also known as "Company Selvan",' Beema Raja explained. 'He was called Company Selvan as he was born when our family was in the custody of the East India Company. Company Selvan had two sons: Thalavai Kumarasamy and Subramaniadurai. Being the eldest, Thalavai Kumarasamy became the next heir and he had a son, Veerpandiadurai, who was my father. I am an only son and the fifth descendant of Kattabomman.'

When I asked him if the other siblings of his grandfather and great-grandfather had sons or daughters, Beema Raja conceded that one or two of his distant cousins might be older than him and, thus, eligible, but they had never vouched for it. 'You don't become a raja just by birth. The true raja is one who spends his life for the welfare of his subjects. And that is exactly how I have lived my life, so I am the most eligible among my blood relatives,' he added.

To substantiate his claim, Beema Raja dug through a folder full of old news clippings from Tamil magazines and fished out a government document dated 5 October 1872, signed by the tehsildar of Ottapidaram. The document stated that Company Selvan, son of Panchalankurichi Polygar Kattabomman, was eligible for government pension, which was passed on to his son, Thalavai Kumarasamy. Reading out those lines to me, Beema Raja said, 'Let them go to court and find out the truth through the court. They won't believe me if I tell them, but the documents will speak for themselves,' he added, before explaining the other contents of the document, copies of which he was glad to give me.

With the inheritance issue sorted at least to my immediate satisfaction, I told him I was curious know why a Polygar's fifth-generation heir was living a life of abject poverty and qualified as a Below Poverty Level (BPL) family.

Beema Raja stared at the wall opposite him for a while before responding to my question. 'It is our curse; we people of royal lineage aren't supposed to work for a living. Our job is to take care of our people. But times have changed ... what more do I say?' he pondered.

When I asked him specific questions about his ancestors, Beema Raja divulged the details, often putting out a disclaimer that everything he was saying was what he had heard from his father and other relatives. According to him, after Kattabomman and his brother Oomaithurai were slain and their armies defeated by the British, the families were lodged in prison for almost seventy years until they were released. By then, Panchalankurichi ceased to exist for all practical purposes, and his great-grandfather was given accommodation and food by friendly families of royal lineage in and around Thoothukudi out of respect for what they had done. 'Some of our acquaintances in Sekkarakudi built a home for us and provided us accommodation for a while. Similarly, other royal families also gave us food and other valuables as a token of appreciation for the service done by my forefathers. It used to be a common tradition for the subjects of a king to go and present their ruler with produce from their farms and a share of their wealth for the protection they were given. Kattabomman was the ruler of ninety-six villages in and around Panchalankurichi, and his past subjects often frequented my grandfather and great-grandfather and shared their produce with them as a traditional practice. Besides, the family received a royal pension from the government until 1958, when it was stopped abruptly. An amount of Rs 50 per month was provided as royal pension, which was distributed among the four children of my grandfather. Thalavai Kumarasamy and my father got just Rs 12.5 from that sum, with which he ran our family,' Beema Raja recalled, as tears rolled down his cheeks.

After '58, with virtually no income, their family struggled to make ends meet. 'Those were extremely difficult times. I lost my father when I was just seven, and since then have been struggling to take care of my family. Only I know the troubles that I have been through during all these years. As children from royal families are not allowed to go to public schools and study with common people, none of my family members have received formal education, including myself and my children. So we could not get jobs or take up a trade to make money,' he continued. Since becoming a teenagers,

Beema Raja had been exploiting his royal lineage, visiting rich and influential families across Tamil Nadu and seeking monetary help for the sustenance of his family. He shared a particular fondness for Coimbatore district, where he claimed many of his benefactors were from.

In 1974, Beema Raja managed to convince former DMK president M. Karunanidhi of his claim to the Kattabomman legacy and was instrumental in the formation of the Kattbomman Santhathiyar Kudiyiripu. It was the high point of Beema Raja's long life; he had got something for his clan and that, to him, was befitting of a ruler. Over the years, a majority of the 202 original allottees sold the land allotted to them, while some have even sold their homes and moved on elsewhere. Even Beema Raja had to sell the 3 acres of land allotted to him during a family emergency and legally holds no property anymore, except the shed that he calls home inside the Kudiyiripu.

Beema Raja and Pethiammal have a son, Ganapathi Raja, and a daughter, Murugadevi, both of whom are also illiterate and were unemployed until recently. Thanks to some benevolent businessmen, Beema Raja managed to get both his children married, but that did not elevate their family condition. So, a few years ago, he set aside his pride and sought former chief minister Edappadi K. Palaniswami to provide government jobs for his two children, citing their BPL status. The Palaniswami government immediately obliged and gave his children jobs at Panchalankurichi Fort as lower cadre staff, due to their lack of education. Now Murugadevi and Ganapathi Raja are workers at the palace their ancestors built, from where they ruled over almost a hundred villages in the vicinity. While Ganapathi Raja has no children, Murugadevi has two sons, Surya, a.k.a. Sakthi Veema Raja, and Sakthi Karthik Selva. Both the boys are now going to a government school in a village near Ottapidaram and are in classes nine and eight respectively.

'Many of my close relatives, including cousins, have married into other castes and have children and grandchildren who went to school and college, and are well-settled in good positions. But we did not do any of that as we believe that royal blood does not engage in such activities. So my relatives and other members of my clan think that I am a madman and a beggar. They mock and make fun of me. But I am not bothered,' asserted Beema Raja. 'I have been doing only what my ancestors have been doing all along. I am working hard for the welfare of my people and spreading the goodwill of my ancestors. I had gone to the late CM Karunanidhi and sought homes for all 202 families of my clan, not just for my family. That was brought by this madman. I went to the state government pleading for a memorial for Kattabomman in Kayathar and the government built a new one. After seeing Kattabomman's statue there, the Goundars in the west decided to build one for Dheeran Chinnamalai. I still go and participate in all government functions as the direct descendant of Kattabomman, who fought the British even before the 1857 Mutiny. I have spent my life spreading awareness about his good work and I am glad. If people think I am useless and mad, I can't help it,' he said, his voice stumbling and grief gripping his throat yet again.

Just about then, Beema Raja's grandson Surya parked his bicycle next to the temple wall and walked in to check on his grandmother. Slightly plump, Surya had shiny olive-black skin that dripped with sweat. Despite his royal lineage, the boy went to a government school with other children from the Kudiyirupu. He looked first at me and then at his grandmother probingly. 'Your grandfather is telling him about the legacy of our family, the history of your ancestors, my child,' Pethiammal said, but the boy seemed disinterested. He asked his grandmother to return to the temple soon and rushed out.

Beema Raja, meanwhile, continued to narrate various anecdotes of meeting rich, influential businessmen/politicians across Tamil

Nadu who have been kind enough to help him with funds and still treat him like a royal. In a way, it was this very quality of his that irked his relatives and other members of the community. Their claim was that he was bringing disrepute to their clan by projecting the Thokalavars as beggars who were rulers once. They were keen on challenging his claim of being the community's representative and wanted to settle the matter once and for all; they couldn't believe that a man like Kattabomman, known for his defiance and pride, could have such a descendant.

'It's not Murugaboopathy alone,' said Beema Raja. 'Now, there is another man who claims to be a direct descendant of Kattabomman. As a youngster, he murdered four men in a brawl over a petty issue. During the trial, he claimed he was of royal blood and couldn't tolerate an insult to his clan. They asked me if he was a descendant and I said yes, just to protect him. Now he claims that the court is convinced that he is the descendant and, thus, goes around saying he is Kattabomman's direct kin,' Beema Raja lamented. 'It's always like that when you are royalty. There are traitors all around. Nothing has changed. We have to fight them all and I will continue to do so,' he told me again.

Pethiammal, who had been quietly listening all along, added, 'Even today, when the collector came this morning, he asked for my husband and paid his respects on behalf of the government. But people of our clan do not do that anymore. They don't pay us due respect at the festival and do not honour my husband, as is the protocol. We have to fight and get it back.'

Meanwhile, drumbeats at the temple gathered momentum and the crowd began chanting religious slogans. My driver walked into the shrine to warn me that if we didn't leave then, we might not be able to get out easily. As I got up to leave, Beema Raja held my hand and asked me to help him by exposing the truth. He got up from the cot, tightened his turban, adjusted his starched kurta and posed for a picture with his wife beside him. Before I clicked the photo, he asked me to wait for him to put on his royal slippers, the fronts of which were curved upwards, resembling like an eagle's beak. The footwear was clearly oversized for him, but the raja slipped his ageing, trembling feet inside them effortlessly. 'Kattabomman was known only for his gambeeram [majestic looks], tough posture and grandeur. We can't let go of that now, can we?' he said. Then he took a deep breath, puffed out his chest, held his head high, curled his moustache and signalled me to take the photograph.

---

Major Bannerman's strategy of making the public execution of Kattabomman a grand spectacle to instil fear among the locals did not just turn out to be a futile exercise but actually backfired, as the British were to realize later. Following the death of Kattabomman, the Company officials lodged his two younger brothers, Sevathaiya and Oomaithurai, who was speech-impaired, in Palayamkottai Jail, along with some of the key lieutenants of the slain Polygar. With the fort razed to the ground, army in disarray and key leaders in jail, the British believed they had solved the Panchalankurichi problem effectively.

But the war was far from over. Just a little more than a year after Kattabomman's execution, a small team of soldiers from Panchalankurichi, armed with lethal weapons, launched an attack on Palayamkottai Jail on 2 February 1801 to free Sevathaiya and Oomaithurai. While the soldiers attacked the prison guards from outside, the prisoners, led by Sevathaiya and Oomaithurai, launched a simultaneous attack within the premises and stormed out of the jail, dashing back to Panchalankurichi overnight.

The British, who were taken by surprise, scrambled together a formidable force and followed the escaped prisoners all the way to Panchalankurichi, only to be shocked by what they saw there. The fort, razed to the ground following the battle with Kattabomman, had been rebuilt in just a few days and was well-guarded by trained soldiers who were battle-hungry. A British Army officer, Col James Welsh, who fought in those battles, recorded the incident in his memoir:[20]

> In the first place, we were opposed by a strong fort, raised as if by magic, in six days and in the second, its defenders, increased beyond all possible calculation, were likely to become the assailants.

He goes on to describe the rebuilt fort:

> An irregular parallelogram, two sides of which were about five hundred feet, and the other two about three hundred feet only, built entirely of mud of a very solid and adhesive quality, presented so very unwarlike an object to the eye that some of our soldiers, at first sight, compared it with a 'kailyard, with a dike about it'. The wall was generally about twelve feet high with small square bastions and very short curtains. A few old guns were mounted in these bastions and the whole was surrounded by a thick hedge of cockspur thorns but no ditch.

The forces met and the British, who weren't prepared to fight such a committed force, had to make a tactical retreat for a few days after the failed attempt to gather reinforcements and heavy artillery from other regions to fight the Panchalankurichi army. The second attack also ended in a pitched battle with an army led by Oomaithurai, as famed a soldier as his elder brother, putting up a stiff resistance that shocked the British. Col James Welsh, describing one of the early

---

20 James Welsh, *Military Reminiscences: Extracted from a Journal of Nearly Forty Years' Active Service in the East Indies*, vol. 1 (London: Smith, Elder, and Co., 1830), p. 55.

days of the battle with Oomaithurai's soldiers, wrote: 'Our total loss for the day was four officers and forty-nine men killed, with thirteen officers and two hundred and fifty-four men wounded. Battle was pitched.'

However, despite the initial setbacks, the British later put together a strong force under General Agnew, and a major battle, known to be one of the largest operations in the south after the Mysore wars, was launched, and Panchalankurichi eventually fell in May 1801. Thousands of soldiers lost their lives but Oomaithurai and Sevathaiya escaped and joined forces with the Maruthu brothers of Sivaganga for a final attempt at regaining their territory. However, even that battle ended with a British victory, and both Oomaithurai and Sevathaiya were hanged along with the Maruthu brothers. The British, once again, razed Panchalankurichi Fort and planted thorns and thistle where the fortress stood to ensure that it could never be rebuilt again.[21]

However, the bravery displayed by the mute Oomaithurai and his soldiers did not go unnoticed by the enemy. In his journal, Col James Welsh described Oomaithurai as 'one of the most extraordinary mortals' he had ever come across and dedicated significant space for the mute warrior:[22]

> A near relation of Cataboma Naig (Oomaithurai), who was both deaf and dumb, was well known by the English under the appellation of Dumby, or the Dumb Brother, by the Mussalmans as Mookah, and by the Hindoos as Oomee, all having the like signification. He was a tall, slender lad, of a very sickly appearance, yet possessing that energy of mind, which in troubled times, always gains pre-eminence; whilst in his case, the very defect which would have impeded

---

21 *VO Chidambaram Pillai*, p. 15.

22 *Military Reminiscences*, p. 131.

> another, proved a powerful auxiliary in the minds of ignorant and superstitious idolators. The Oomee was adored, his slightest sign was an oracle, and every man flew to execute whatever he commanded. No council assembled at which he did not preside; no daring adventure was undertaken which he did not lead. His method of representing the English was extremely simple: he collected a few little pieces of straw, arranged them on the palm of his left hand to represent the English force; then with other signs, for the first time, he drew the other hand across and swept them off, with a whizzing sound from his mouth, which was the signal for attack; and he was generally the foremost in executing those plans, for our annihilation. Whatever undisciplined valour could effect, was sure to be achieved wherever he appeared; though poor Oomee was at last doomed to grace a gallows, in reward for the most disinterested and purest patriotism.

He also referred to the soldiers of Panchalankurichi as the 'hardiest and bravest' of all the southern Polygars, whom he generalized as a race of rude warriors.

Oomaithurai was also loved by his people, who considered him their saviour. An incident during the final battle for Panchalankurichi highlights the popularity of Kattabomman's sibling among his subjects. On 24 May 1801, the fort fell into the hands of the British yet again, and Oomaithurai and Sevathaiya, who had been severely wounded in the battle, managed to get out of the fort but collapsed near a small village a few miles off Panchalankurichi, covered in blood, along with some of their troops. Some of the women from the village went in search of family members among the wounded men to bring them home. An elderly woman who found her severely injured son was about to bring him home, when he asked her to take Oomaithurai, who also lay wounded next to him, instead. Legend is that the mother let her son die in the fields but took Oomaithurai home to nurture him back to health. 'He was present as active as usual on 7th and 10th June and was taken alive at the conclusion of the campaign, and hanged along with his gallant and ill-fated relation, on the tower erected in the plain before Panchalankurichi, now the only monument of that once-dreaded fortress,' wrote Col Welsh in his war diary.[23]

While Beema Raja's claim as a direct descendant of Kattabomman might or might not be true, the selfless contributions of Oomaithurai, Sevathaiya and thousands of the brave soldiers of Panchalankurichi, whose valour was admired and respected even by their enemy, is the rich heritage that Murugaboopathy and other members of the Thokalavar community are unwilling to concede to a single family.

---

The most popular destination on Beach Road, Thoothukudi, besides the beach, are the grand grounds of the Basilica of Our Lady of Snows. Originally built in the sixteenth century, when members of the Paravar community in this region converted to Christianity, the church is believed to have protected Christians in this city for almost four and a half centuries now. Members of this coastal Catholic community, comprising mostly fisherfolk, consider the church their second home and grew up listening to the hymns of their beloved Snow Mary protecting the people of their Pearl City even from thunderbolts and other natural calamities. As a natural consequence, most mothers love to add the prefix 'Snow' to their daughters' names to remind themselves that they are all Snow Mary's children. In the year 2000, when Vanitha, a fisherwoman from Uvari, near Tiruchendur, and her husband, Jackson, from Thoothukudi, had their third child, they named her Snowlin

23 *Military Reminiscences*, pp. 130–31.

because they considered their only daughter born after two sons a gift from Snow Mary.

Vanitha and Jackson live just a few 100 metres from the Thoothukudi coast on a congested street too narrow for cars to pass through. As was often the case with most outsiders searching for an address in this part of town, my attempts to reach the home of Vanitha and Jackson landed me only at the front gates of the Basilica of Our Lady of Snows. But the rest of the journey turned out to be easy—all I had to do was ask for 'Snowlin's home'. From auto rickshaw drivers to tea shop owners, everyone knew Snowlin's residence, and they were only glad to direct me to the modest two-storey home where Vanitha and Jackson lived with their sons, Godwin and Johnraj, daughters-in-law and grandchildren. Their only daughter, Snowlin, had been shot dead by the Tamil Nadu police—she was among the thirteen people killed in the police firing during the riots that ripped apart Thoothukudi on 22–23 May 2018. Snowlin was a few months short of eighteen when a bullet pierced the back of her skull and burst out, drilling a hole through her face.

As I walked through the narrow streets adjoining Beach Road, it was easy to see that the homes, although cramped together, often with common parting walls, flaunted affluence, with tall compound walls at the entrances, CCTV cameras facing the road and the living rooms visible even from the road. In comparison to the rest of the colony, Vanitha and Jackson's home was modest. A narrow entrance led me to an approximately 8 by 8 feet living room, where a bare-bodied, middle-aged man with a silver-grey goatee beard and a slightly heavyset woman were lying down on the tiled floor. Though my contact had informed them ahead of my arrival, the exact time hadn't been mentioned, and it was clear that the couple weren't prepared to receive visitors when I walked in and introduced myself apologetically.

Vanitha, who appeared to be the more loquacious between the two, immediately brought out a plastic chair for me to sit on, while she and her husband preferred the floor. Until a rogue bullet drilled an unfillable hole in their lives, Vanitha sold idlis outside their home and Jackson went fishing on the high seas, like his ancestors had done for centuries. 'My husband has not gone fishing for four years now. He has lost the strength to go out to sea and frequently complains of chest pain whenever we talk of Snowlin,' said Vanitha. And how does he not think of her for even a minute? Their living room is full of photographs of her: Snowlin clinging to her mother as a baby; Snowlin, wearing a bright blue saree and matching jewellery, posing with her friends just before going to a wedding; a collage of Snowlin smiling, blushing, looking serious, laughing; and even a portrait of the teenager in a sombre mood.

But the most poignant photograph among them lay behind a glass panel that was locked. Vanitha opened the panel and handed the photograph to me. In that portrait, Snowlin was not draped in a fancy saree or salwar, she hadn't glossed her lips, plaited her hair, and she certainly wasn't posing—the young woman was holding a placard and marching aggressively, as if heading for battle. 'This is the last photo taken of my daughter, recorded on someone's phone camera during the riots. Minutes after this photo was taken, the police shootout began and our Snowlin was killed. An unknown person sent this to us a few days later,' Vanitha said, and broke down. She wiped away the tears with the pallu of her saree and said that their Snow Mary must have taken her along. 'The bullet entered through the back of her skull and came out through her mouth. It bore a hole in her face,' she said, still looking at the framed photograph, and broke down once again. 'I took her to the meetings; if only I hadn't, none of this would have happened.' Vanitha became inconsolable and Jackson rushed out of the room, wiping tears from his face with both hands.

As a devout Christian, Vanitha visited her church, the Basilica of Our Lady of Snows, regularly and also participated in prayer meetings as often as she could. During one such visit, after finishing her prayers,

Vanitha was talking to other members of the church, when she came to know about the protest against the Sterlite plant by the people of Kumarettiyapuram. 'At church, we were told about the harmful effects of the effluents let out by the factory and the suffering of the people of the village. I was moved. A few days later, there was a meeting at church about the ongoing protest and I learned more about the issue. I am usually passionate about such people's movements and try to attend any such meeting organized by the church. On that particular day, I took Snowlin along with me as she was also genuinely concerned about people's welfare,' Vanitha told me.

Snowlin had temporarily discontinued her studies after completing class ten due to certain health issues. After recovery, she was keen on going back to school again and wanted to become a nurse. 'Originally, she wanted to be an air hostess. So we made some inquiries and found out that she had to study further to quality for the job, and so we started making arrangements. But the family was not in favour of the flying job and instead enrolled her in a six-month course for nurse practitioners. Snowlin completed the course and was even helping out our neighbours and acquaintances by cleaning minor wounds, tying bandages, etc., when they needed it. After the nursing course, she joined tailoring classes to make use of her free time. It was around that period that I took her for the anti-Sterlite meetings,' Vanitha recalled.

After hearing about the fisherfolk's protest against the Kudankulam Nuclear Power Plant and the anti-Sterlite protests that had been going on for a long time, Snowlin became passionate about those issues and told her parents that she wanted to study law. She began taking private classes to prepare for the class twelve board exam.

'But she was not alive to find out the results of the exam,' said Jackson, now back in the living room. 'Had she been alive, she would have almost completed her law degree by now.'

'She was always like that,' her mother intervened. 'Very stubborn once she made up her mind. When I took her to the meetings against Sterlite, Snowlin was moved and became a regular at every protest meet I was invited to. She got really involved in the issue and genuinely wanted to make a difference.'

When Vanitha came to know of the proposed march to the Thoothukudi collectorate on 22 May 2018 to mark the 100th day of the anti-Sterlite protests, she volunteered immediately, like several other members of the church. At around 7 a.m. that day, Vanitha, her elder daughter-in-law, Snowlin and even her granddaughter, who was just a toddler, assembled at the spot along with thousands of people from the neighbourhood. Vanitha carried her granddaughter in her arms, while the two younger women held placards and began their march to the collectorate along with the others at 9 a.m. or so. 'Everything was fine until we reached the VVD Signal. The march had been peaceful. We were just raising slogans and walking,' she recalled.

At the signal, an altercation ensued between some transgender activists and the police, following which clashes broke out. 'The police began a lathi-charge and people started running helter-skelter. The crowd split into two groups; while one group ran towards the collectorate, the other group retreated. Since I was carrying the child, I was lagging behind and got stuck with the group that retreated, while my daughter-in-law and Snowlin were with the group that marched to the collectorate. I remember stones being pelted at us, and a few vehicles were set on fire. My immediate concern was to protect the baby from the violence, and so I rushed inside the compound of a nearby home to take shelter. While I was there, I heard the gunshots and my heart sank instantly. Even in movies, if there's a shooting scene, I usually turn away from the screen as I don't like violence. Here I was hearing gunshots and my daughter and daughter-in-law were stuck in the crowd that the police were firing at indiscriminately. I tried to carry the child and go see what was happening on the other side, but the retreating crowds from the collectorate prevented me. They thought I was mad to go inside with a child when the police were shooting people down. As more shots were fired, people started running for their lives,' Vanitha recalled, her demeanour now stoic.

While the women had gone out to protest against Sterlite, most of the men had gone to work as usual. Jackson was at the port, engaged in casual labour, his sons also out for some other work, when the violence broke out. Godwin, who saw the shooting on TV, immediately rushed to the collectorate and managed to spot Vanitha and the baby. By then, he had also heard from other residents of their neighbourhood that something had happened to Snowlin. 'Godwin told me that Snowlin had been injured in the clash and had been taken to the hospital. At that moment, my stomach churned; I knew something bad had happened to my girl. But I put on a brave face and returned home with my granddaughter,' Vanitha said.

At home, Vanitha was trying to feed the baby some biscuits because she hadn't been fed all morning due to the chaos, when she noticed neighbours walking up to her home, peeping inside and then walking away. They said nothing. 'Then a policeman came and told us that Snowlin was hurt.' Vanitha broke down yet again.

'Later, we got to know from others present at the shooting that she initially took a rubber bullet to the forehead while inside the collectorate grounds. She had turned around to run, when a live bullet pierced her skull,' Jackson finished for his wife.

Four years had passed but the scars remained fresh. The state government had since offered a government job to their eldest son, Godwin, besides sufficient compensation to the bereaved families of all the victims of the violence. Jackson went to work at the port now but still hadn't found the strength to get back to the sea. Vanitha had also accepted what had happened as God's will and was trying hard to move on. 'But what I can't really bear is the talk among some of my neighbours that we are living off the blood of our daughter. Some people here think that we have made crores of rupees as compensation for our daughter's life and come asking us for money. If we refuse, they say all kinds of things,' Vanitha poured out, tears gushing down her cheeks. 'I can put up with any suffering, but the gossip about our family and my Snowlin's death is the worst.'

Since the violence, Vanitha and her husband had been visited multiple times by several politicians, activists and government officials. The family had also made amends with the police over those four years. 'I don't know exactly who shot my daughter, but for my second son's wedding, I invited the Thoothukudi SP, collector and DSP too. They all came for the wedding and blessed my son,' Vanitha added. 'When I had gone to the SP's office to invite him for the wedding, he apologized to me for what had happened and told me that shooting Snowlin or anyone else had not been their intention. He assured me that the job of the police was only to protect the people. I did not know how to respond to that. I still don't!'

# Idinthakarai, Tirunelveli District

THE DRIVE TOWARDS VALLIYUR FROM NAGERCOIL along the scenic coastal highway, past dozens of sleepy fishing hamlets, was bumpy for the most part, with roadworks forcing frequent detours and delays. But for the natural beauty, there was nothing on either side of the road worth writing about: Just a few shacks selling essentials, beyond which were vast tracts of vacant land dotted with palm trees and some ramshackle houses. The landscape, however, underwent a dramatic transformation as I reached the Chettikulam area, where the Anuvijay Township, the residential quarters for employees of the Kudankulam Nuclear Power Plant (KKNPP), was located to my right. The sprawling township was going through constant expansion, with several new blocks under construction in addition to the thousands of apartments and sea-facing villas that had already been occupied by the staff. To my left, a variety of supermarkets, restaurants, pizzerias, bakeries, retail stores, two-wheeler retail outlets and even swank beauty parlours, most with flashy neon billboards, dotted the roadside. Beyond the pizza joints and retail outlets, a number of one- and two-storey independent homes had come up in the past decade in what used to be a barren, useless landscape with just palm trees and thorny bushes—qualifying this neighbourhood as a thriving suburb of Nagercoil.

After a few minutes, we rode past the well-guarded campus of the KKNPP, soon to become a nuclear park. Just beyond the plant, a name board to my right welcomed me to Idinthakarai village. I exited the highway and headed in the direction pointed by the name board on a smooth, tar-topped road with colourful, single- and double-storey homes on both sides that led me all the way down to the Our Lady of Lourdes Church in Idinthakarai village. As I proceeded to the church, I drove past at least half a dozen parked sedans, including a black Mercedes-Benz decorated with roses and tulips, ready for a just-married couple. The neat roads, concrete homes and cars provided an overall sense of cleanliness and comfort that used to be uncommon in remote fishing hamlets in this part of the state.

If I had to zero in on a single factor that could have stirred the people of Thoothukudi to stand defiantly against a corporate giant like Sterlite Copper, at a time when even elected governments would shy away from such a face-off, it ought to be the precedent set by the gritty residents of this insignificant, unknown fishing hamlet, approximately 120 kilometres south of Thoothukudi. The unrelenting protest by the residents of Idinthakarai had forced the world to take notice of their fight against a nuclear plant built by the Government of India in collaboration with the Russian government. The anti-nuclear protest in Idinthakarai–Kudankulam, which peaked in 2012 and lasted more than 1,000 days, eventually fizzled out but remains a historic example of what a determined group of individuals can achieve by grabbing the attention of a nation of over a billion people with their peaceful resistance movement. Naturally, my journey of exploring people's right to dissent in a democracy had brought me to that quiet village caressed by the emerald waters of the Bay of Bengal.

When I had arrived in Idinthakarai ten years ago, when the anti-nuclear protest was at its peak, I had landed in an agitated, impoverished village without a single motorable road and just one or two concrete houses—the remainder of the dwellings had been just shacks then. All the roads leading to the Lourdes Church, next to which was the venue of an indefinite hunger strike, had been blocked by the villagers, who placed huge boulders and smaller rocks on these roads, to prevent the police and other government officials from entering the village. If any outsider, except media professionals, had dared to enter the village back then, they were welcomed with stones, pieces of rock and, at times, even Molotov cocktails. When I managed to breach the boulders and flying missiles and somehow reached the village, I had been welcomed by empty streets and deserted homes, as the entire village—men, women and children—had gathered at the protest venue, where they would be till dusk, demanding the closure of the nuclear plant next door. Reporters and camera persons from across the country were busy updating their audiences on the villagers' every move. Beyond the church, the winding road ended in an open fish market that was also a boat landing, where blue nylon fishing nets were strewn around haphazardly. To my right were two yellow dome-shaped structures with giant chimneys jutting out from them and reaching for the sky.

In ten years, only that view had remained unchanged in Idinthakarai. On that sultry afternoon in May 2022, upon reaching the boat landing, I found a couple of old fishermen, eyes fixated on their nets as they tried to untie the knots. I walked up to them and asked for the panchayat president, Sahayaraj, who was an active anti-nuclear campaigner and one of the leaders of the protest ten years ago. One of the men directed me to a two-storey house away from the shore but not too far from the church grounds.

When I reached the house, I found a couple of roosters sitting on plastic chairs that had clearly been put out in the portico for visitors. I rang the doorbell and waited. A young girl wearing jeans and a black T-shirt came out and informed me that Sahayaraj had gone to Tirunelveli and would be back only in the evening. I told her the purpose of my visit and asked if there was anyone else I could speak to. The girl went inside again, checked with her family and told me that it would be better to wait and speak only to him if I wanted to know the truth.

With no other immediate agenda, I walked around the village aimlessly, past more concrete houses and petty shops, when I found a fat old man seated on a bench outside his blue-and-violet home, among the few single-storey cramped buildings in the village. I noticed that he, too, was curious about my presence on his street, so I walked up to him. He invited me to sit next to him when I explained my visit to Idinthakarai ten years ago to cover the riots. 'I just wanted to see the village now as I was passing by,' I told him.

'What do I say now, nothing has really changed,' the man said, sulking. 'We protested with all our strength but the government did not shut down the nuclear plant. Hot water is still let into the sea, close to our shore, as a result of which our catch has become small. Yes, we still go about our lives, but there isn't enough to fulfil even our basic needs. When we don't get enough fish, vendors bring them from the Kollam market in Kerala for us to buy and eat. Such is our plight.'

'But the village definitely appears more prosperous,' I pointed out.

'All that is mostly through our own efforts. Most of the young boys don't like to fish here anymore as it is unprofitable. So they now go to other countries to fish. At least 1,000 boys from this village and the surrounding hamlets are now fishing for big companies in Saudi Arabia and other Arab countries. Many others have joined the merchant navy. They send money home and their parents build better houses. One thing is for sure, we have not benefitted from the protests. Some people got houses; some have got jobs at the nuclear plant too, but those numbers are very few. Most of us haven't got anything from the nuclear plant or from the protests against it,' he said, and asked me to go around the village and double-check if he was telling the truth.

I thanked him and continued wandering down the narrow roads and bylanes, ending up outside the Idinthakarai Public Library, now converted into a government fair price shop. The unique distinction of that stretch of road is that the first country bomb of the 2012 protest had exploded outside the house I now stood at—taking the stir to the next level. A few buildings away, two men were seated on plastic chairs put out on the road and were busy chatting. One of them was dark, pot-bellied and had thick black hair and an equally black moustache, while his shorter, sturdier friend had thick curly hair and a thin moustache that had already turned grey. When I passed them, they offered me a chair next to them. The shorter man introduced himself as David and was more loquacious than his neighbour and friend Sandiyar, who appeared to be the more thoughtful one.

'We tried ... we tried really hard and managed to get the attention of the entire world, didn't we?' David said. 'But the protests were still a failure, as you can see. The nuclear plant is not just functioning but expanding too. The good thing is today everyone knows about Idinthakarai and the stubborn nature of our people. We should have continued the fight but mistrust and infighting spoiled it for us,' David elaborated.

His friend Sandiyar, who belonged to the ruling DMK party, cautiously intervened with his list of woes regarding the way the protests were handled. 'Too many rumours and stories were being passed around. Everyone used to say he got 5 crore and she got 10 crore and so on. After a point, we did not know whom to believe and whom not to. But we got nothing. It's not that the government did not offer us anything; they did bring a package of 500 crore to please us. But we refused the homes they promised to build for us and the jobs they wanted to provide. We did not want those luxuries when our main reason behind wanting the plant closed was not considered. In the end, so many people who already had homes and money got more and became richer. Only about five or six genuinely poor people have got homes and one of them is right here,' he said, pointing at a pale blue two-storey home right opposite his. 'This man and his children were suffering. It's good that they took the home and money, but we don't need it. We don't want their money,' he reiterated.

But just a minute or two later, Sandiyar reversed his stance. 'We should have taken the money first. After we refused, the people of Kudankulam benefitted from the government's kindness and their town saw a lot of development. The state government even promised a government hospital in Idinthakarai, but since we rejected it, the hospital was built in Kudankulam. It's those people who benefitted from the schemes,' Sandiyar clarified.

Both David and Sandiyar took active part in the protest and claimed they were tricked into ending it using the annual church procession as a reason. 'The token protest in Idinthakarai continued for over three years, with at least a few men and women sitting in the venue every day. But some did not want it to keep going. When the annual church festival was underway and the chariot procession had to pass through the protest site, the village committee dismantled the shelter temporarily. But after that, a group of villagers did not allow us to build it again, saying that the protest was meaningless as the government went ahead with whatever it wanted anyway,' David recalled.

By then, two women had also joined us and narrated interesting anecdotes of the hunger strike and how they had protected their leaders from the police and other agencies. 'Now, after all these years, we are only left with police cases. Most of the young men here have been slammed with cases, as a result of which they are unable to go abroad now. That's the biggest problem here now,' said one of the women.

I asked them if they would participate again if there was a similar protest now, with the government planning to open the third and fourth nuclear plants soon.

None of them gave me an affirmative response. 'We have lost a lot: Daily earnings, peace of mind and, most importantly, our children's future, with so many cases raised against them,' said David. 'We still oppose nuclear plants but no longer have the stamina for another fight only to benefit others. We were used,' he added.

'I have been active in politics all my life but now I truly feel politics is only for crooks. Only crooks succeed in it,' rued Sandiyar, rubbing his bare belly and looking up at the sky as if the answer to their concerns lay among the stars.

---

On my way back from Idinthakarai, I met Sahayaraj, president of the Idinthakarai panchayat, at a restaurant in Valliyur. He had just returned from Tirunelveli after a peace meeting with the collector and was surrounded by half a dozen supporters, including two women. After exchanging pleasantries, he insisted that all his supporters be present with him during our interaction and picked a corner table for six, where we all settled down.

Sahayaraj was fifty-five years old but looked at least a decade younger. After his wife had passed away recently, he spent most of his time at his sister's place, which was where I had gone earlier in the day. While his eldest son was in the merchant navy, the younger one was pursuing a degree in commerce at a local college. Among the very few residents of Idinthakarai who had travelled around the world, Sahayaraj had been actively involved in taking up social causes since his youth. Ten years ago, when the anti-nuclear protests were at their peak, Sahayaraj had brought his entire family to participate in the hunger strike, including his minor children, and had insisted that they all participate in the protests despite facing resistance. But he swore never to do such a thing again. 'It has left a bitter mark on me. I was branded a traitor among my people, and it has taken so many years to win their trust again,' said Sahayaraj as his associates nodded earnestly.

'I got involved in the movement in 2009,' he recalled. 'I had recently returned from an overseas stint when I heard about the People's Movement Against Nuclear Energy and their efforts to highlight the perils of nuclear energy in Kudankulam. Back then, the leader of the movement, S.P. Udayakumar, and a few other anti-nuclear activists had been regularly organizing protests and awareness campaigns in the coastal villages, which were attended by just about fifty men and women. They had been doing that for several years and I volunteered to join the movement with my entire family, as I believed nuclear energy was bad and we didn't want a nuclear plant right next to our homes. During those days, the protest meetings hardly attracted a decent crowd. At one such meeting, Udayakumar told me that the movement would strengthen only when the fisherfolk were roped into the protests. I am from Idinthakarai village and had reasonable clout with the locals. So I went to the village and talked to my people about the ill effects of the nuclear plant, and the difference was visible at the next meeting—a huge crowd had gathered and made the district officials and police take notice. It was our first success,' he recalled.

Following that victory, members of the anti-nuclear movement joined hands with other NGOs and like-minded people to organize a larger protest in Kudankulam village, where the plants were set up. But the police took note of the development due to the crowds and refused them permission. When they decided to go ahead with the stir, the police asked them to delay the protest for fifteen days, promising a solution by then. However, when that did not happen, the various groups involved in the protest decided to shift the next stage of the protest—an indefinite hunger strike—to Idinthakarai, where they felt they were safer due to the proximity to the sea. After a lot of deliberation, the protestors zeroed in on a vacant plot of land next to Lourdes Church and began the hunger strike with the participation of about 125 men and women, mostly from the village.

For the first two days, the hunger strike turned out to be a low-key affair, with hardly any media paying heed to their protest, but for a few local channels, and only a handful of police personnel monitoring the developments. By the third day, some of the women swooned and collapsed, and their resilience began to garner media attention. As the days went by, the protest intensified, and in a week or so, the Idinthakarai anti-nuclear protests grabbed headlines across the state and Udayakumar emerged as the leader of the most potent anti-nuclear movement in south India.

'By the eighth or ninth day, the state government agreed to negotiate with us and sent a team headed by the district collector. The collector even called me personally and updated me on the safety measures at the plant and also said that the government was willing to give us anything we wanted, including shifting this entire village to another shore with better amenities. They promised us colleges, hospitals and everything else. I thought it was a good deal. If the lives of my fellow villagers got better, that was good for us. So I went back to the protest committee and said I was willing to compromise if a good relief package was assured. But Udayakumar and the others did not agree, and, instead, some of the committee members spread rumours that I had taken money and had been bought,' said Sahayaraj, as his associates continue to nod. 'Everyone in Idinthakarai was made to believe that I took money and had changed sides. Even these folks did,' he said, pointing at a hefty older man to his right, who nodded in agreement. 'They missed an opportunity to do some good for the people who fought so bravely. The government was willing to give them everything: Money, homes, develop the village using CSR funds and even relocate them to a different village. But our leaders refused and instead stressed only on the closure of the nuclear plant. Had they struck a deal when we were strong, it could have been good for the villagers. Instead, nobody got to benefit from the proceedings. The plant is operational and the villagers have nothing to show for their brave fight. It was a colossal failure.'

After that rift, Sahayaraj claimed to have stayed away from the rest of the protest, as he was labelled a traitor by his people. 'Those were difficult times. With these outsiders staying on in our village for so long, the unity among our fisherfolk got destroyed. Everyone suspected one another and there were so many fights among us. It was a bad phase. Now the truth is out. What have the protestors gained ... nothing! Had they listened to me, we would have got something. Now, you go to the village and see for yourself. Nobody trusts the leaders of the protest as they have seen their true colours. Today, all the villages surrounding Idinthakarai have prospered but our plight remains the same,' Sahayaraj lamented.

Before we parted, I asked him if there was any possibility for a similar protest now, with two new plants on their way. 'It's very unlikely; our people feel used and do not trust anyone much. At one point they even suspected me and tried to accuse me of taking money. They have all suffered a lot because of this. Most of our children cannot get jobs as the police have slapped sedition cases against us [the Supreme Court later intervened and provided relief]. If there has been any progress over the past ten years, it is due to our own efforts and has nothing to do with the government,' he clarified.

As I got up to leave, Sahayaraj came close to me and said that the one change brought by the protest was that their people had become exposed to the world. 'Now, all our children go to schools and colleges and are aware of how we were exploited. You see, in ten years, we will solve all our problems on our own,' he told me with a thumbs-up gesture before getting into his car.

After several failed attempts to reach the anti-nuclear activist and leader of the 2012 Kudankulam protests, S.P. Udayakumar, for about two days, I finally managed to catch up with him on a sunny morning in his family home, adjacent to the Parakkai junction in Kottar, Nagercoil. Now in his sixties, Udayakumar lived with his aged parents, spending most of his time taking care of them. As a scholar, academic and active campaigner against nuclear energy, Udayakumar had lived and worked in different parts of the world, including the US, where he did his PhD, before returning to India. Over the past decade, he had also dabbled in politics by joining the Aam Aadmi Party and contesting in the 2014 Lok Sabha polls, and later forming a party of his own, Pachai Tamizhagam (Green Tamil Nadu). He had contested in the 2016 assembly elections as a clean energy campaigner. At the peak of the 2012 protests, Udayakumar became a household name in Tamil Nadu as well as the rest of the country, appearing on national and international media outlets on a daily basis. When I told him about our last meeting ten years ago, outside Lourdes Church in Idinthakarai—when he had been surrounded by thousands of people, including fisherfolk, activists, journalists and even college students—he confessed with a smile that he didn't recall interacting with me. 'It was a very stressful time and I was constantly giving interviews to journalists,' he pointed out. And he was right, as I had managed to sneak him out of the pandal for just about ten minutes or so, before his supporters shooed me away along with the other journalists. In comparison, the interaction in his ancestral home, with just his aged father watching me from an adjacent room, presented a man who was about as stoic as anyone can be.

When I asked him about his take on the genesis of the anti-nuclear protest and its outcome a decade later, Udayakumar expressed disappointment, as while the three-year-long struggle had managed to raise awareness and debate about nuclear energy and its use, nothing concrete was accomplished. 'The third and fourth plants are now coming; there are also talks of a fifth and a sixth unit and two more units are being discussed in collaboration with the National Thermal Power Corporation,' he said. 'But we have been writing to the government and lobbying officials to stop the expansion and bring out a transparent nuclear waste disposal strategy. The work continues.'

Recalling his role in the protests against KKNPP, Udayakumar clarified that his association with the anti-nuclear movement began in the late 1980s—soon after the Chernobyl disaster in 1986. 'Even back then, there were talks of bringing about a nuclear plant in Kudankulam and a handful of activists were already trying to reach out to villagers to alert them of what's coming. But I was not very active and moved to the US for further studies. When I returned in 2001, there were talks between the then Indian Prime Minister and Russian President about reviving the Kudankulam plant. Around that time, I decided to take on an active role and we [anti-nuclear activists] got together in Madurai and started the People's Movement Against Nuclear Energy [PMANE]. But we did not do much more than visit one or two coastal villages and meet the parish priests who brought together a few villagers, to whom we explained nuclear energy and its ill effects. Often, we also met members of youth forums, women's collectives and other groups to spread the message. It was a very low-key activity and went on for about ten years,' he recalled.

The big trigger for the revival of PMANE and the anti-nuclear movement, according to Udayakumar, was the Fukushima nuclear disaster in March 2011, which once again revived fears of having a nuclear park in the neighbourhood. 'I was happy as well as sad about the incident. Sad as so many suffered and happy that the issue was brought to light again and that people were getting to know of the perils of nuclear energy. That incident took us to the second phase of our struggle. I returned to Nagercoil in June 2011 and we organized a one-day protest in Kudankulam. But just around

200 people turned up and we were disheartened,' Udayakumar remembered.

Just a few weeks after that, sometime in July 2011, the hot run for reactors I and II and the Kudankulam plant were conducted, which resulted in a lot of smoke and hot water being released from the plants. The villagers, from the coastal hamlets as well as from those inland, panicked and got together to protest against the plant soon after the hot run was completed.

Udayakumar had then just returned from a trip to Fukushima and Hiroshima, where he got to see the impact of nuclear disasters first-hand. 'I received a call from a woman in Kudankulam who claimed that about 1,000 people had gathered at the church to protest against the plant and asked me to head it. They were aware of me and PMANE due to our regular visits and lectures,' he recalled, in between taking phone calls and attending to the needs of his father, who had by then come to the living area and sat on a chair a few feet away from us. 'I wasn't sure of what was going on but went anyway. As the woman had said, a crowd had gathered and I spoke to them about what I saw in Fukushima. They told me that now they were very clear about wanting to shut down the plant at the earliest. The parish priest of Idinthakarai was also present and assured me that hundreds of fisherfolk were willing to protest for the cause. They asked me if I could lead them and I agreed without thinking too much about what I was getting into,' he said, recalling that moment with a smile.

Among some of the perpetual issues in this part of the state is the ongoing rivalry between the Nadar community and the fisherfolk. Several brutal conflicts have marred the relationship for decades and continue to stir trouble every now and then. But the nuclear threat appeared to have brought the two communities together for a change. 'We spoke to people in Idinthakarai and Kudankulam about working together and formed a struggle committee with people from different communities. I even spoke to my friends elsewhere in the country and abroad who had led similar protests on the most effective approach. After receiving suggestions from all quarters, we decided to go for a peaceful, non-violent struggle, as I am an admirer of Gandhi and I felt it was the best form of protest in our country. The other leaders also agreed and on 16th August we held a one-day demonstration in Idinthakarai, which was well-attended,' Udayakumar said.

With the one-day stir turning out to be a success, the protestors decided to follow it with two more days of a sit-in protest in Kudankulam to continue the momentum. However, on 18 August, the third day of the protest, the police approached Udayakumar and the other leaders and urged them to give up the stir because some religious festivals were around the corner. The police and district administration sought fifteen days to get answers from the state government for their demands and asked the protestors to disperse until then. 'We agreed to the proposal and waited for fifteen days. Even then, I faced resistance from some groups, who wanted us to disregard the police request and continue our protest. But that would have only ended up in clashes with the police and been a futile exercise. Instead, during those fifteen days, we travelled across the length and breadth of the coastal villages and spoke to the people about a longer, more serious protest if the government did not decide to shut down the plant. As expected, we got no response from the state,' Udayakumar told me. The struggle committee then fixed a date in September 2011 for the next one-day hunger strike and, depending on its success, planned to continue the fast as a chain protest. They also decided that Idinthakarai would be the most ideal location for the hunger strike as it was on the coast, so the police would find it difficult to unleash violence or foil their plan. The one-day hunger strike turned out to be a huge success, following which a chain hunger protest was announced.

'This phase of the protest was largely carried forward by women, who braved the odds and rushed to the pandal every morning. They used to sit there without even sipping a drop of water. Now, fisherfolk are hard-working people who are used to eating well. When they stopped eating for more than a day, some of them began to swoon; and when women started falling sick, the media channels rushed to the spot and the movement gathered momentum. From that point onwards, there was no looking back,' recalled the anti-nuclear activist.

The seaside protest attracted like-minded people from far and wide. Youth groups, school and college students, NGOs, political parties, etc., flocked to Idinthakarai from across the state and even from Kerala to express solidarity with the protestors, and some participated in the hunger strike for a day or two before returning to their routine lives. Discussions at the national and international level began on how to handle the protest and what would happen to the nuclear plants that the Centre had invested so much in. Anti-nuclear talk became a national debate, with Udayakumar and his beaming smile becoming the face of the movement.

'From the beginning, I was very clear that we would launch only a non-violent campaign. If we resorted to violence, they would unleash it at a larger scale and finish us off. It would be that simple,' Udayakumar revealed while tending to his now persistently coughing father, who was also keenly observing our conversation.

But there were several in the struggle committee who weren't very confident about the Gandhian way and soon, as Sahayaraj had also alluded to, fissures began to erupt within the committee, with several of the leaders wanting to resort to some form of violent resistance. Udayakumar, Sahayaraj and anyone else who had led the protestors were accused of softening their stance for personal benefits, which eventually broke the mettle of the fisherfolk as well as the inlanders. The intensity of the stir fizzled out soon afterwards.

Ten years later, Udayakumar was well-aware of how a section of people in Idinthakarai viewed him. While there were those who still vouched for him, there were also dozens who felt he had betrayed them for personal gains. 'I don't want to say anything in this regard. My actions should speak and they will. If I had taken a bribe, I would have had to stop opposing the nuclear plants, but I have not, and the people of Kudankulam and Idinthakarai will soon find that out. Only time will make them understand what we accomplished together, as well as my stance,' he said, before our conversation drifted off to other unrelated topics.

---

On NH44, approximately 18 kilometres from Udayakumar's home, is the Gandhi Memorial in Kanniyakumari—my final destination. You could call it the southernmost tip of India, as NH 44—which begins in Jammu and Kashmir and cuts through Punjab, Madhya Pradesh, Uttar Pradesh, Andhra Pradesh and Telangana before entering Tamil Nadu for its final stretch, extending all the way to Kanniyakumari town—comes to an end at the Gandhi Memorial, beyond which lies the Indian Ocean. As the bus I was travelling in entered the coastal town, a renowned tourist destination with people from across the country visiting throughout the year, a mild drizzle began to fall on the dusty road. The bus passed several landmarks as it went through the town: Kanniyakumari Railway Station, the wax museum, Our Lady of Ransom Church, Kanchi Adi Shankara Math and the road leading to the pier facing Vivekananda Rock. It also passed a government museum, a couple of air-conditioned bars running discounts for beer and half a dozen hotels on either side of the road before finally halting at the entrance to the Gandhi Memorial.

The Gandhi Memorial in Kanniyakumari is unlike other such memorials built for the Mahatma. It was there that the ashes of the Father of our Nation were kept for a last public display before they were immersed in the Indian Ocean, according to his wish. The building also boasts certain unique architectural feats. Drawing inspiration from the Odisha style of architecture, the central spire of the building has a height of 79 feet, which is symbolic of the age of Mahatma Gandhi at the time of his demise.

When I got there at the end of this long and tiring journey, which had begun at the Sabarmati Ashram in Ahmedabad on a weekday afternoon in February 2022, a significant number of tourists were already present inside the memorial, walking leisurely past the various photographs depicting significant moments from Gandhi's life. In between those portraits were also quotes from his writing that continue to inspire thousands even today. On the wall at the far end of the memorial, facing the sea, was the framed text:

> I am writing this at the cape in front of the sea, where three waters meet and furnish a sight unequalled in the world. For this is no port of call for vessels. Like the goddess, the waters around here are virgin.
>
> 15-1-1937 M.K. Gandhi

Despite all these years, those words remain poignant and fresh like the ocean behind the wall on which they are framed.

After looking at all the photographs, portraits and other memorabilia, I came out of the main hall and hung around at the entrance for a while, just to soak in the serenity of the building. A middle-aged north Indian couple—a light-framed man wearing a long-sleeved shirt and trousers and his heavyset wife draped in a saree—walked past me, admiring the portraits. The man stopped and asked his wife if there were any more destinations on their checklist. She immediately pulled out a piece of paper from her handbag, on which was written a list of go-to spots in Kanniyakumari, with a blue tick mark next to most of the items. 'No, this is the last,' she confirmed. 'Let's hurry then,' the man said, and the couple skipped the rest of the portraits and walked out of the entrance. Outside the main hall, an elderly Tamil couple and their young son were seated on stone slabs, discussing the price of the idlis they had eaten that morning. The son claimed that he had bought five idlis for Rs 20, while the mother argued that she got only four of them and that he should have told her in the morning that five idlis cost Rs 20. She wanted him to be more careful when coming to tourist places like this.

A few other tourists stretched out their legs while resting on the pavement outside the main hall, perhaps after visiting other attractions in Kanniyakumari, which were all within a radius of less than a kilometre. I walked past them along a paved walkway, towards the rear of the memorial, which juts out over a rocky shore. Giant waves crashed relentlessly against the huge rocks before splitting into tiny droplets that hung in the air for some time and then evaporated in the heat of May. To my right was a row of tattoo shops with names like XXX Tattoos, A2 Tattooz, SS Tattoos and so on, which attracted dozens of backpacking young tourists eager to leave an imprint of their visit to Kanniyakumari on their bodies. Above me, on the balconies of the first and second floors of the memorial, young couples clung to each other tightly, as if afraid that the strong sea breeze would separate them. One such couple, likely to be in their thirties, were trying hard to take a selfie, or rather a usie, with the Thiruvalluvar Statue in the backdrop, but could not seem to get the perfect frame. The woman's dupatta flew out of the frame every time the man stretched forward to take a selfie, and she would turn around to grab it, missing the perfect shot. After she had adjusted the dupatta once more, the man stretched his hand forward for another attempt, but the gusty wind blew the dupatta away yet again.

# Acknowledgements

SEVEN YEARS IS A LONG TIME TO HOLD ON TO AN IDEA ON one's own. Countless people have helped through these years as this book took shape from a vague, almost impossible-to-accomplish concept to the form in which it is today. I thank each and every one of them for believing in me.

I would like to extend special thanks to Dr Sudarshan Iyengar, former vice chancellor of Gujarat Vidyapith, for his valuable insights on Gandhism and its relevance today; Ankit Patel from Unnao for taking time off work to help me understand life in his hometown; anti-nuclear activist S.P. Udayakumar; environmental crusader Prof. Fatima Babu; and so many other activists from southern Tamil Nadu for sharing details of some of the most difficult phases of their lives with me without any hesitation.

As has been the case with my previous books, I owe a big thanks to my agent Kanishka Gupta and his team at Writer's Side for this book too and for bring my writing career this far. I thank Sohini Basak and Rahul Soni from HarperCollins India for believing in my proposal and signing me on, and my editor Tanima Saha for guiding this book through the later stages of publishing.

Most of all, I thank my family and friends for supporting me throughout this incredible journey.

# About the Author

**Pradeep Damodaran** is the author of the critically acclaimed *Borderlands,* which was shortlisted for the Raymond Crossword Book Award for Non-fiction in 2017. His first book was *The Mullaperiyar Water War,* published in 2015.

# HarperCollins *Publishers* India

At HarperCollins India, we believe in telling the best stories and finding the widest readership for our books in every format possible. We started publishing in 1992; a great deal has changed since then, but what has remained constant is the passion with which our authors write their books, the love with which readers receive them, and the sheer joy and excitement that we as publishers feel in being a part of the publishing process.

Over the years, we've had the pleasure of publishing some of the finest writing from the subcontinent and around the world, including several award-winning titles and some of the biggest bestsellers in India's publishing history. But nothing has meant more to us than the fact that millions of people have read the books we published, and that somewhere, a book of ours might have made a difference.

As we look to the future, we go back to that one word—a word which has been a driving force for us all these years.

Read.